AF478276

SHAPING A LIBRARY:
WILLIAM L. CLEMENTS AS COLLECTOR

BY

MARGARET MAXWELL

Nico Israel/Amsterdam

1973

Printed in the Netherlands

ISBN 90 6072 631 6

TABLE OF CONTENTS

LIST OF ILLUSTRATIONS

Frontispiece: William L. Clements (1861-1934); by Herman Hanatschek.

(between pages 176 and 177):

PREFACE

William L. Clements represented the best in the American business man. Inventor, manufacturer, and banker, he yet gave himself freely in public service to his home city and state. All kinds of civic committees and unpaid offices found him an active participant. He was also the ideal university alumnus: a graduate who kept on educating himself, who developed a deep respect for scholarship, and who served his university as regent for twenty-four years and as generous benefactor. Rounding out his interests, he was devoted to his church, loved good music, and enjoyed professional sports and travel.

Yet above all he will be remembered as a discriminating collector in the field of early American history. What began as a hobby became a consuming quest. With consummate taste and erudition, he formed a basic collection which he presented to The University of Michigan along with a handsome building to house it. His collection could be – and has been – filled in and expanded by the University and by friends who caught his vision of a research library for scholars.

It is with Mr. Clements' career as a collector that this study is concerned. Mrs. Maxwell has carefully examined his papers and those of his associates to identify his bibliophilic trail through more than three decades of collecting here and abroad. She has interviewed family and friends. In slightly different form, her work was accepted as a doctoral dissertation at The University of Michigan in 1971. It is particularly appropriate that in the fiftieth anniversary year of the opening of the William L. Clements Library her narrative should be published.

Ann Arbor, Michigan
1973

HOWARD H. PECKHAM,
Director,
William L. Clements Library

INTRODUCTION

The period between the Civil War and the depression of the 1930's saw the emergence on the American scene of the private collector as library builder; men of wealth such as J. P. Morgan, Henry E. Huntington, Henry C. Folger, John Carter Brown, and William L. Clements combined business interests with a life-long, consuming passion for rare books. In conjunction with certain erudite book dealers who guided the growth of their collections, they ranged widely, bought on a grand scale, and through the scope of their acquisitions determined the future trends in book collecting.

The late nineteenth and the early twentieth centuries have truly been called the golden age of the book collector. The dispersal at auction of such collections as the Brinley, Harrisse, Menzies, Brayton Ives, and Robert Hoe in this country and the Henry Huth and Christie-Miller libraries in London brought opportunities that have not been repeated. The collectors mentioned above took advantage of the books that poured onto the market to form libraries which stand today as monuments to their creators. It is significant that these men had no intention of breaking up the collections they had fashioned. Each of them either deeded his library to a university or set up a private foundation for its preservation as a library for advanced research.

Among the first of the great collector-library builders was John Nicholas Brown, who in 1900 left the library of Americana chiefly collected by his father, John Carter Brown, to Brown University. Included in the deed of gift for this remarkably complete collection of classic Americana was provision for the erection of a building at a cost of $150,000 and a trust fund of $500,000 for maintenance and enlargement of the collection. The John Carter Brown Library served as a model for William L. Clements' library, not only through the notable rarities included in it and made known to the public through two printed catalogs (1865–71 and 1878–82). Acting under the influence of George Parker Winship, who had been John Carter Brown's librarian from 1895 to 1914, Clements used much of the Carter Brown administrative setup, including an independent director working under a five-man Committee of Management, for his own library.

The library presented to the public by J. P. Morgan, Jr. (1867–1943), in New York City in 1924, was a collection of rare books and manuscripts ranging from ninth-century Coptic manuscripts, medieval illuminated manuscripts, and incunabula including a strong collection of Caxtons, to original nineteenth-century manuscripts of such authors as Sir Walter Scott and Charles Dickens. Started by J. P. Morgan, Sr. (1837–1913) in the last years of the nineteenth century and the first part of the twentieth, it was further built to strength in the decade following his death by the younger Morgan. He gave *carte blanche* to his librarian, Belle Da Costa Greene, to acquire any desiderata that might come on the market, at any price.

Morgan and Miss Greene found a formidable opponent after 1911 in the person of Henry E. Huntington (1850–1927). Huntington, nearly as wealthy as Morgan, had begun his collection in a modest fashion about the turn of the century. Despite his purchase of the E. D. Church collection in 1911, for $1,200,200, he was virtually unknown as a collector until after the Robert Hoe sale of that year, when he carried off almost 40 percent of the entire Hoe collection. A private purchase of the Beverly Chew collection of English literature followed in 1912, for $500,000. Other collections that Huntington secured *en bloc* in the next decade included the Frederick R. Halsey collection of English and American literature for $750,000, the Duke of Devonshire's collection of plays and playbills and the Devonshire Caxtons for $1,000,000, the Earl of Pembroke's incunabula for $100,000, the Bridgewater House Library of books of the English Renaissance period for $1,000,000, and the Americana portion of the Christie-Miller (Britwell Court) Library for $350,000.

Huntington, also an art collector, housed this collection at his home in San Marino, California. His books he kept in his crowded private library in New York City until after the completion of a separate building to hold them in San Marino. In 1920, his collection of approximately 100,000 volumes was transferred to San Marino, and given, along with an endowment for its maintenance, to the state of California for scholarly research.

The William L. Clements Library of Americana, although not realized on so grand a scale as the collections of Morgan and Huntington, is representative of the achievements of the private collector as library builder in the first half of the twentieth century. Clements, although well endowed with financial resources, was no match for such giants as Morgan and Huntington, and he thus had to shape his library with care, rarely buying *en bloc*, but rather watching and waiting for individual books to appear on the market, then weighing values in order to place each book 'in proper relation to others of its kind.'[1] He decided very early in his collecting career to limit the sphere of his activity to Americana. Clements was not a pioneer in the bibliographical wilderness; others before him such as Harrisse, Winsor, Evans, Sabin, Church, and Brown had studied, collected, and made catalogs of books that they considered significant landmarks in American history. The libraries of E. D. Church and John Carter Brown, emphasizing the most important source books for American history, are known as 'classic' libraries of Americana, and it was on these libraries that Clements determined to model his own.

A classic library of Americana takes as its natural point of departure Columbus and his discovery of America. The collector of Americana seeks to acquire cosmographies and geographies such as those of Pomponius Mela and Claudius Ptolemy, Caius Julius Solinus' *Polyhistor*, and Pierre d'Ailly's *Imago Mundi*, all known to have influenced Columbus' thinking about the then known world. The cornerstone of every great library of Americana is, of course, the Columbus letter to Ferdinand and Isabella telling of his discoveries. The earliest versions of this appear today in the printed editions, the Spanish (Santagel) letter, and the Latin (Sanchez) letter, both dated 1493. Accounts of the later voyages of Columbus and his contemporaries, including those of Amerigo Vespucci, were immortalized by an obscure teacher of geography at the college of St. Dié in the Province of Lorraine, Martin Waldseemüller. Waldseemüller in 1507 wrote an account principally of the four voyages of Vespucci (*Cosmographiae Introductio*) in which he proposed that the name 'America' be given to the newly discovered western lands.

Cortes' letters to Charles the Fifth, printed and widely distributed in the sixteenth century, set forth the Spanish conquest of Mexico from the conquistadors' point of view. Far more sensational and more widely read was a series of nine tracts written by a Dominican friar, Bartolomé de Las Casas, describing the cruelty of the Spanish conquerors toward the Indians. These tracts, printed at Seville in 1552 under the title *Brevissima Relacion de la Destruycion de las Indias*, were pivotal in shaping the image of Spanish cruelty that has colored accounts of the conquest from that time to the present.

The English caught the excitement of exploration and discovery in the New World after the 1497 voyage of John Cabot through a number of writers such as Peter Martyr, Richard Hakluyt, and Richard Eden, who compiled accounts of travel which were immensely popular in the sixteenth century. In Germany, in 1590, Theodor De Bry began his remarkable compilation of folio travel books, reprinting and illustrating individual accounts of voyages to the new world and to the East Indies. Of signal importance in the De Bry *Voyages* was the reissue in 1590 of Thomas Hariot's *Virginia*, an account of the first English settlement of the new world on Roanoke Island, first published in London in 1588. Even more popular was a similar collection of narratives of travel and exploration begun by Levinus Hulsius of Nuremberg in 1598. French exploration and colonization in the new world was chronicled in the annual reports sent by the Jesuit priests to their superior general in France between 1632 and 1672. These reports, known as the Jesuit Relations, are of paramount historical importance, particularly for Canadian and Great Lakes history.

The seventeenth century produced landmark books in the settlement of each of the original American colonies. Hariot's *Virginia* (1588) was followed by Captain John Smith's *True Relation of Virginia* (1608) and by the extremely rare *Brief and*

True Relation of the . . . North Part of Virginia – actually New England – written by John Brereton in 1602. Brereton's *Relation* and another early description of New England, James Rosier's *True Relation of the . . . Discovery of the Land of Virginia* (1605), are of such supreme importance as 'firsts' in New England history that the two volumes together are called 'the very two eyes of New England history.'

With the publication of Nathaniel Morton's *New-Englands Memorial* (Cambridge, 1669), English colonists in the new world began to issue their annals at home as well as in London. The calendar of Americana from this point is filled with significant titles: Winslow's *Tracts*, Bradford's *History*, Winthrop's *History of New England*, the religious works of the great Puritan divines John Cotton and Richard, Nathaniel, Increase, and Cotton Mather, John Eliot's Indian tracts, all important for New England history. In the middle colonies we find Daniel Denton's *Brief Description of New York*, Samuel Smith's histories of New Jersey and Pennsylvania, and William Penn's tracts and letters describing the province of Pennsylvania. The Dutch side of the transfer of the colony of New Netherlands to British control is told in *Kort en Bondigh Verhael* . . . (1667). Important in chronicling the early settlement of the southern colonies is Coxe's *Carolina* (1741), Martyn's *Georgia* (1741), and Filson's *Kentucke* (1784).

The French and Indian wars are chronicled by many contemporary writers, including Major Robert Rogers, Thomas Mante, and Captain John Knox. By 1763, English dominance of the new world seemed assured, but French resentment smoldered until it burst into flame during the latter part of the American Revolution, when France actively supported the rebellious colonists.

Important source material giving both sides of the American

Revolution abounds. Hundreds of pamphlets and tracts written before and during the Revolution influenced and often inflamed public opinion concerning events of the day. Essays by James Otis, Samuel Adams, John Adams, Thomas Paine, John Dickinson, and Samuel Seabury gave the American colonists' point of view, while supporters of the Tory party in Great Britain, including John Wesley and Dr. Samuel Johnson, spoke for the other side.

The discovery period, the period of travel and exploration, the colonial period, and the American Revolution, a time span roughly between 1493 and the end of the eighteenth century: this is the province of the 'classic' collector of Americana. Within this span he attempts to gather not only rare original printed and manuscript sources in pristine condition, but also material of historical significance to the development of America. This pattern of collecting served as the foundation for the William L. Clements Library of Americana.

1   William L. Clements, *The William L. Clements Library of Americana at The University of Michigan* (Ann Arbor: The University, 1923), p. iii.

The following abbreviations will be used in footnotes:

GL: General Library, The University of Michigan, Ann Arbor.
MHC: Michigan Historical Collections, The University of Michigan, Ann Arbor.
MHC #1–MHC #19: Clements Library Archives, Michigan Historical Collections, in nineteen boxes.
WC: William L. Clements.
WLCL: William L. Clements Library, The University of Michigan, Ann Arbor.

I

THE FORMATIVE YEARS

April in Michigan is an uncertain month at best, and Monday, April 1, 1861, was stormy in Ann Arbor, a day with snow flurries alternating with gray, penetrating sleet. In the house on the south side of Catherine Street, a block north of the Washtenaw County Court House, where James and Agnes Clements lived, a baby had just been born. William Lawrence Clements they named him; he was their sixth and last child. He was not quite two weeks old when Fort Sumter fell to the Confederate armies, heralding the start of the Civil War.

William Clements' father, James Clements, had come as a young man from Abingdon, England, and settled in Thompsonville, Connecticut, where he met and married Agnes Houston Macready. A gas engineer, he and his family came to Ann Arbor in 1858 to lay gas mains for the Ann Arbor Gas Light Company. He settled permanently in Ann Arbor and soon occupied an imposing Victorian baroque mansion constructed for him about 1863 on the northwest corner of Madison and State Streets, opposite the University campus and just south of his good friend Judge Thomas M. Cooley's home.

Many of William Clements' boyhood memories centered about this house. Entrance to the house, which was surrounded by a white picket fence, was gained through a gothic arched doorway surmounted by a peaked tower three stories high. Four tall brick chimneys marked fireplaces that furnished heat both upstairs and down; this meant chopping wood and carrying it to keep the woodbox filled. But in another way young Clements was lucky; his father had tapped the water line – the first running water in Ann Arbor – that had fortuitously been laid between the Clements' house and Judge Cooley's place over to President Angell's house on the campus in the spring of 1871. This pipe line saved him much pumping with an old hand-pump.

James Clements was away from home much of the time during his son's boyhood and youth. Together with a group of prominent business and professional men, he had by 1872 diversified his original interest in the Ann Arbor Gas Works to include the establishment of gas works in Leavenworth, Kansas, and in the Michigan cities of Port Huron, Lansing, and Bay City.

More important, however, was the purchase in Bay City by this same group of a run-down and practically bankrupt foundry, John McDowell's Bay City Foundry and Machine Shop, in 1873. The foundry, with James Clements as vice-president, was renamed the Industrial Works. The new firm confined itself at first to repair work for saw mills and to the manufacture of piping for Bay City salt manufacturing firms. Within ten years, however, the Industrial Works began the manufacture of railroad steam shovels and other heavy auxiliary railroad equipment, which were to be the firm's specialties during the long period in which first James Clements and after him his son William guided its growth.

By 1868, James Clements was boarding in Bay City during the week and spending his weekends in Ann Arbor. It seems likely that he liked the little city of Ann Arbor and enjoyed the cultural advantages of the University enough to be willing to endure the rigors of weekly commuting from Bay City to Ann Arbor. The city and the University were to play an important part in molding the character of his youngest son.

William Clements' world as he approached his teens was bounded chiefly by the city of his birth, an Ann Arbor almost doubled in size in the years since his father had first set eyes on it, numbering 9,000 population in 1872. Industries flourished; along the Huron River stood woolen, flour, plaster, paper, and saw mills. He and his friends if they walked north on Broadway to the bridge could hear 'the sounds of water wheels, steam engines, and cupola bellows, daily groaning under the weight of their ceaseless tasks in smithing, melting, forging, and turning the rougher materials of iron into millshafts, wheels, etc.'[1] Ann Arbor boys were avid baseball players in the 1870's, and young Clements and his friends played baseball regularly on Saturday afternoons. Sundays he remembered as pleasant days, days in which the entire Clements family attended services at St. Andrew's Episcopal Church, sitting in the pew reserved for them. On long summer Sunday afternoons about 1875, the Clements family would join their neighbors the Cooleys for buggy rides into the country and the woods about Ann Arbor.

The young William Clements felt a profound veneration for Judge Thomas M. Cooley, whose 'dignity, . . . reserve, . . . unprejudiced, kindly advice, [and] . . . keen interest in earnest effort' made a lasting impression on him. Randolph G. Adams, first director of the Clements Library, who knew Clements well in his later years, attributed Clements' life-long habit of working while others slept to Clements' observations of the Judge's habits while the two were neighbors. Clements' room at home overlooked the Judge's study, where at midnight a 'light would

16

show him in relief, and the everlasting movement of his pen.'[2]

Although James Clements was away from home so much of the time, he seems to have had considerable influence on his son. He evidently had a good library that reflected his own interest in American literature. William Clements later described his father as 'a devotee of the writings of Benjamin Franklin and those curious New Englanders who styled themselves "The Harvard [sic – Hartford?] wits." ' Here, in his father's library, the young Clements seems to have picked up the germ of his interest in Americana. He said of himself in those years,

I was literally apprenticed, before my teens, to 'Poor Richard's Almanac.' 'Twas in the blood, I suppose, to take enthusiastically to that home provender. American history, starting as my task, just naturally extended into a pleasure which seemed to become absolutely my chiefest joy, though, perhaps, I should confess that occasionally I could divide my enthusiasm so far as to omit battlefields and congresses and territorial expansions when along came Saturday's baseball orgies.[3]

About this same time in his perusal of his father's library he came upon a copy of Carlyle's *Inaugural Address at Edinburgh*, delivered April 2, 1866, on his installation as Rector of Edinburgh University. Carlyle's advice to the students, emphasizing diligence and honesty in study and reverence for those older and wiser than they were, and his statement that 'the true University of our days is a Collection of Books,'[4] seems to have made a tremendous impact on Clements, so much so that Randolph Adams claims the address was 'a guiding light of his life.'[5]

A week before his death some sixty years later, as he lay seriously ill in a Detroit hospital, William Clements' thoughts turned again to the Carlyle essay. Speaking to Randolph Adams, who was visiting him at the hospital,

He said that he wished the library [Clements Library of Americana] to be a source of inspiration for the development of an appreciation by the University students of aesthetic values and a reverence for their superiors. He expressed the wish that every undergraduate of the University be compelled to read Thomas Carlyle's address to the students at the University of Edinburgh on these subjects.[6]

William Clements applied for admission to The University of Michigan in September 1878, and took the regular examination given candidates for the degree of Bachelor of Science. The examination began with the writing of an essay of at least two pages, which was graded on spelling, punctuation, capitalization, grammar, and paragraph division. In 1878, prospective freshmen could choose to write on either the story of Brutus, from Shakespeare's *Julius Caesar;* the story of Amy Robsart, from *Kenilworth;* or the story of Tiny Tim, from the *Christmas Carol.* Clements was also examined in history, geography, arithmetic, algebra, geometry, French, natural philosophy (physics), geometric drawing, zoology, and botany. Clements entered the Department of Literature, Science and the Arts of the University at the age of seventeen, in a freshman class totaling 172 students, including thirty women. There were 441 students in the Department, and 1372 students in the entire University.

The University campus, like the city of Ann Arbor, had seen much progress and growth in the years since William Clements' father had first come to Ann Arbor. The most impressive building on the campus was University Hall, which 'with its front of 347 feet, and its dome rising to a height of 140 feet from

18

the ground,'[7] connected Mason and South Halls. University Hall housed President Angell's office and the campus chapel on the first floor; the second story was mostly taken up with a large auditorium seating 3,400. A new brick museum building was constructed in 1880 while Clements was a student; this stood just south of University Hall and helped to relieve congestion in other classroom buildings which had hitherto stored the University's extensive collections in mineralogy, geology, and zoology.

The first separate library building on the campus was not built until 1883, the year following Clements' graduation. During the years he was a student, the library was still housed in a room in the law building; in 1878, it contained 26,000 volumes, with 8,000 pamphlets. The library boasted a catalog surprisingly full and useful considering cataloging practices of the day; it consisted of two parts,

a catalogue of titles on slips, arranged in the alphabetical order of the names of the authors, and a catalogue of the subjects treated in all the books and reviews and magazines in the Library.[8]

Clements' experiences as a student seem to have been typical of those of well-to-do young men of his time. He paid the regular admission fee of $10, and his tuition amounted to $20 annually. Since he lived at home, he did not need to worry about board and lodging with a private family, which the 1878–9 *Calendar* estimated would cost from $3.00 to $5.00 per week. He joined Chi Psi fraternity, one of the oldest fraternities on campus, and was a member of The University of Michigan Shooting Club.

Two of the commonplace books that Clements used for copying literary excerpts that appealed to him have survived from this period. Dated February, 1879, and January, 1880, they contain lengthy extracts in Clements' neat longhand from books and contemporary periodical articles which do not seem to be related in any way to his class work and doubtless are representative of his other interests at the time. Subject interest is divided between literary and political quotations; the question of universal franchise (for men only, of course) seems to have interested him. Several excerpts from the 1879 book deny the idea of the 'equality' of all men and thus their inherent right to the franchise. A large proportion of the copied extracts reflect Clements' interest in the life and works of Sir Walter Scott, an interest maintained throughout his life.

A number of sentimental love poems occupy a good deal of space in both the notebooks; one quatrain in the 1879 book may be original:

If . . . were all that she seems,
If her smile were all that I dream,
Then the world is not so bitter
That a smile could make it sweet.
Lines to . . .

A name at the end has been carefully erased. Immediately following,

When he loved, he loved with the whole energy of his strong mind. When death separated him from what he loved, the few who witnessed his terrible agonies trembled for his life and reason . . . . He succeeded in inspiring in a virtuous woman, born his superior, a passion fond even to idolatry.

20

These noble sentiments the youthful Clements carefully identified, as he did each passage he copied. These lines were from Macaulay's *William of Orange*[9].

Clements seems to have been a good student; he routinely completed the requirements for the degree of Bachelor of Science, which included mathematics, French, German, English, philosophy, physics, general chemistry, zoology, botany, drawing, history, mineralogy, and geology. In line with this interest in engineering, he took extra courses in mathematics and drawing, the latter being taught by Charles S. Denison. Denison, whom the students called Lord Chesterfield, was a perfectionist in all things, an immaculate dresser who often appeared in class attired in a Prince Albert coat, carrying a cane and gloves. He expected the same sort of perfection from his students in drawing.

The coming of Mortimer E. Cooley, on leave from his post as Assistant Engineer, U.S. Navy, in the fall of 1881 to teach in the newly established Department of Mechanical Engineering meant a final year for Clements of intensified course work in mechanical engineering, pattern making, molding, founding, machine construction, and other practical aspects of his future profession. Cooley occupied a small brick building erected for the new department that year at a cost of about $1500, not including the outlay for necessary machinery and equipment. Cooley remembered Clements in after years with pride and affection:

Mr. Clements was my first student in Mechanical Engineering, and my only student the year I came to Ann Arbor, in 1881. I mention this with some pride, because it is not often that an engineer has taken so great an interest in Americana.[10]

Clements' course pattern during his university career shows an unusual concentration in history for a student majoring in mechanical engineering; he took four history courses, none of which was required for graduation. These included the political history of America from the settlement at Jamestown to the adoption of the Articles of Confederation, taught by Assistant Professor Richard Hudson, and three courses offered by Professor Charles Kendall Adams, a well-known historian who later was President of Cornell University and of the University of Wisconsin. These were the political history of England after Napoleon I; the government of England; and the rise and development of Prussia. The last-named course, which Clements took during his junior year, is the only one in which Clements ever failed. This is probably a ready explanation for the fact that Clements expressed little liking for Charles Kendall Adams in later years.

In English, Clements took two required courses in rhetoric during his freshman year under Isaac N. Demmon, a scholar and a lover of rare books. Clements respected Demmon so much that, after he became the chairman of The University of Michigan regents' library committee, he appointed Demmon as first curator of rare books in the University Library. But it was through a semester's course in Chaucer that Clements met Moses Coit Tyler, whose books on the literature of colonial and Revolutionary America had a great influence many years later on the development of Clements' collection of Americana.

The formal study of American literature in the classroom was unknown when Clements was a student. Tyler's research in American literature began as an outgrowth of his work in English literature. His *The History of American Literature, 1607–1765*, a two-volume work published in November, 1878, was a pioneer work based entirely on original source material which Tyler had assembled at considerable cost and effort. Tyler's intensive study of colonial American literature continued during the period that Clements knew him, but at this particular moment Tyler seems to have made little impression on Clements. Later in his life, with his own collection of Americana already well developed, Clements paid tribute to Tyler and to his pioneering histories of American literature. Randolph Adams said that Tyler's picture remained on the wall of Clements' study until his death.

William L. Clements graduated with the degree of Bachelor of Science from The University of Michigan on June 29, 1882, and soon thereafter took himself to Bay City, where his father, then vice-president of the Industrial Works, had a position waiting for him, the newly created office of Chief Mechanical Engineer.

The Industrial Works when Clements entered the firm was undergoing a period of financial trouble. The closing of some of the Bay City lumber mills in the 1870's had led to a shift in emphasis at I-W about 1880 from mill-related manufacturing to the construction of heavy-duty railroad steam shovels. But the railroad shovels, although well made, did not prove to be commercially profitable. James Clements found a valued advisor and confidante in his neighbor Judge Cooley, who combined astute business judgment with knowledge of the law and who had a personal interest in the success of I-W because of his own heavy financial investment in the corporation. Clements conferred with Cooley on 'business matters . . . more or less perplexing'[11] nearly every weekend that he managed to spend in Ann Arbor, and Judge Cooley made a number of trips to Bay City to look into the problems of the firm. During the early part of the year 1882, Cooley said with cautious optimism,

My interests in the Bay City Industrial Works are the most considerable I have any where & for a long time they have occasioned all the associates a good deal of concern . . . . We have in round numbers property of the value of $175,000 and owe $100,000. At present we are apparently making $1000 to $2000 a month. We are manufacturing steam excavators, & if they prove satisfactory, as they now promise, we shall reduce our debts largely this year.[12]

The Industrial Works had a good product. Finding interested buyers with ready cash proved to be the problem. James Clements, who had left shortly after Cooley's Bay City visit on a trip to push sales of the shovel in railroad centers of the eastern seaboard, reported, after canvassing Boston and New York City, 'Business is rather quiet here . . . .Hope we will get some orders in during the coming month.'[13] Back at the Bay City plant in April, 1882, Clements voiced his discouragement with prevailing business conditions.

Our shovel this year appears to be a great success at least so far as the manufacture is concerned. *[roman mine] If we had sent this shovel out last year, I have no doubt our shop would have been filled with orders . . . . I hope we shall get a chance to get some out. We are building six [but] not receiving many enquiries. The condition of Railroad matters is bad at present and they are not making any new expenses. We have got up a* good steam shovel *and we must now get up a good line of Derricks and hoisting machinery. After that our property will be good and we shall find plenty of business at paying prices a great part of the time, even should they cease to cut lumber.*[14]

Derricks and hoisting machinery – could this further diversification of the Industrial Works production be the answer to

24

their problems? Several shovels were sold, and some were leased to railroads for roadbed operations. The firm solicited testimonial letters from satisfied shovel customers evidently for advertising purposes. But despite all efforts, 'the shovel business deteriorated into a matter of selling almost entirely to irresponsible contractors,'[15] from whom they had difficulty in collecting.

Meanwhile, the ailing firm's new Chief Mechanical Engineer, perhaps catching a hint from his father's suggestion of April, 1882, that the Industrial Works might add 'a good line of Derricks and hoisting machinery' to its business, was working on the problem of building a workable heavy-duty crane. The Industrial Works Fiftieth Anniversary booklet credits William L. Clements at this early period with 'immediately recogniz[ing] the fundamental limitations of [previous] cranes, their very short rotating arc and fixed radius, and in an order for three wharf cranes for the New York Central Railroad [built late in 1882, he] embodied new principles that are the basis of all Industrial cranes as we know them today.'[16]

But business continued slow; Judge Cooley on December 18, 1882, sent a sharp letter to Charles R. Wells, since the death of his father Ebenezer Wells earlier that year, both secretary and treasurer of the Industrial Works. Reminding him that he, Cooley, had invested considerably more than $100,000 in the firm, he told Wells that he must direct the Industrial Works with more 'personal energy, determination, and careful supervision of the business' than he had evidently shown previously. It was up to Wells, said Cooley, either to make a success of the business or to sell it.[17]

An attempt at internal reorganization was made. Cooley recorded in February, 1883, that

Mr. [James] Clements came in [this] evening with ... the

manager of the Ottawa Iron Works . . . . Mr. Clements proposes to endeavor to secure him for manager of the Industrial Works. We both like his appearance very much, and we shall secure him if possible.[18]

But a change in management did not seem to be the answer. Judge Cooley continued his conferences with Clements in Ann Arbor several times each month, and noted in his diary that on Sunday, July 15, 1883, he had 'had a long talk with Mr. Clements about Bay City interests, my concern in which begins to look of questionable value.' On August 26, he voiced his opinion that 'the affairs of the Industrial Works . . . are very loosely and inefficiently managed,' and noted Charles Wells' suggestion related to him by James Clements that William Clements should 'go into the works as manager and displace the present superintendent.' Cooley wrote Wells the next day, 'advising him to take the responsibility of reorganizing the Industrial Works on his own judgment, with a view to greater efficiency and economy.'[19] Evidently Wells took Judge Cooley's advice, for at some time during the fall of 1883, William Clements was appointed Superintendent of the Industrial Works.

As William Clements moved into a position of greater responsibility in the Industrial Works, Thomas M. Cooley noted that his conferences with James Clements regarding I-W matters often now included the younger Clements. A midyear 1884 appraisal of his financial standing, however, led Cooley to state,

I have been scanning over my interests in manufacturing enterprises, and they stand about as follows: Industrial Works, Bay City – Stock, par value $20,000. Actual value, nothing.[20]

Financial problems at the Industrial Works reached a critical point by the end of 1884. Judge Cooley noted on November 30,

It is proposed to fund the debt [of the Industrial Works] and issue bonds for the amount. Four parties, [James] Clements, [George] Kimball, [Charles R.] Wells, and [Edgar A.] Cooley [T. M. Cooley's son, a Bay City lawyer and one of the principal stockholders in the firm] are now endorsers and it is desirable that they be relieved from this personal responsibility. The works have never made any profits.[21]

At sometime either late in 1884 or in 1885, the Industrial Works was reorganized, with James Clements as president and C. R. Wells as secretary-treasurer. This reorganization seems to have solved many of the problems of the company. James Clements was an effective administrator; by the year 1886 the Industrial Works began to prosper.

During this year the steam wharf crane, with further improvements, was mounted on a four-wheel railroad car and used around the plant to handle heavy castings and machinery parts. This was the forerunner of the modern locomotive crane, which has become such an invaluable piece of equipment in American industry.[22]

1886 was a banner year for William L. Clements personally as well. On October 5 and December 7 he submitted to the U. S. Patent Office for registry under his name two original inventions, a pile driver and a portable rail saw plant. The Industrial Works Fiftieth Anniversary booklet states that 'the portable steel rail saw ... even today with but few developments is standard equipment for its purpose.'

A laconic notation in T. M. Cooley's diary on September 4,

1886, gives a hint of some important personal interests that the youthful inventor and budding industrialist William L. Clements was pursuing. Cooley said,

Mr. W. W. Young, banker of Pittsburgh, writes me a letter of inquiry regarding W. L. Clements who he says is courting his daughter.[23]

Mail service in the late nineteenth century was obviously superior to that to which we are accustomed today; Young's letter was dated on a Lawrence Bank of Pittsburgh letterhead only the day before. It read as follows:

Pittsburg, Pa.,
Sept. 3rd. 1886

Hon. T. M. Cooley
Ann Arbor, Mich.

Dr. Sir

I take the liberty of addressing you for the purpose of getting some information as to the character and standing of Mr. W. L. Clements of 'Industrial Work' [sic] Bay City Mich. – having been informed that you know all about him – he is visiting on [sic] of my daughters with whom he became acquainted at school in your city, and as we know nothing of his antecedents, are at a loss to know how to recieve [sic] him. We would treat any information you might give us (my wife & self) as entirely confidential and be very greatfull [sic] for it – Will you please let me hear from you and much oblige.

Yours truly,
W. W. Young

P.S. Please consider this confidential. WWY[24]

It would be interesting to know Thomas M. Cooley's reply. Whatever Cooley said must have impressed Young favorably, however, for on February 8, 1887, William Lawrence Clements and Jessie Newton Young were married in a fashionable ceremony at the Shady Side Presbyterian Church, Pittsburgh, Pennsylvania.

Sometime before their marriage, the young couple may have been in Syracuse, N.Y., because they had matching photographs taken at a Syracuse photographer's studio. The solemn expression of the thin, dark-haired William L. Clements, with his Chi Psi fraternity pin prominently displayed on the vest of his black broadcloth suit is matched by that of Jessie Young, who, with her luxuriantly curling hair wound tightly about her head in a coronet braid and a double row of brass buttons marching down the front of her high-collared brocaded dress, fixes her gaze on eternity with an air of serious purpose.

February 8, 1887, turned out to be 'one of the rainiest, muddiest, and most unpleasant evenings we have experienced this winter.' The wedding, held at eight p. m., was attended by 'fashionable representations of Pittsburgh Society, a greater portion of the ladies being in full evening dress.' Jessie Newton Young, 'the charming little bride,' wore 'an exquisite dress of faille francaise, the front one mass of lace, a tulle vail [sic] covering her from head to foot.' Carrying a bouquet of bridal roses and lilies of the valley and a pearl inlaid fan, she was escorted by her father to the altar, where six ushers, four brides-maids, and the groom awaited her. Following the ceremony, continued the newspaper account, the bridal party

with about fifty relatives and friends proceeded to the residence of Mr. Young on Penn avenue, East End, where a reception was held. The house was beautifully decorated with vases of long stemmed roses, narcissus and lilies of the valley. Toerge's orchestra was in attendance, and a supper, perfect in every detail, was served from the Duquesne Club.[25]

William and Jessie Clements left for Bay City as soon as the reception was over, where they moved into a fine residence on the southwest corner of Center Avenue and North Johnson Street.

The year 1887 drew to a close with no further events of note; the Industrial Works prospered, and the Clements-Cooley conferences became less frequent and less urgent. On Sunday, April 22, 1888, T. M. Cooley and James Clements, old friends and associates of thirty years' standing, sat together after dinner and talked. In the course of their conversation, Cooley reached a decision about his holdings in the Industrial Works. He wrote in his diary later that evening,

After he [James Clements] left I wrote C. R. Wells that he and Will Clements now had the Industrial Works well in hand, and would find their life work there: that my work would be elsewhere, and I would sell them my stock at 50¢ on the dollar, payable $1000 down and $1000 a year thereafter at 6 pr. cent. interest with the stock as collateral. I should be greatly rejoiced if this offer were accepted, though I should lose by it at least $10,000, with many years interest.[26]

And indeed, William Clements and Charles R. Wells, together with a third man, Ernest B. Perry, who began his career with I-W following his graduation from The University of Michigan in June 1889, did find their life work there, assuming control of the firm after James Clements' death in 1895.

A period of moderate growth and financial stability in the

affairs of the Industrial Works was punctuated happily for William and Jessie Clements by the birth of William Wallace Clements on September 2, 1889, and Eliza Moody Clements on September 9, 1891. But the year 1891 began a period of nation-wide financial depression.

Then, after a dull year,

came an opportunity that seemed like Good Fortune herself. A contract was secured with the Exposition Company to supply a number of cranes for erecting and freight handling at the World's Fair in Chicago in 1893. The cranes handled all of the heavy work of the exhibits and were given a splendid showing with much public-ity at the exposition, finally being awarded first prize and a gold medal.[27]

But the Columbian Exposition year of 1893 proved a disastrous one for business all over the United States. During the course of the year, 554 banks failed.

Before the crisis ran its course, railroads representing one-fourth of the total capitalization of the industry went into receivership .... Railroad failures were accompanied by curtailment of coal and iron production, and there was a chain reaction of unemployment, business failures, strikes, and riots.[28]

During the fall of 1893, as business conditions worsened, William Clements went to the Chicago Exposition in hopes of selling some of the I-W cranes. He slept in the cab of one of the cranes, rather than spend the money for a hotel room, but was unsuccessful in making any sales. Ernest B. Perry made a similar trip to the Exposition between December 14 and December 20, 1893; he also had a few nibbles, but made no sales.

In the midst of the worst financial crisis to affect the Industrial Works since he had assumed the presidency, James Clements' wife, Agnes Macready Clements, died, on October 8, 1893, of Bright's disease. Clements' old friend, former *Michigan Argus* editor Elihu B. Pond served as pallbearer, along with ex-Governor Alpheus Felch, Judge T. M. Cooley, E. D. Kinne, President James B. Angell, Philip Bach, Professor P.R.B. Du Pont, and Mr. Treadwell.

It seemed to James Clements that his seventy-four years weighed heavily on his shoulders, as financial conditions in the Bay City Industrial Works grew worse. Ongoing obligations at I-W were met by issuing bonds backed by the personal guarantee of Industrial Works officials, and the immediate financial crisis at the Bay City plant was alleviated. But this, as everyone knew, was only a stop-gap measure. He continued his heavy schedule of sales trips and travel from Ann Arbor to Bay City and elsewhere on Industrial Works business. November 12, 1895, found him at home in Ann Arbor, nursing a bad cold which had kept him housebound for several days. Before going to bed that evening, he went over in his mind some of the things that needed doing at the plant, and he took the time to write a letter to his son in Bay City.

November 12, 1895

W. L. Clements

My dear son,

I am very sorry to hear Jessie is so poorly. I don't think you are to blame, for you have done everything you could for her comfort and quiet.

In relation to the Pullman Crane I would sell if I could do so without a loss. I don't think that I can go over to Chicago this week; at least it will be Friday before I can go. I have got a bad cold, getting my feet wet in Bay City, have not been out since I came home. But hope to do so tomorrow. If anybody except Nichols goes to Chicago, Wells or Perry will have to go at this time. You had better change the specification from the friction to possitive [sic] clutch or any other changes needed before signing any contract. There is very little in the price book about that machine. I have returned all the papers, not having any use for them here.

Your affectionately,

James Clements

James Clements[29] died later that night. As the account in the *Washtenaw Evening Times* the next day told it,

He retired to bed in good season, but later as his daughter [Mary A. Clements] passed his door she thought he breathed heavily, and going into the room found him unconscious. A physician was telephoned for but before he could arrive Mr. Clements had breathed his last. His death is believed to have been caused by an apoplectic or paralytic stroke.[30]

James Clements' death precipitated a series of crises at the Industrial Works. As summarized in the Industrial Works Fiftieth Anniversary booklet,

Stockholders were generally dissatisfied and the directors were called upon to make good their guarantee of the bonds. Somehow it was done, new stock being issued to the men who retired the bonds, with the result that within the year the entire assets and liabilities, principally the latter, had been forced into the hands of two men, Mr. W. L. Clements and Mr. C. R. Wells.

Mr. Perry had in the meantime become so necessary to the company that he was, at the time of this reorganization, taken into the firm. The final division of duties was most logical, Mr. Clements succeeding his father to the presidency, Mr. Wells continuing as Secretary and Treasurer, and Mr. Perry becoming General Manager.

Under the astute management of the Clements-Wells-Perry triumvirate the Industrial Works entered a long period of growth and profit. I-W became world famous for the heavy-duty crane that William L. Clements helped build in 1882. The medal-winning 1893 twelve-ton crane developed from the prototype 1882 crane was soon dwarfed by giant cranes of increased capacity, culminating in the two-hundred-ton crane of 1923 that

could reach over a prostrate locomotive, and, with cables and hooks protruding from a curved snout, pick up the whole mass bodily and place it somewhere else or roll away with it suspended.[31]

As for William L. Clements, he seems to have taken a less active part in the operations of the Industrial Works as he grew older, even though he remained president until his retirement in 1924. Ernest B. Perry would seem to have been the moving force behind the profitable operation of the Works, leaving Clements free to a great extent to pursue other interests. Chief among these, beginning in the early years of the twentieth century, was the building of a remarkable collection of Americana.

NOTES

1 Ann Arbor, *City Directory*, 1872, pp. 66–67.
2 Clements, 'Sketch of the Life of Judge Isaac Marston,' *Michigan History*, I (July, 1917), 5.

34

3   Henry Alloway, 'Bye the Bye in Wall Street,' *Wall Street Journal*, January 15, 1935.

4   This essay is to be found in many editions. cf. Thomas Carlyle, 'Inaugural Address at Edinburgh,' in his *Works*, Centenary edition. New York, AMS Press, 1969, v. 29, 449–83.

5   Randolph G. Adams to Miss Larson of the Business Historical Society, April 4, 1938.

6   'Memorandum of a conference between Mr. Clements and Mr. Adams at the Jennings Hospital, Detroit, October 31, 1934.' WLCL, 'Ruthven file, Clements Will I.'

7   *Regents' Proceedings*, 1870–76, p. 203.

8   Michigan. University. *Calendar*, 1878–79, p. 12.

9   These notebooks are in the WLCL.

10 M. E. Cooley to W. F. Russel, May 21, 1926, in 'Clinton Enquiry File,' WLCL.

11 T. M. Cooley, Diary, January 22, 1882.

12 *Ibid.*, February 5, 1882.

13 James Clements to Cooley, March 30, 1882, Cooley Papers.

14 *Ibid.*, April 12, 1882.

15 Industrial Works, *Fiftieth Anniversary booklet*.

16 Judge Cooley notes in his diary entry for May 15, 1883, that James Clements 'has just returned from New York where he had been on business connected with supply of machinery for the N.Y. Central R. R. Co.'

17 Cooley Papers.

18 Cooley Diary, February 25, 1883. The individual referred to may be Mr. Dill, 'not only a good mechanic, but quite an inventive genius,' who according to the I–W *Fiftieth Anniversary booklet* came to I–W as superintendent about this time from *Toronto*.

19 Cooley, Diary, July 16, 1883; August 26, 1883; August 27, 1883.

20 Cooley, Diary, July 30, 1884.

21 *Ibid.*, November 30, 1884.

22 Industrial Works, *Fiftieth Anniversary booklet*.

23 Cooley, Diary, September 4, 1886.

24 Cooley Papers. Photostat in WLCL, Clements folder.

25 Quotations and information on the Young-Clements wedding are taken from five different unidentified Pittsburgh newspaper accounts of the event, in Jessie Y. Clements' scrapbook, belonging to her daughter, Betty C. Finkenstaedt, Hyannisport, Massachusetts.

26   Cooley, Diary, April 22, 1888.

27   Industrial Works, *Fiftieth Anniversary booklet*.

28   Jennings B. Sanders, *A College History of the United States*. Vol. II: *1865 to the Present* (Evanston, Ill.: Row, Peterson, 1962), p. 38.

29   James Clements to William Clements, November 12, 1895, Clements folder, WLCL.

30   *Washtenaw Evening Times*, November 13, 1895.

31   Herbert G. Watkins, 'Memories of a Michigan Town,' *Bay City Times*, August 14, 1949, p. 7.

II

THE MAKING OF A BIBLIOMANIAC

In October, 1924, more than forty years after his graduation, William Lawrence Clements, recent donor of a great collection of Americana to The University of Michigan, was asked to address the Michigan Library Association. He took this opportunity to analyze himself as well as his collection, and concluded that he might well have contracted a fully developed case of bibliomania. With a touch of wry humor, he proceeded to classify the symptoms of the disease, first described, as he pointed out, by that incurable bibliomaniac Thomas Frognall Dibdin in 1809.

If a man is even moderately enthusiastic, and has actually collected a sufficient number of books to make a foundation of a library on a specific subject, he, by general understanding among his co-sufferers, has been inoculated with the disease and has a case of Bibliomania, the severity of which increases or decreases in direct proportion to the patient's enthusiasm and self-sacrifice to attain the end he has in view. Friends of the patient look upon him pos-

sibly with sympathy, but always with an eye of pity, and members of his family speak of his trouble with indignation and sometimes shame, if his excesses in purchasing rare books, even though entirely within his subject, encroach in any way upon the normal activities of the family and upon the expenses connected therewith. For these reasons, I believe the genuine book collector ... has grown of necessity to be a timid individual in the eyes of his friends, though he may at an important sale of books surprise all by his boldness. He will even seek the craftiest methods of depositing books on the shelves of his library. Before becoming addicted myself, I can well remember how one of the first bibliomaniacs I knew used to come home with a loaf of bread under one arm, and a book concealed in his coat pocket.[1]

Bay City, a raw and hustling lumbering and industrial town in the late nineteenth century, was an unlikely place to uncover a full-fledged bibliomaniac, and Aaron J. Cooke, a small, middle-aged dry-goods store owner, hardly a likely prospect. But as William Clements made 'the acquaintance, the closer acquaintance, and finally ... the friendship of Mr. A. J. Cooke,'[2] he discovered a man with a consuming passion wholly unrelated to mundane matters of carpets and linoleums, a man who used his buying trips to New York City to haunt rare book shops and to attend auctions, a man who kept a quotation from Erasmus over one of his bookcases, 'If I have any money, I buy books; if there is any left, I buy food and clothes for the family.'

Aaron J. Cooke had come to Bay City two years before James Clements had arrived to set up the Gas Company, in 1866. A veteran of the Civil War, he had been employed when he was sixteen by a carpet merchant in Lyons, N.Y. 'with a flair for rare books and laces,' who loaned him books and encouraged his reading.[3] In Bay City, he and a Mr. Langworthy established

38

the firm which later became Cooke & Co. On trips to New York for his firm

he often bought books, many of which he sold to his friends for just what he had paid for them. With this money, like a revolving fund, he bought more books. . . . He wanted people to appreciate good books and he spread the gospel by making available, at cost, a type of books [sic] otherwise unavailable in a very small midwestern town.[4]

Cooke also formed a fine library of his own, rich in Americana and other volumes from the sales of Brinley, Barlow, Menzies, and other great nineteenth-century book collectors. This library was his chief delight.

Together with a local banker, Byron E. Warren, Cooke started the first circulating library in Bay City three years after his arrival. By the time William L. Clements came to know Aaron Cooke, the Bay City Library Association had been merged with the Board of Education Library to form the Bay City Public Library. Cooke was, not unnaturally, one of the original members of the Board of Trustees, serving in this capacity until he was appointed Librarian in 1898.

Cooke's daughter, Fanny Cooke McCabe, said that books went with her father to his dry-goods stores and that he used to read to his clerks on rainy days when business was slack. Cooke found his most notable convert, however, in the youthful industrialist William L. Clements, who 'frequently . . . would call at the Cooke home at Madison and 10th and be taken by Mr. Cooke to his library on the second floor for their discussion . . . After one of these occasions, Mr. Cooke predicted that Mr. Clements would go far in his knowledge of books.'[5]

But old age, with its attendant pains and illness, crept upon

Aaron J. Cooke, and by May, 1904, he asked the Public Library Board to accept his resignation as Librarian. This they refused to do, tendering him instead a four-month paid vacation in the hope that he would regain his health. He was back at his post in the library by October, little better for the rest, and he resigned from the library two years later. But Cooke had already made a more painful decision. In 1903, 'with regret and sadness never to be forgotten, he confided the collection he had been many years in forming to [William L. Clements].'[6] Heading the list of titles which he was turning over to Clements was a short poem in his own handwriting:

Books I have loved so well, my love so true
Tells me 'tis time that I should part from you,
No longer, selfish, hoard and use you not,
Nor leave you in the unlettered dark to rot,
But into alien keeping you ensign –
Hands that love books, fear not, no less than mine.[7]

Clements considered this first major acquisition the foundation of his library of Americana. When he gave his library to The University of Michigan twenty years later, he said of Cooke's collection,

It contained about a thousand volumes, mostly well selected histo-
ries of the thirteen original states, together with a few books of
discovery using Hakluyt of the year 1600 and the Eden of 1577 as
focal books. Many of these volumes were from the library of
William Menzies, sold in 1875 [sic. November, 1876] and those
who know about his books will realize that these acquisitions were
sure to be most beautiful and perfect copies . . . There was a har-
mony and method in the formation of the Cooke collection which

40

study revealed, and interest in it was soon strengthened. Under Mr. Cooke's guidance, until his death [in November, 1907], the Library was conservatively added to whenever important books were offered in the auction sales or book market.[8]

Without doubt Aaron J. Cooke influenced Clements' later collecting activities in the field of Americana. A check of auction records and book dealers' invoices in the Clements Papers for purchases before 1903 show that, although he had caught the fascination of reading auction catalogs and submitting bids and although he frequented bookstores on trips that took him to New York and other cities, he had no fixed direction or purpose in his book buying. Beginning June 8, 1897, the date of the earliest invoice, he submitted bids to Bangs and Company, auctioneers, of New York City. Bangs' invoices for 1897 and 1898 record numerous small purchases of miscellaneous books, including such widely diverse authors as Hans Christian Andersen, Charles Darwin, Henry Fielding, Oliver Goldsmith, Washington Irving, James Anthony Froude, and Shakespeare, well-chosen standard authors typically to be found in the usual nineteenth-century 'gentleman's library.' Clements paid between two and three dollars per volume on an average for his early auction purchases, which in 1898 totalled approximately $200.

This same period saw similar transactions, small purchases of miscellaneous books, from Charles F. Libbie and Company, Boston auctioneers. Following the pattern set by his mentor, Clements evidently bought books on consignment for Bay City friends on occasion; a note in his handwriting on the Libbie invoice for May 3, 1898, indicates that '$30.00 of the above [total bill of $43.13] pd. by H[enry] Clements,' William Clements' older brother, a Bay City resident. In a similar fashion, eleven items totalling $230.67 purchased at an auction of 'Elegant, rare, and curious books,' Bangs and Company, April 10, 1901, were divided among E. B. Perry, W. L. Clements, his brother Henry Clements, and a Mr. Norris, all of Bay City. An idea of the extent of Clements' early book purchases may be gained from the fact that by May 23, 1901, two years before he acquired Cooke's collection, Clements' personal library, composed principally of miscellaneous standard authors, was of such size and value that he insured it for $1,500.

In 1899, Clements became one of the directors of the First National Bank of Bay City. He must have been well acquainted with Byron E. Warren, cashier and director, friend of Aaron J. Cooke, and collector of Washingtoniana. Sometime during this early period, Warren sold Clements sixteen signed letters, including autographs of George Washington, Samuel Huntington, Lafayette, Jefferson, Bushrod Washington, James Madison, Aaron Burr, and Alexander Hamilton, for a total of $68.50. Also included in the transaction were twenty books, including ten from the library of William Menzies, dealing with George Washington and dated between 1800 and 1879, for $107.25. Six hundred and twenty-four examples of English etchings and engravings at $521.93 brought the total bill to $697.68.

After he purchased the Cooke library of Americana in 1903, William Clements' book-buying habits underwent a rather dramatic change. At the Anderson Auction Company's March 16, 1904, sale of 'Choice and fine books including a small collection of Rare Americana,' Clements acquired a set of books for $20.70 which marks the beginning of his serious study of the bibliography of Americana; this was Sabin's *Dictionary of Books Relating to America*, parts 1–50 in nine volumes. The auction catalog noted that the list price was $250, so without doubt Clements felt he had acquired a bargain. And indeed he had, as Sabin and other bibliographies of Americana became his familiar companions and guides in the furtherance of his bibliographic education.

During this same month, Clements made his first purchase from the firm of Francis P. Harper, New York City. He may very well at this time have met Francis Harper's partner and younger brother, Lathrop Colgate Harper, who was to have a decisive influence a few years later on the growth and direction of his collection. From the Harper brothers Clements bought Major André's narrative for $40 and the Grolier Club Washington portraits for $50, both substantial acquisitions.

Within two weeks he had made a fairly extensive purchase of books on American history from C. F. Libbie, Boston auctioneers, who sold the library of Alfred S. Manson on April 6, 1904. At this sale he acquired two Washington portraits and Peter Force's *Tracts* (Washington, 1836), together with a number of reprints and late nineteenth-century secondary works on New England colonial history.

Although the records do not show such acquisitions at this time, William L. Clements' library evidently included some incunabula. About 1905, he met the redoubtable George D. Smith, book dealer extraordinary, the man who within the next decade was to make a permanent niche for himself as Henry E. Huntington's principal agent. Clements sold Smith a collection of incunabula.

It is likely that Clements was in Boston in February, 1905, and that he attended the sale of Arthur Mason Knapp's library at C. F. Libbie's. Here he acquired the 1625–26 five-volume *Hakluytas Posthumus; or, Purchas his Pilgrimes* ... London, W. Stansby, for $141.50. The auction catalog noted the copy as 'fine copy except map of Virginia is in facsimile.' Clements kept his first copy of *Purchas's Pilgrims*, and it remains in the Clements Library as an interesting commentary on Clements' later discriminating taste and avoidance of imperfect copies, or 'cripples', wherever possible. The catalog card for this edition notes that the volumes have 'many imperfections.'

The only transaction that has been preserved from the year 1907 is an attempted trade with A. C. McClurg, Chicago, of Peter Force's *Tracts* (1836) which Clements had acquired for $60.00, in exchange for the 1814 edition of Lewis and Clark, which McClurg listed for $60.00. McClurg was not anxious to make the trade, but he offered to trade for Coxe's *Carolina* (1826) carried in his catalog for $48.00, and to sell Clements the $60.00 Lewis and Clark outright. This proposition Clements accepted.

The McClurg transaction was the only purchase for which records have survived between 1907 and 1911. A number of factors probably served to turn Clements' mind from book collecting. Aaron J. Cooke's death in November, 1907, put an end to the friendly, informal exchange of bibliographical information so stimulating to Clements' collecting activities. But probably more important was the economic crisis. As in the financial depression of 1893, the panic of 1907 seems to have started with banking and finance, and spread to industry generally. As a director of the First National Bank and president of the Industrial Works, and a heavy stockholder in each, Clements probably felt a financial pinch. He also began the building of his beautiful home, Garra-Tigh, in Bay City at about this time. Such luxuries as rare Americana had to wait for better days.

In late summer or early fall of 1908 a chance after-dinner conversation at the home of Mr. and Mrs. James B. Shearer of Bay City precipitated a chain of events which was profoundly to affect Clements' life for the next quarter-century. George A. Marston, brother of Mrs. Shearer and Bay City attorney, was a guest at the Shearers' with William L. Clements. As Marston remembered the incident a number of years later, he said,

'Mr. Clements, why aren't you a candidate as Regent to succeed Mr. [Frank W.] Fletcher [whose term expired December 31, 1909]?' His reply was, 'George, I would rather be Regent of The University of Michigan than governor of the state or have any other position.'

Marston investigated the situation, and discovered that Judge George P. Codd was the only other new candidate for regent on the Republican tickct. Two places were open. He appealed through his brother, Thomas Frank Marston, a member of the State Board of Agriculture, to Governor Fred M. Warner for his support of Clements' candidacy. Governor Warner agreed to back Clements' nomination on the condition that Frank Marston would resign from the State Board of Agriculture if Clements were elected; Governor Warner felt that only one person from a given city should be in a state office controlling any state schools. The State Board of Agriculture at this time controlled Michigan Agricultural College (now Michigan State University). Frank Marston agreed, and he later resigned his position.

With the backing of Governor Warner, Clements' nomination at the Republican State Convention at Grand Rapids, February 12, 1909, was virtually assured. As reported by the *Ann Arbor Daily News,*

Mr. W. L. Clements . . . in whose candidacy for regent Washtenaw took a deep interest because he was an Ann Arbor boy and splendidly equipped . . . had a clear field . . . and was an easy victor by a unanimous vote.[9] *–*

William L. Clements, gratified by his nomination, wrote Claude H. Van Tyne of The University of Michigan History Department, as soon as the convention was over,

I little supposed when my name was proposed for regent . . . that there would be any results. My friends, however, pushed this matter to a finish and it seems that the only thing left is the verdict of the voters in April.[10]

The verdict of the voters on April 6, 1909, was clearly in favor of both William L. Clements and George P. Codd as new regents of The University of Michigan, with terms beginning January 1, 1910. Clements' tenure as regent lasted twenty-four years; during this period he became a powerful and moving force in University affairs.

Regent Clements' first official activities involved him in the dedication exercises for the newly completed Alumni Memorial Hall, which took place May 11, 1910, and in decisions regarding the transfer of the University art collection from the aging and overcrowded University library building to that Hall. His dual role as member of the Buildings and Grounds Committee and the Library Committee involved him in planning for proposed changes in the old library building, which for some time had proved overcrowded and a potential fire hazard. This rather routine assignment grew in the next decade into plans for a new, fireproof library building for the University, and also for a separate building to house the collection which he would give to the University. But in 1910, such plans were as yet far from Clements' thinking.

A second major responsibility was placed upon Regent Clements with the reading of a letter from the executors of the estate of former Regent Arthur Hill. By terms of Mr. Hill's will, the University had been left $200,000 for the construction of an auditorium. Regent Clements as chairman of the Buildings and Grounds Committee had overall charge of plans for the building. In the months between October, 1910, and the formal opening

46

of Hill Auditorium on June 25, 1913, he spent much time in travel, inspecting auditoriums in St. Paul, Minneapolis, Chicago, Brooklyn, and Boston, among other places. Clements regarded Albert Kahn of Detroit, the architect who had designed his spacious home in Bay City in 1908, as the most able architect in Michigan, 'a master of the art of concrete construction,'[11] and he added his strong recommendation to the Board of Regents' decision to employ Kahn for the auditorium. By September, 1911, Regent Clements and architect Kahn had settled on a plan: 'a modification of Thomas Orchestra Hall [Chicago] in its platform and stage arrangements, and . . . very similar to St. Paul Auditorium in its gallery arrangement.'[12] Overriding regental desires for a deep stage suitable for operatic and stage performances, Clements pushed through his original plan for an 'exceedingly plain structure' in which 'simplicity must be the word,'[13] and he held building costs down by careful planning and the elimination of unnecessary frills. Hill Auditorium has stood for sixty years as a monument to Clements' and Kahn's wisdom and good judgment.

Two of Clements' fellow-regents, Junius E. Beal of Ann Arbor and Lucius L. Hubbard of Houghton, Michigan, were collectors of rare books, and during the long terms of office shared by the three men they became fast friends. Beal, already on the Board of Regents when Clements began his tenure in 1910, collected incunabula. Hubbard, who joined the regents a year later to fill the unexpired term of Regent Chase Osborn, just elected Governor, had a strong collection chiefly in Americana. It would seem that Hubbard's enthusiasm revived the dormant collector's spirit in Clements and brought him again into activity in the book world.

The book collecting world may never again see a year like 1911, 'that Annus Mirabilis in American bibliographical annals,' as W. N. C. Carlton called it.[14] The dispersal of the Robert Hoe library at the Anderson Auction Company in New York City in four great sales between April, 1911, and November, 1912, caught the fancy of the public as well as the attention of the greatest collectors and dealers in the United States and abroad. Wide publicity in the popular press cast an aura of glamor about the major actors in the drama: Alfred Quaritch and Benjamin Maggs of London; Madame Theophile Belin of Paris; Dr. Joseph Baer of Frankfurt-on-Main; George D. Smith of New York; Walter M. Hill of Chicago – the world's outstanding book dealers were there for the initial bidding. Among collectors present were Beverly Chew, Brayton Ives, Harry and Joseph Widener, Henry C. Folger, and H. F. DePuy. Also present was one not yet so well known, a man of great dignity, tall, with a high forehead and piercing blue eyes, whose companion, short, stooped, with a bristling moustache and bald head, must have provided a startling contrast. The two men, Henry E. Huntington and his agent, George D. Smith, were destined to make bibliographical history that night.

As at other famous sales, there was an atmosphere of suppressed tension throughout the hall as Sidney Hodgson of London stepped up to the auctioneer's desk. . . . The climactic moment came with Item no. 269, the vellum copy of the Gutenberg Bible, and a battle of giants ensued for the possession of this incomparable rarity. Smith started with a bid of $10,000. When $20,000, the highest previous price brought by a copy of this Bible, was reached, a chorus of whispered 'oh's' and 'ah's' floated through the room. At $30,000 Quaritch dropped out, and from that point on 'GDS' and Joseph Widener wrestled mightily for the beautiful volume. When, amid a breathless silence, the great prize fell to the former for $50,000, a burst of enthusiastic applause rang throughout the

48

*hall. Then from all directions came cries of 'Who is the buyer?'
There was a quick exchange of signals between 'GDS' and the
auctioneer, followed by the latter's announcement that the
purchaser was Mr. Henry E. Huntington, whereupon the applause
was renewed with great heartiness.*[15]

The battle of the books in the Anderson Auction rooms was
watched with interest by William L. Clements and Lucius L.
Hubbard, but they took no active part in the first round of the
contest. Hubbard frankly told his New York agent, Frederick
W. Morris, before the sale that he felt that most of the items in
the first Hoe sale were beyond his means, and that he thought the
other three parts of the sale would 'contain books that come
nearer being in my class.'[16]

The second part of the Hoe sale was scheduled for January 8
and January 15, 1912. Items were on display during December
in the Anderson Auction Company's book exhibition room.
On Dececember 4, 1911, Hubbard wrote to Clements,

*Just before the last Hoe sale you expressed a wish that we might
go to New York together and look over the books. I have made
arrangements to see the books still remaining unsold, and plan
to go to New York right after the Regents' meeting and spend a
day or two book hunting. . . . It will be at least something of an
education to see so many fine books. Won't you join me, or at
least be ready to go if nothing unforseen should arise to prevent
our joint trip?*[17]

Clements responded with enthusiasm, in two letters, the first
dated December 7:

*I should indeed like to look over the balance of the Hoe collection.
. . . I have before me two catalogues . . . and there are a great*

many items in them which I would like to have but fear they will go at prices beyond what I would care to pay.

and on December 9:

I have spent two evenings looking over the Hoe catalogues. . . . It is the first time I have ever seen such a complete lot of Eliot tracts. . . .

It has occurred to me that with letters from University authorities stating that both of us were Regents of the University we could get permission to visit the J. P. Morgan collection. What do you think of getting such a letter and at least trying to examine it?[18]

The two men left for New York on December 17, armed with a letter from the custodian of the Hoe collection giving them access to the collection, and a promise of entrée to the Morgan library. The most significant event of Clements' trip with Hubbard, however, was not his inspection of the Hoe and Morgan libraries, interesting though he found them. On December 20 he reestablished his contact with Lathrop C. Harper, just starting as an independent rare book dealer. From Harper, Clements purchased seven books, all significant acquisitions in Americana, for a total of $1010 net, or $875 with discount. These included the 1620 *Declaration of the State of the Colonie and Affairs in Virginia* ($150), *Sir Francis Drake Revived*, 1626 ($250), and Thomas Morton's *New English Canaan*, 1637 ($275), a book that had caused a scandal when it first appeared and had landed its author in jail. All seven books, fine, clean, beautifully bound copies, found permanent places in the Clements Library of Americana.

Regents Clements and Hubbard returned from their bibliographical pilgrimage shortly after December 20, much interested in what they had seen of the Hoe and Morgan collections. Neither of them attended the second Hoe sale, but each submitted bids to the auctioneer. Clements wrote to Hubbard on January 6,

I am sending in a bid today upon some of the books in the Hoe collection. My bid is very conservative and I hardly expect to get anything.[19]

Hubbard also telegraphed bids on three items, but as the first week of the sale progressed, he eyed the prices the Hoe books were bringing and wrote with some discouragement,

I think ... that you can cancel your expectation if you believed you would get even a single item.[20]

Hubbard's pessimistic prediction seemed likely to be fulfilled as dealers and collectors battled prices to new highs. The press caught the excitement as the second sale began. 'Embattled hosts are spurring over the plain, the master of the lists is calling, and the tourney is well underway,' proclaimed the *New York Herald* on January 14. 'Henry of Huntington has not couched lance with any man, but they say that his shield is borne by his squire and that he gives the sinews of war. . . . The Bibliophile Bowmen are taking long shots at everything in sight.' The *Herald* continued with a concise definition of the bibliophile:

The dyed-in-the-wool bibliophile, the worshipper of the half bound calf, the vellum idolator ... invests in books because of their rarity, of the associations which they have with the past. . . . A bibliophile is a man who pays dear for the mistakes of other men

after they are dead. It is fine to fall down and give thanks before a first edition, but sweet and proper it is to have the first issue of a first edition with a mistake on the title page.[21]

But 'Henry of Huntington,' or rather his 'trusty squire' George D. Smith, was shortly to enter the field, and by the end of the second part of the Hoe auction, Smith had established himself as one of the foremost rare book dealers in the country, while his client was known as a collector to rival even the great J. P. Morgan. As at the first Hoe sale, 'GDS' was the heaviest purchaser, his successful bids totalling $152,000. Bernard Quaritch of London acquired $123,000 worth of books, including a paper copy of the Gutenberg Bible, which went for $27,500. Walter M. Hill of Chicago, agent for the Newberry and other libraries, was third heaviest buyer, with $123,000.

Among the giants at the second Hoe sale sat Lathrop C. Harper, not yet as famous as Smith, Quaritch, and Hill, but well enough known to the book buying public to take his place with the immortals caricatured by the *New York Herald* on January 14, 1912. The chief participants in the 'Bloodless Battles for Books,' Arthur Hoe, A. S. W. Rosenbach, A. Eisemann, Major E. S. Turner, Arthur Swann, George D. Smith, Bernard Quaritch, and Lathrop C. Harper, sit in solemn cartoon dignity, while the shades of Grolier, Gutenberg, and Aldus look on in benign astonishment at the prices their books have brought at auction.

As for Clements, he made four successful bids at the second Hoe sale, none of them for Americana. At the January 9 session he acquired the 1478 Nuremberg Bible, Koberger's fourth edition, for $200 and a copy of the Geneva or 'Breeches' Bible of 1583 for $65. The second session netted him a red and black vellum missal pontificales, a sixteenth-century manuscript, for

$350. Rather as an anticlimax, a $3 bid on January 18 made him the owner of Alex Dalrymple's *A Collection of English Songs* (London, 1796).

Toward the end of January, 1912, Hubbard visited Clements in Bay City on his way to Florida. When he returned to his home in Houghton in March, Hubbard wrote to the book dealer with whom he did most of his business, Robert E. Stiles of Henry Stevens, Son, and Stiles, London, asking him to send Clements a catalog.

Stiles' response, indicating that he had sent a copy of the Stevens *Rare Americana Catalogue*, was the start of Clements' dealings with the senior partner of the firm, Henry N. Stevens. Like Clements' American dealer, Lathrop C. Harper, Stevens became a trusted friend and advisor, and it was through Stevens in the 1920's that Clements acquired most of the major manuscript collections that absorbed his interest during the later period of his collection building.

Clements' experiences with sales and exhibitions in New York City had served to refocus his interest in book collecting, and Lucius Hubbard's admiration of the books already in the Bay City home, particularly the William Menzies books from the Cooke collection, may have turned his ideas seriously in the direction of concentrating on Americana. Evidently in response to a letter from Clements, Lathrop C. Harper, from whom Clements had made a substantial purchase of Americana on December 20, wrote the following April: 'I enclose a brief list of the books. I made a close guess they figure a little over $23,500.'

The list was indeed a remarkable one; it consisted of 140 books, including such key items in American history as Anne Bradstreet's *Tenth Muse* (1650) priced at $1,500; Filson's *Kentucke* (1784) without the rare map ($250); Bernard Romans'

Concise Natural History of East and West Florida (1775) for $650; Humphrey Norton's *New-England's Ensigne* (1659) for $450; Luke Fox's *Northwest Fox* (1635) and Thomas James' *Strange and Dangerous Voyage* (1633) for $450; Sir Richard Whitbourne's *A Discourse and Discovery of New-Found-Land* (1620) for $300; Adriaen Van der Donck's *Beschryvinge van Nieuw-Nederlant* (1656) for $900; Samuel Smith's *History of the Colony of Nova Caesaria, or New Jersey* (1765) for $750. An uncut, blue paper copy of William Smith's *The History of the Province of New-York* (1757) was priced at $1,500; Lescarbot's *Histoire de la Nouvelle France* (1609), $750; William Penn's *Some Account of the Province of Pennsylvania in America* (1681) for $750; Cotton Mather's *Magnalia Christi Americana* (1702), large paper copy with errata, $650; Captain John Smith's *True Travels, Adventures, and Observations* (1630) for $500; Linschoten's *Discours of Voyages into ye Easte & West Indies* (1598) for $300; John Lawson's *A New Voyage to Carolina* (1709) for $500; the 1520, 1522, and 1526 editions of Varthema's *Itinerario* for $300; Hakluyt's *Voyages* (1589) for $400; a vellum copy of François du Creux's *Historiae Canadensis* (1664) which was compiled from the yearly *Relations* of the Jesuits, for $400; nine of the famous and influential Las Casas *Tracts* (sixteenth century) for $500; Laudonnière's *L'Histoire Notable de la Florida* (1586) for $500; and Sabellico's *Enneades* (1498) in two parts for $300. Many of the volumes were large paper, uncut copies; most were handsomely bound in morocco, a number by Pratt and Riviere, and all were virtually perfect copies with no 'cripples' among them.

Clements seems to have taken only a few days to consider the list before he set off for New York City to confer personally with Harper. It was an auspicious time, as the third part of the Hoe sale was to start on April 15. But before the sale Clements and Harper had a long conference, in which they talked through Clements' plans for the future of his library. As Harper said some years later, 'When in 1912 [Clements] outlined the Clements library to me it seemed that he had visualized the impossible.'[22] But Clements with his 'impossible' dream had come to the right man at the right moment. The long list of books which Harper had sent was from the Americana library of Newbold Edgar, New York lawyer and clubman, which Harper had just purchased. By the end of his stay in New York, Clements had agreed to purchase the 140 titles from the collection, for a total of $23,555, which with a 20 percent discount came to $17,500.

Neither Harper nor Clements kept a record of the conversation in which they formulated a plan for the guidance of Clements' future collecting activities. It is evident, however, from the direction which Clements' collection took immediately thereafter, that Harper probably suggested the Elihu Dwight Church library as a model. The Church collection of approximately 2,000 titles had been virtually unknown until the Church catalog, consisting of five volumes of Americana and two volumes of English literature, came out in 1908. This catalog, made by George Watson Cole, librarian of the Church collection, included a checklist of locations of other copies of works in the collection, based on a survey of one hundred collections made by Cole in 1903. 'These catalogs ... introduced the modern science of comparative bibliography.'[23] Harper admired the Church library, considering it in many respects the ideal 'nugget' collection of Americana.

A second library, considerably larger, also served as a model from the first for Clements: the John Carter Brown Library. The two editions of the John Carter Brown Library catalog, 1865–71 and 1878–82, had made Brown's collection of Americana famous, and its influence is evident in the books that Clements early sought to add to his collection. As for Harper's opinion, 'the image of the John Carter Brown Library was behind everyone whom Mr. Harper counseled'.[24] With these two libraries of Americana as models, William Clements set the goals for his own collection of Americana.

The third part of the Robert Hoe sale started on April 15, 1912, while Clements was still in New York City. By a tragic coincidence, this same date saw the sinking of the Titanic. Among those lost with the vessel was Harry Elkins Widener, a wealthy young collector who, had he lived, might have rivaled Huntington in the range and scope of his activity.

Clements evidently attended at least the first two days of the Hoe sale with Harper, who as his agent procured three Bibles for him. On April 17, Clements and Harper drew up the formal agreement for the sale of the Newbold Edgar collection. Presumably Clements then left New York and did not attend the final days of the sale. Harper wrote to him on April 27, 1912;

The Hoe Sale is over and the high prices maintained until the end. . . . I secured for you however lot 2057, Antiphonarium, for $175.00 which was very cheap.[25]

With this trip, Clements laid the foundation for an association with Harper beyond the ordinary customer-dealer relationship. Clements learned to trust Harper implicitly; he sought his advice through the years on most of his major purchases even when he was buying from other dealers; Harper in his turn gave freely of his vast erudition. As he said many years later to Randolph G. Adams, first Director of the Clements Library,

When one sees the Library and knows what is being done you can realize what a remarkable man Mr. Clements is. . . . And I

56

who both admire and love him, feel very grateful to you for the important part you are playing in it all.[26]

The rest of the year 1912 saw a steady increase in Clements' additions to his collection. From Harper stock in October he acquired sixty-eight items totalling $3,000, including Smith's *History of Virginia* (1632), $290; Lescarbot's *Nova Francia* in English translation (1609), $270; and Cortes' *La Praeclara Narratione* (1524), $250; all significant acquisitions. The fourth Hoe sale, held in November, proved a disappointment, with desirable items bid to figures far beyond Clements' means. Among the books which he had hoped to secure was a copy of the Church catalog, which he felt he needed badly. He confided to Hubbard:

I am at present arranging for a complete and careful cataloging of the Americana in my library, and consequently I feel much in need of either this catalogue or the Carter-Brown catalogue. I can get a Carter-Brown, but I would prefer the Church.[27]

With purchases totalling close to $24,000 for the year 1912 alone, Clements had reason to feel that his collection justified a catalog, although this was not to be a reality for two more years.

The year 1913 was marked by the steady growth of Clements' collection, with the addition of some significant rarities. He was evidently in New York City on January 23, when he made his first transaction with one of the older dealers in rare Americana, Robert H. Dodd of Dodd and Livingston. From Dodd he purchased the 1632 edition of Champlain's *Voyages*, along with a five-volume set of the John Carter Brown Library catalog, for $775. As he had mentioned to Hubbard, the Brown catalog together with the Church catalog gave him the models he would need for his own catalog.

Two days later, Clements purchased twenty-one items from Harper for $2829.50, including Cabeza de Vaca's *Relacion* (1555), $500; Lescarbot's *Histoire de la Nouvelle France* (1618), $200; and Maximilianus' *De Moluccis Insulis* (1523), an account of Magellan's circumnavigation of the world, for $350. A note in Clements' handwriting on the invoice for these purchases indicates that he and Harper probably had a bibliographical conference regarding his collection and its catalog. As further additions to his working tools he noted, 'Would like Ford's *New England Primer*, working copy of Winsor's *History*, Hildeburn's *Bibliography of Pennsylvania, Bibliography of New France*'.[28]

The sale of the Edward N. Crane library of Americana at the George H. Richmond Literature Company, New York City, on March 24, 1913, was one of the most important rare book auctions held in the United States that year. Harper served as Clements' agent, acquiring fourteen items for him, including three rarities: Champlain's first *Voyages* (1613), $955; Gabriel Thomas' *Historical and Geographical Account of the Province and Country of Pennsylvania and of West-New-Jersey in America* (1698), $745; and Roger Williams' *The Bloody Tenent Yet More Bloody* (1652), $440.

The dispersal of the Henry Huth library by Sotheby and Company, auctioneers, in London between 1911 and 1920 was an event at least as important to book dealers and collectors as were the Hoe sales in New York. Clements made many of his finest acquisitions either directly from the Huth auctions or by purchase from dealers' stock after the sales. Harper, in London to attend the sale, served as Clements' agent and managed to secure four highly desirable items for his client; George Fox's *An Answer to Several New Laws and Orders Made by the Rulers of Boston in New England* (1678), $101.75; William

Hilton's *A Relation of a Discovery Lately Made on the Coast of Florida* (1664), $750; Robert Hayman's *Quodlibets* (1628), $264; and one of the star items of the Huth library, the Latin (Gabriel Sanchez) translation of the Columbus letter to the Spanish Court, published in Rome by Stephan Plannck, in 1493.

The Columbus letter came into Harper's hands in a rather roundabout fashion. Offered for sale at the second Huth auction beginning June 5, 1912, it was purchased by B. F. Stevens & Brown, London, for £210. When Clements, who had been introduced to Stevens & Brown by Theodore W. Koch, University of Michigan Librarian, in January, 1913, inquired as to whether the firm had a set of Stevens' facsimiles available for sale, they replied that they did have such a set, in twenty-five volumes, half red morocco, for £84. As an afterthought, the next week they wrote again, offering Clements a number of items of rare Americana, among which was 'Columbus. Epistola. 4 leaves. 33 lines to a page; described by Major as the earliest edition. £350.' This was the Huth copy which they had purchased the year previous. Clements expressed interest, but other matters took his attention, and at length he received a letter from the firm stating that the 'owner' of the Columbus letter had a customer in London for it, and had removed it from the store. The mysterious 'customer' seems to have been none other than Harper, who, knowing that Clements wanted the letter, purchased it from Stevens & Brown and sent it along with the items from the third Huth sale, pricing it at $1,650.

Clements was delighted with his latest acquisition. He wrote to Stevens & Brown as soon as he received it. Noting that Harper had been Stevens & Brown's 'customer,' he said, 'I am very glad to get this letter, for while it is not the rarest possibly of the two Rome editions, it will, I believe, maintain its value'.[29]

An item that Clements also commissioned Harper to bid on at the third Huth sale was undoubtedly the star of the Huth Americana collection. This was an unassuming little quarto volume by a sixteenth-century Englishman, Thomas Hariot, a member of the first expedition to colonize Roanoke Island off North Carolina in 1585. Hariot had returned after a year on Roanoke Island and had written a description of the new territory to encourage others to venture forth. This first book by an Englishman describing the first English colony in America appeared in London in 1588 under the title *A Briefe and True Report of the New Found Land of Virginia*. Of it Henry N. Stevens said,

The little quarto volume of Hariot's Virginia is as important as it is rare, and as beautiful as it is important. Few English books of its time, 1588, surpass it in either typographic execution or literary merit.[30]

Clements himself was even more emphatic as to its value.

Hariot of 1588 is the star of all Americana, for it is such a nearly accurate and well written account of what is now the United States. For typographical execution it is unexcelled even today.[31]

Not only is Hariot's *Virginia* of 1588 significant as a historical and typographical landmark; the little volume is among the rarest of Americana. No copies are known today to be in private hands; six copies are extant, the imperfect Stevens-Lenox copy in New York Public Library, the Oxford Bodleian Library copy, the Grenville copy in the British Museum, the University of Leyden copy, the Drake-Quaritch-Kalbfleisch-Lefferts-Church copy in the Huntington Library, and the Huth copy in the third Huth sale in 1913. No copy has been sold since then.

But Harper did not obtain the Huth Hariot at the sale. Clements' limit of £1200 had been too low. A terse cable from Harper to Clements on June 12, 1913, told the story: 'Prices high. Hariot £1300. Quaritch.' Bernard Quaritch, a prominent London dealer in rare books, had obtained the prize.

Clements seems to have dropped the matter for the next few months, until a chance meeting in Philadelphia with Dr. A. S. W. Rosenbach, one of the most colorful rare book dealers of his time, brought the subject to the fore again. As he later described the meeting to Quaritch,

Some time ago I happened to be in Philadelphia and there met Dr. Rosenbach. He told me he had in his vaults the Huth copy [of Hariot's Virginia*] and made me an offer upon it, in which I was not interested. Later I understood the copy was in Chicago and I happened to hear later that it has been refused by two parties on account of the high price. Since my original bid I have had nothing to do in the matter of this book with any book dealers, excepting to hear what they had to offer.*[32]

Bernard Quaritch had found it difficult to dispose of his hard-won prize and had turned it over to other dealers on consignment. After Clements' meeting with Dr. Rosenbach, he wrote directly to Quaritch, asking if he would consider $7,500 for the book. In less than two weeks Quaritch accepted.

Clements, however, had not actually meant his feeler as a firm offer, and he wrote frantically to Harper for advice. What did Harper consider a good price for Hariot's *Virginia*, considering that it had been turned down by the John Carter Brown Library and the Edward Ayer Library on account of its high price? A prompt reply from Harper suggested that, since Quaritch seemed to be having difficulty selling the Hariot, Clements should 'make a stiff offer of £1400.'[33] But Clements meanwhile had decided that he wanted the Hariot, even at a higher figure than Harper's suggested £1400 ($7,000). He closed with Quaritch for $7500, and on May 2, he wrote Harper,

I found upon my return from New York a package from Bernard Quaritch containing Hariot's Virginia. I have examined this very carefully; it collates exactly with the Church catalog, and with the exception of some repairs in the corners of the title page and some of the headlines cut into, it seems to be a perfect copy. Quaritch purchased it for Mr. Huth, he reports to me, about sixty years ago. Livingston states that this copy was probably the Heber copy sold in 1825. The binding is a good deal faded, but this is an unimportant matter. Altogether it seems a great acquisition to my library.[34]

And indeed it was a great acquisition. It remains today the greatest single rarity in the William L. Clements Library.

As Clements' collection of Americana grew in size and importance he began thinking seriously of making a full-scale printed catalog of it. That the Church catalog with its many facsimile reproductions and full bibliographical description and collation should serve as a model for his own seems to have been taken for granted from the first. However, the best means of carrying out his ideas presented many problems. George Parker Winship, whom Clements met at the John Carter Brown Library on May 31, 1913, suggested the answer to one of them: a practical means of making title-page facsimiles. Clements had scarcely returned to Michigan when Theodore W. Koch of the University Library had a caller.

Mr. R. J. Swanton, representative of the Commercial Camera Company, Rochester, N.Y. . . . called this afternoon. . . . Their

New England representative had informed them that some member of the Board of Regents was interested in this apparatus as a means of reproducing title pages of rare books, etc. From the context of the letter I inferred that this was the outcome of your recent visit to the Carter Brown Library.[35]

Clements purchased a photostat machine, and by August he wrote to Hubbard;

I have had a man working all summer in making titles for my proposed new catalogue. I enclose a sample of a few facsimile title pages. I think there will be from four to five hundred facsimiles made before I have finished. Then will begin the collation, which I presume will take the greater part of the winter.[36]

Clements' first meeting with George Parker Winship in May had another important outcome; possibly at Winship's suggestion, Clements hired his first full-time librarian, Miss Florence Brown. Miss Brown evidently had had no professional library training or experience, and Clements suggested that she take the summer course in library science at Columbia University before coming to Bay City. But before she embarked on her studies, he wanted her to have some idea of rare books and libraries, so he asked Winship to show her the John Carter Brown Library. Miss Brown began her duties about the first of October. Her first work consisted of collating the books from Clements' collection against the Church catalog, and copying the description from Church if it fit the Clements copy, noting any variations. Each bibliographical description was typed on a separate sheet, with space left for facsimiles to be pasted in afterward. The completed entries, arranged chronologically, were fastened in three large bank ledgers. This preliminary three-volume edition was limited to three copies, an original and two carbons, one for Clements himself, one for The University of Michigan General Library, and one for Clements' most important book dealer, Lathrop C. Harper.

In February, Clements wrote to Harper,

The catalogue progresses slowly but surely. As I stated, I am having photographed and mounted the most important maps to accompany many of the books. This has been an extensive piece of work taking much time, but I think it adds a great deal to the catalogue. It is something in which Church is entirely lacking and I think is more important than the title pages.

By April Clements could say,

I am rather thinking of sending a set of my catalogues to you that we may look them over together when I am in New York and possibly at the same time consult Mr. [Wilberforce] Eames [bibliographer, New York Public Library].

Technical problems preliminary to printing the catalog occupied Clements in the next few months. He reported to Harper that he was making reduced half-tone photostats of

moderately rare but important books . . . These halftones will be reproduced in the text with brief collations and in contrast to the more important books of great rarity which will have full size . . . facsimiles reproduced on a full page with complete collations adjoining.[37]

Several catalogs of private collections, printed on a less lavish scale than the Church catalog, commended themselves to him

64

as possible models for the printed catalog. He noted with admiration the typography of the Brayton Ives catalog printed by Theodore Lowe DeVinne, but he preferred his own half-tone photostatic title page reproductions to the Ives catalog's exact line electrotype face setting of title pages. By August, Clements was able to report that

Miss Browne [sic] has completed the collations of all the rare books and the card catalogue has been completed of others belonging to the collection. The facsimiles have been made and altogether the work is now completed up to the critical and analytical part. ... I think up to this point the work has been very thoroughly done. I am not sure, however, how well she is prepared to do the critical work.[38]

George Parker Winship had warned Clements of this difficulty the year before in Providence. Making detailed bibliographical descriptions of rare books, especially with the Church catalog as a model, was comparatively easy, but Clements' dream was to go beyond Church and to appraise the books in his collection from a critical and historical standpoint, not only as rare artifacts but as textually important documents. 'Appraisal,' warned Winship, 'has been the dream of every catalogue maker I ever talked with, but I do not think of a case where it has been done satisfactorily.'[39]

And this difficulty, together with the expense of printing, seems to have brought the project to a halt, although it remained in Clements' mind as something he would like to do for many years. The European war by the fall of 1914 was seriously affecting business in the United States. Economic problems caused Clements to curtail his book buying. The printing of the full-scale facsimile catalog would have to wait for better days.

But a request by the Michigan Historical Commission to see his collection made the printing of a brief checklist of the most significant rarities seem desirable. Using the titles collated for his facsimile catalog as a basis, Clements said,

I am having a list made of about 400 of the most important books I have. I intend to print a few copies especially for the Michigan Historical Commission which I expect to entertain in Bay City.[40]

In November, the catalog appeared, beautifully printed on deckle-edged rag bond, and illustrated with a photograph of Clements' spacious oak-beamed library at his home, Garra-Tigh. Entitled *Uncommon, Scarce and Rare Books relating to American History during the Discovery and Colonial Periods, together with other Americana from the Library of William L. Clements, Bay City, Michigan,* it was not the catalog Clements had envisioned when he began, but it served as an impressive introduction to the scope of his collection, known hitherto to only a few people. It included approximately 400 titles out of his collection of about three thousand books. These were arranged chronologically under the general headings 'Discovery and Colonization Periods,' 'Religious Works,' 'French and Indian War,' 'Poetry and Drama,' 'Indians,' 'Pennsylvania and Other Colonies, Provinces, or States,' 'Colonial Laws and Charters,' 'The Revolution,' 'Travel in North America and Early Western History,' 'Washingtoniana,' 'The More Important Historical Collections and Transactions Relating to American History,' and 'Bibliography of American History.'

As 'appropriate to the unsatisfied effort of any would-be collector of Americana,' Clements quoted Sabin's phrase from the title page of his *Dictionary of America*, 'A painful work it is, I'll assure you, and more than difficult, wherein what toyle hath

66

been taken, as no man thinketh, so no man believeth, but he hath made the triall.' Clements might well, at that point, as had Sabin, have been referring to the trials attendant on catalog making.[41]

The members of the Michigan Historical Commission met at Clements' home all day on December 2, 1914. Clements described the event to Harper the next week.

After holding a business session during the morning they spent the afternoon examining the library and in the evening we had a dinner and reception. All went off beautifully and I think . . . altogether it was an enjoyable occasion . . .

The members of the Commission are all well informed on early Americana. Each of them has a subject which he has especially studied, and altogether I never met a body of men who were so interesting. Everyone of them has written something about the subject in which he is most interested, and while my collection is not in line with the work that any of them have done, yet I am sure the library was intensely interesting to them.[42]

NOTES

1   W. L. Clements, 'Some Rare Americana,' *Michigan Library Bulletin,* XVI (January-February, 1925), 3.

2   Clements, 'Some Rare Americana,' p. 3.
WC to A. E. Newton, March 29, 1930, MHC #2.

3   [Agatha Jennison Greene?] 'Biography of Aaron J. Cooke,' typescript [1930?], MHC #9.

4   James Shearer II, 'Bay City and the Clements Library,' *Michigan History Magazine,* XXXVII (September, 1954), 257.

5   George Wight Cooke, A. J. Cooke's son, quoted by James Shearer II, 'Bay City and the Clements Library,' p. 262.

6   Clements, 'Some Rare Americana,' p. 4.

7   The list, with Cooke's poem, is in Clements Papers, v. 11. The books on the list are recorded, presumably in Cooke's handwriting, in such an informal fashion that it is impossible to ascertain exact editions or titles which were included in the transaction. Prices are included, and are extremely reasonable, as, for example, 'Drake-Indians, $9.25; Las Casas – Voyages & Discoveries, $15.; 2 Hakluyt, $85.; New England Primer, no charge; Columbus letter, $1.50; Mourt's Relation, $3.25; Columbus Landfall, $1.; Hariot – Virginia, $20; Brereton's Virginia, $1.50; Hutchinson – Mass. Bay, $1.85; Hutchinson – Papers, $16.50 Durrett – Filson, $1.20; Eden, 1st 3 Eng. books. $4.50,' etc. Also included are two cancelled checks from Clements to Cooke, dated December 23, 1904, and February 23, 1905, totaling $487.35. The list in the Clements papers is evidently only a part of the total number of books Cooke sold to Clements. It totals approximately 500 books, and Clements said Cooke sold him about 1,000.

8   W. L. Clements, *The William L. Clements Library of Americana at The University of Michigan* (Ann Arbor: The University, 1923), p.v.

9   'Republican State Convention at Grand Rapids,' *Ann Arbor Daily News*, February 13, 1909, p. 2.

10   WC to Van Tyne, February 15, 1909, Van Tyne Papers, MHC.

11   WC to Hutchins, March 18, 1911, Hutchins Papers.

12   WC to Beal, September 11, 1911, Beal Papers.

13   WC to Hutchins, March 18, 1911, Hutchins Papers.

14   W. N. C. Carlton, 'Henry Edwards Huntington, 1850–1927,' *American Collector*, IV (August, 1927), 165.

15   Carleton, 'Henry Edwards Huntington,' p. 167.

16   Hubbard to Morris, April 17, 1911, Hubbard Papers, Rare Book Division, The University of Michigan Library.

17   Hubbard to WC, December 4, 1911, Hubbard Papers, MHC.

18   Clements to Hubbard, December 7 and 9, 1911, Hubbard Papers, MHC.

19   Clements to Hubbard, January 6, 1912, Hubbard Papers, MCH.

20   Hubbard to Clements, January 11, 1912, Hubbard Papers, MHC.

21   'The Bloodless Battles for Books of the Bibliophiles,' *New York Herald*, January 14, 1912, Section III, p. 4.

22   Harper to R. G. Adams, June 26, 1928, MHC #14. Charles F. Heartman claimed that Clements even at this early date had formulated his idea of giving his collection to The University of Michigan. 'In

the spring of 1912 Mr. William L. Clements outlined to Mr. Harper his intention of forming a great historical library to be presented to the University of Michigan.' (Heartman, 'Lathrop Colgate Harper,' *The Americana Collector, I* (January, 1926), 142). If this is accurate, it is interesting to speculate that the seed of Clements' gift, not to come to fruition until 1923, might have been planted by Lucius Hubbard during his visit to Clements' home in January, 1912.

23 Gerald McDonald, 'Elihu Dwight Church,' in *Grolier 75* (New York: Grolier Club, 1959) p. 14.

24 Douglas Parsonage to Margaret Maxwell, December 9, 1970.

25 Harper to WC, April 27, 1912, Clements Papers.

26 Harper to Adams, June 26, 1928, MHC #14.

27 WC to Hubbard, November 25, 1912. Hubbard owned a copy of the Church catalog, which after some negotiation he sold Clements for the amount he paid for it, on condition that Clements would sell him his uncut copy of Lewis and Clark (1814) as part of the deal. (Hubbard to WC, November 27, 1912, Hubbard Papers, MHC.)

28 Harper invoice, January 25, 1913, Clements Papers.

29 WC to Stevens & Brown, July 28, 1913, Clements Papers. This proved to be a gross understatement, as a survey of recent auction records will demonstrate.

30 Quoted by Randolph G. Adams in his introduction to the facsimile edition of Hariot's *Virginia* (Ann Arbor: Clements Library Associates, 1951), p. xvii.

31 WC to Adams, September 30, 1925, Adams Papers.

32 WC to Quaritch, March 21, 1913, Clements Papers.

33 Harper to WC, March 16, 1914, Clements Papers.

34 WC to Harper, May 2, 1914, Clements Papers.

35 Koch to WC, June 11, 1913, Koch Papers.

36 WC to Hubbard, August 23, 1913, Hubbard Papers, MHC.

37 WC to Harper, February 25; April 2; May 27, 1914, Clements Papers.

38 WC to Harper, August 13, 1914, Clements Papers.

39 Winship to WC, June 26, 1913, Clements Papers.

40 WC to Harper, October 27, 1914, Clements Papers.

41 Clements, *Uncommon, Scarce, and Rare Books relating to American History during the Discovery and Colonial Periods* ... (Bay City, Mich., 1914), p. [2.] Hereafter referred to as Clements, Checklist, 1914. The quotation from Joseph Sabin appears on the title page

of his *A Dictionary of Books Relating to America, I* (New York: J. Sabin, 1868). Sabin was quoting Anthony à Wood, *The History and Antiquities of the Colleges and Halls in the University of Oxford* (Oxford: Clarendon Press, 1786–90), Preface.

42   WC to Harper, December 9, 1914, Clements Papers.

III

THE UNIVERSITY LIBRARIAN

More than a year before the meeting of the Michigan Historical Commission in Clements' home, William L. Jenks, a member of the Commission, had visited Clements. In January, 1914, he wrote to President Harry B. Hutchins,

Last October while in Bay City I had the pleasure of making two visits to Regent Clements' library. It is a magnificent collection, without any doubt the finest of its class in this section of the country.

In conversation with Mr. Clements upon my asking him what disposition he intended making of it he said he had thought of presenting it to the University, but expressed some fear that it might not be properly cared for and maintained. *[roman mine]*

It is, of course, obvious that such a library containing very rare and very valuable books, beautifully bound, is not adapted for the use of ordinary students, but the possession by the University of this library, taken in connection with the acquisition by

the City of Detroit of the Burton Library, would make Michigan the possessor of very unusual resources in the line of historical material, and the University would be far in the lead of any of the Western Universities.

It would seem that some arrangements could be made which would meet with reasonable requirements of Mr. Clements. The keeping of it intact as a special library, and the surrounding of it with such conditions as to care, maintenance and use, that would forever protect it.

This situation may be entirely familiar to you, but I am writing you upon the chance that it may not, and in the hope that the necessary influence can be exerted so Mr. Clements will carry out that idea and the University secure the collection.[1]

It is evident that William Clements, though he was thinking of the possibility of giving his collection to the University, had no idea at this time of erecting a separate building to house it. Nor at first did he envision its administration under anyone but the University Librarian. But Theodore W. Koch, University of Michigan Librarian since 1905, seems to have been curiously unaware of any plans for a gift to the library on the part of Regent Clements. In fact, until Clements replaced Regent Harry C. Bulkley as chairman of the Regents' Library Committee in January, 1913, it appears that Koch did not even know of Clements' interest in rare books. Despite several friendly overtures on Koch's part, Clements kept their relationship on a strictly business basis, never sharing book talk or news of his own acquisitions. For a number of reasons to be detailed later, Regent Clements neither liked nor trusted the University Librarian.

Theodore W. Koch was a scholar, a productive although not a profound writer, and a lover of books. Characterized by

President Harry B. Hutchins as 'a thoroughly educated man,' Koch had 'a wide knowledge of books and of libraries ... [was] gentlemanly, accommodating, [got] on well with the members of his staff, and [had] a keen appreciation of scholarly work.'[2] But all these sterling qualities counted for little in the eyes of Clements. As President Hutchins put it,

This gentleman is at the head of large business interests and insists upon everything with which he is connected being conducted in a businesslike way.... Naturally he is interested in library administration and was much troubled by Mr. Koch's failure to run the business side of the library in a businesslike way.[3]

Theodore Koch's apparent ineptness as a library administrator long antedated Regent Clements' tenure on the Library Committee. He failed to call regular faculty library committee meetings. He was inattentive to such housekeeping details as shabby floors and worn carpeting. But to Regent-Collector Clements, who viewed the books in his own collection as valuable artifacts to be handled only by properly accredited individuals with reverent care, Koch's seeming lack of interest in the physical condition of the books under his charge was a serious matter. Not only were the books dusty, but in many cases the bindings were in sad need of repair. And, unlike other libraries of which Regent Clements had knowledge, The University of Michigan Library had no provision for segregating the more valuable books from the rest of the collection. Clearly the situation was one that needed to be corrected before Regent Clements could consider giving his already outstanding collection of Americana to the University Library.

A small step was taken when the regents authorized funds 'for the purchase of a case or two for rare books.' But alas,

Koch failed to understand the intent of the regents' communication about the appropriation, and instead of spending the money for fireproof metal rare book cases, he spent it for fireproof cases for library records and the shelf list, much to the annoyance of the chairman of the Regents' Library Committee. That seems to have ended the matter for the year 1913, but the next year, Regent Clements tried again. At the February 18, 1914, meeting of the faculty library committee, he presented his ideas of proper rare book facilities and protection for maps in the library. Another meeting with the Faculty Library Committee on March 26 led to plans for a section of the library stacks to be set apart for a rare book section.

After the meeting, Librarian Koch busied himself with preliminary plans for the remodeling of the proposed rare book area. But his efforts to take the initiative in dealing with the Art Metal Construction Company in regard to fireproof stacks ran afoul of the adamant chairman of the Regents' Library Committee. Regent Clements obviously lacked confidence in Koch's ability to handle even a small project, and he informed Koch sharply that the Art Metal Construction Company was to deal with Mr. Marks, Superintendent of Buildings and Grounds, rather than with the librarian.

Seemingly still undaunted, Theodore Koch immediately thereafter left on a self-appointed tour of several Eastern libraries which might serve as models for the University Library's rare book conservation project. In his letters to Regent Clements following his return, he reported on ideas he had gleaned in regard to stacks and book storage for rare books. However, to all intents and purposes, his unofficial library tour was ignored in subsequent plans for remodeling.

Theodore Koch left Ann Arbor at the end of April, 1914, for Leipzig, where he had been asked by the American Library

Association to prepare the A.L.A. exhibit for the German Library Association meeting in May. He was back in the library by mid-June, having toured enough European libraries to provide himself with ammunition for a half-dozen descriptive articles and generally, according to his own account, having covered himself with glory.

But the prophet in his own country was politely ignored. Not until he read of it in the newspapers did he learn that the regents had appropriated money for further remodeling of part of the stack area for the protection of rare books. Although he wrote to Regent Clements suggesting some problems to be considered in deciding the capacity of the new section, the regent had his own ideas. 'I think,' said he to Regent Hubbard,

a combination of the vault system in closed cases will solve the problem for us. All books will be carefully protected but the rarest of them will be doubly protected by grilled door cases in each of the vault rooms.[4]

Bids were let on equipment for the proposed Treasure Room on August 25, and work went forward on the project without interruption and with a minimum of 'interference' on the part of the librarian.

By the middle of April, 1915, the remodeled quarters for 'reserved books' were ready, and Koch reported to Regent Clements that he had begun moving books into the area. Noting that catalog cards would have to be marked to show the new location of the books, he said, 'I should think that this would be part of the work of the proposed custodian or curator.'[5] If Koch hoped by this comment to learn the identity of the new curator, he was mistaken. Clements' reply was noncommittal.

'As to the administration of this section of the library,' said he to Koch, 'the Library Committee at this time is not prepared to make any definite plans.'

Perhaps the Committee had not made plans, but Regent Clements had. He had determined to appoint Professor Isaac N. Demmon, chairman of the Faculty Library Committee, long-time member of the English Department and a man who bore Theodore Koch considerable ill will. Clements acted in full realization of the problems likely to result from such an appointment. He wrote to President Hutchins,

Referring to the appointment of Professor Demmon as Curator of rare books in the library, my intention, which may or may not receive the approval of the Board, was to have Professor Demmon to take entire charge of this section of the library, and not to be dependent in any way upon Professor Koch, for I believe any association between these two men would lead to disagreement. At the same time my idea, upon consideration, was to have Professor Demmon, through his work in this department, create an interest in the rare books of English literature which the University possesses and in other branches through lectures, informal talks with advanced students and others, so that in reality this department would assume a definite line of work. [6]

As to the consequences which might arise from the friction between Koch and Demmon, Clements was not particularly concerned. He had already determined that Koch must be replaced as Librarian.

While Theodore Koch was abroad, the large-scale plan for a major library enlargement, dormant since 1910, was revived. President Hutchins appointed Professors Isaac N. Demmon and Karl E. Guthe – but not Librarian Koch – to visit

76

with a Committee of the Board of Regents several of the most modern libraries for the purpose of studying the latest improvements in library methods and in library buildings preliminary to the preparation of plans for an addition to our General Library stacks.[7]

It is possible that the library tour was deliberately planned to be carried out in Koch's absence, but one delay followed another, and the trip, scheduled originally for June, was postponed until later in the summer and then dropped until Regent Clements revived it in November. In a letter to President Hutchins, he said,

I am sure this visit will be of benefit from an administration standpoint. . . . It seems to me that our library is one of the weakest parts of the University. Considering the age of the library it is not nearly so extensive or complete as many other institutions not nearly so old.[8]

But after all his preparation, Regent Clements did not make the inspection trip with the others. He had gone to New York on business, intending to join the committee in the East. A heavy cold, together with the fact that Dr. Hubbard, who had planned also to go, was not able to be with the group, made him forego his part of the investigation.

By the end of December, Regent Clements had 'arranged with Mr. Albert Kahn to make some sketches and submit estimates.'[9] On January 7 and 8, 1915, members of the Library Committee met in Detroit in Kahn's office to consider the library plans. These were based on the new Widener Library at Harvard but were somewhat simpler in details. By the time of the January regents' meeting, Clements and Kahn were ready with floor plans, and the regents moved ahead with 'A Bill making an appropriation for a new library building and for a model school for The University of Michigan,' which they presented in February as a suggestion to the Legislature in Lansing. They asked for a total appropriation of $650,000: $350,000 for the library building, and $300,000 for the model school, half to be available in 1915 and half in 1916.

The week following the regents' meeting, Clements expressed his views to President Hutchins:

The needs of the University for a new library I believe to be urgent. The library has long been neglected and I believe the statement can be made that for a University of its age ... that it is the poorest equipped of any of its competitors. Many of its most valuable books are stored in a mill constructed, that is, highly inflammable type of building. The stacks are inadequate in capacity for proper classification or for holding the books we even now own.

Above all the Library has no professors' study rooms, or students seminary rooms, now recognized by all Universities as a prime requirement. I suppose we could assume an attitude of passiveness and use what we have, but I am profoundly convinced that we are not doing our duty as executives of the University in not doing our best to rectify these deficiencies and secure if possible a modern library building with ample stack capacity, fireproof in construction, and containing the necessary seminary and study rooms.

A further statement in the same letter refers to continued friction between Professor Demmon and Librarian Koch, and is prelude to Koch's next major, and seemingly innocent, error that was to be held against him by the regents as another example of his lack of foresight, if not downright stupidity. Clements went on,

When in Ann Arbor I had a talk with both Professor Demmon and Librarian Koch, and I impressed upon both of them the necessity of keeping out of all controversies relative to the library. . . . Librarian Koch absolutely denied Professor Demmon's statement that he, Koch, had stated that the University did not need further library facilities, but Librarian Koch stated to me in my conversation with him that he thought the sentiment of the Alumni for the old library building would oppose its demolition even for something that was better fitted for library uses and modern requirements. I exercised great patience in not stating plainly to our Librarian what I thought of such ideas. The library building was constructed after I left the University. There can be little sentiment on account of its age, and Librarian Koch knows well enough, if he knows anything about modern libraries, that it has passed its days of usefulness and efficiency.[10]

Although warned by Clements not to talk officially about the library building plans, Koch could not keep still. He may have felt that if he made a statement favoring the demolition of the old library building and the construction of a new one, he might mollify the wrath of the chairman of the Regents' Library Committee. At any rate, two weeks later he wrote Clements,

The University of Michigan Daily has asked me any number of times as to what the plan is for the remodeling and enlargement of the library building. I have consistently refused to talk for publication, but now that everybody else is talking I gave them an interview which will probably appear in tomorrow's issue.[11]

Two days later, Koch wrote again, enclosing a copy of the *Michigan Daily* article, and suggesting that copies of the article might be sent to members of the University Committee of the State Legislature as he felt that this 'might help the good work.' Regent Clements replied, giving somewhat grudging approval.

There is nothing in the article which you have written that would not be perfectly proper to publish, except that I notice Mr. Kahn's name mentioned in connection with the preliminary plans, etc. Mr. Kahn has had nothing to do with this work as an architect, other than by my special request. I think it quite inadvisable to make a statement whereby inference might be made that Mr. Kahn was to be the architect, especially at this time.[12]

Assured as he thought of Clements' approbation, Koch began to enlarge on his original plan of simply reprinting the *Michigan Daily* article of February 14. He decided to rewrite it for the *Michigan Alumnus*; the article appeared in the March, 1915, issue, just at the moment that the State Legislature was considering the University appropriation bill. But far from 'helping the good work,' it nearly wrecked the careful strategy of the regents to win legislative approval of their bill. On April 1, the unwitting Koch was called to President Hutchins' office. Unfortunately Koch had chosen to include with his article three illustrations: the Wisconsin State Historical and University Library and the Ohio State University Library as 'suggestions for Michigan's proposed new library' and a charming cut of the ivy-covered Michigan University Library building, with its clock tower and rotunda as the backdrop for two small knickered boys posed against the rail fence. Since the appearance of the article announcing the imminent demolition of this picturesque structure, Hutchins had received a torrent of protest – mostly from members of the State Legislature who

were criticizing us severely for proposing to tear down so good a building as your illustration showed the library to be .... It is a fact that [the article] did have an unfortunate influence upon several members of the Legislature.[13]

Koch's unfortunate article did not kill the University bill; on April 21, after much hard work on the part of the regents' committee, the bill was reported out of the legislative committee for the full amount. But the regents did not forget the incident. And as far as Regent Clements was concerned, he had had enough. He wrote from New York City to President Hutchins,

Professor Koch applied for the position of Curator at Harvard [after Luther Livingston's death in December, 1914. George Parker Winship had been appointed to the post by this time.] I think this would give us an opportunity to look for another man to take Professor Koch's place, and get a stronger man at the same time, and with this view, remembering your suggestion of the gentleman now assistant in Washington, I have planned to go to Washington and have a talk with him. I believe his name is Mr. Bishop, and if, upon receipt of this letter, you agree in general to the above plans, I will go to Washington and meet Mr. Bishop if you tell me where he can be found.[14]

William Warner Bishop was no stranger to The University of Michigan. An 1892 graduate of the University, he was in 1915 superintendent of the Reading Room at the Library of Congress. He knew President Hutchins well enough to ask him for a letter of recommendation in December, 1913, for a position at Columbia University. For some reason, Bishop did not after all leave his position at the Library of Congress, and just as the latest crisis involving Theodore Koch was erupting on campus, President Hutchins telegraphed him, asking him to represent The University of Michigan at the twenty-fifth anniversary of Catholic University, Washington, D.C., on April 15. Bishop was unable to accept the invitation because of a conflicting engagement, but this may have been the incident that brought his name before Regent Clements. At any rate, in response to Clements' letter, Hutchins telegraphed,

Heartily approve plan. Hope you will see Bishop. He is Superintendent of Reading Room, Library of Congress. Graduated here in 1892.[15]

Addressing the Founder's Day observance at the William L. Clements Library in 1941, Bishop recalled this first meeting with William L. Clements. He particularly remembered his visitor's penetrating knowledge of rare books and manuscripts and the searching questions that he had asked his guide on his 'attitude toward the care and consultation of these treasures intrusted ... to the superintendent of the Reading Room.' Bishop also remembered that Clements had 'hinted rather broadly that there might be a vacancy at Ann Arbor in the post of librarian of the University, but said nothing more.'[16]

Regent Clements returned to Bay City, where good news greeted him; on April 27, the University appropriations bill had passed the State Senate. Theodore Koch, unaware of Regent Clements' trip to Washington, wrote jubilantly to Regent Hubbard, expressing gratification over the granting of funds for the extension and remodeling of the University Library, and prepared to visit a number of universities 'which,' he wrote to Clements, 'will be of great help to me in my study of the problem of recent university library architecture.'[17] By the end of May, he reported that he had either visited or had written to the librarians of practically all the new university library buildings in the country, asking for suggestions.

But more than a week before this, at Regent Clements' invitation, the Board of Regents had met privately for dinner at the Detroit Athletic Club. It is fairly certain that among the university matters that came up for discussion was the problem of what to do about Theodore Wesley Koch. After the formal regents' meeting the following day, Clements wrote Regent Walter H. Sawyer,

I believe a meeting like the one in Detroit once in a while is very good for an exchange of views. I want to thank you and tell you that I greatly appreciate the action of the Board, for which you are responsible, in reposing confidence in me for a proper disposition of the Library matter. Such action puts a person on his 'mettle,' to do the best. I assure you all important matters will be referred to the Board.[18]

The regents had collectively agreed to consider Koch's dismissal, and had referred the matter to Regent Clements' committee, with power to act.

Regent Sawyer had been delegated to receive Theodore Koch's library budget reports. In March, Sawyer wrote Koch,

I received your summary of payroll distribution for the library for the month of February and was interested in the results; however, I would make the suggestion that this be further amplified by giving the detailed statement of items under each head, to whom the amount was paid, or for what it was paid. Take for instance the *heading 'Main Reading Room,' the expenditure for which was $462.50. I would itemize the expenditures under this as I have indicated above, and so on down the list. With the skeleton you have made you can supply the details which it seems to me will make the business end of the library intelligible to the Board of Regents.*[19]

But Koch was unwilling to follow these instructions; from his answer it would seem that he felt that the regents needed fewer, rather than more, details than he had presented in his report.

Sawyer evidently held his peace until Koch presented his comparative analysis at the regents' budget meeting held the day before the regents' dinner at the Detroit Athletic Club which Clements had organized for private discussion of 'university matters.' Later in the summer, Koch in a letter to Regent Sawyer reviewed what had happened.

You and I had some correspondence last February and March in regard to the matter [of library budget], and I wrote the University of Wisconsin, Minnesota, and Illinois for figures which would help us in the comparative analysis which I had in mind.

I had this material with me when I met the Library Committee of the Board of Regents at its Budget meeting in May, but the interview took a turn that made it inadvisable to present this information. In fact, I have been severely criticized for having tried to put it over the Board by quoting figures of this sort. I think you have known me long enough to know that this was farthest removed from my intentions.[20]

Sawyer's position in the matter would seem eminently reasonable. Summarizing the incident as he saw it, he said to Koch,

Sometime during the spring after my visit with you at the house, you sent me a suggestive scheme of budget distribution in your department. In reply to this I advised you that there should be further subdivision of expenditures. To this I had no reply, and in fact the idea I had in mind was not realized. My purpose in advising you as I did was not only for the relief of the budget committee, but in the interest of you and your department. It is unnecessary for me to repeat that the most annoying thing with which the budget committee has ever had to contend with was the library sheet, and there was always much unpleasant discussion of it. I had hoped to, by the suggestion which I made clear the way for a better relationship between the library administration and the board of regents. Toward this end I do not seem to have been successful, and I sincerely regret the circumstances.[21]

Two days later at the meeting of the Board of Regents, Isaac N. Demmon was officially appointed curator of rare books. Referring to other matters discussed at the meeting, Clements said to Regent Beal,

I appreciate more than I can tell the confidence reposed in me by the Board of Regents in referring the Library matter to my committee as they did. . . . I try to have no prejudices, and I assure you every matter of importance will be reported to the Board before a decision is made. . . . I think if we contemplate calling Mr. Bishop now in the Congressional Library, that his services will be most desirable. I will have something to report at the next meeting of the Board.[22]

Theodore Koch, the man most vitally concerned in the regents' deliberations, seems to have been totally unaware of their proceedings. And as the regents furthered their plans for the new library building by choosing a faculty committee consisting of Isaac N. Demmon, Dean Karl Guthe, and Professor R. M. Wenley to tour university libraries in search of ideas, the absence of the University Librarian from the committee seemed to many people inexplicable. President Hutchins in evident embarrassment wrote Regent Clements, asking, 'Do you think that Librarian Koch should be appointed [to the committee along with Professors Demmon, Guthe, and Wenley]?'[23] Clements sidestepped the question. He said,

All or any of the men referred to [Demmon, Guthe, and Wenley], making up the committee for consultation upon library matters are entirely agreeable to me. The all important conclusion to be reached is the arrangement and design for the building. I am, however, greatly in doubt as to our friend Koch. We should decide to do something relative to him very soon: Either keep him or make some arrangement to get rid of him.[24]

There is no doubt that Regent Clements, at least, had made up his mind as to what was to be done, although he continued to hedge to President Hutchins:

What to do with Mr. Koch is a most perplexing and disagreeable matter. At this time when we need the advice of a thoroughly competent librarian, we have no confidence in Mr. Koch. I am in favor of deciding the matter one way or another at an early date.

And, almost casually, he said,

I expect to be in Washington on the 24th inst. and I may have an opportunity to see Mr. Bishop while there.[25]

86

Clements left Ann Arbor immediately after the regents' meeting. William Warner Bishop described Clements' visit with him on June 24 as follows.

Late in June without any previous warning Mr. Clements appeared again in my office, asked for a private interview, and offered me, on behalf of the Regents and President Hutchins, the post of librarian of the University of Michigan, my alma mater. Naturally, I was pleased and very much surprised. He told me Mr. Koch was very far from well and was retiring from the position of librarian. I remember that I insisted that he should talk to Dr. Putnam. He demurred – said that in business when you stole a man from another firm, you kept quiet about it until the agreement was made. But he acknowledged that Dr. Hutchins had told him he ought to call on Putnam, and so he did.[26]

On his return, Regent Clements reported the results of his visit to President Hutchins.

I spent last Thursday morning [June 24] in the Congressional Library with Mr. Bishop and Mr. Putnam . . . I feel decidedly that with what is before us in the way of administration of a new library, that the abilities of Mr. Koch are far from satisfactory. The administration of his library is not up to the standard, and while it may seem in one way a cruel proposition to dismiss him, it is nevertheless true that the interests of the University demand such dismissal. We should put this dismissal to him in the best way possible, giving him leave of absence, or by any other gentle means ridding the University of his services . . .[27]

President Hutchins' reluctance to serve as hatchet man is evident in his reply:

I suppose that Librarian Koch must go. The situation is certainly an embarrassing one. I agree with you that he is not a good administrator and that it is really for the interest of the library that another man be selected. We may as well take the matter up with him without delay and have it disposed of.[28]

But the regent was determined to push the matter through to a conclusion. He replied,

Relative to our friend Mr. Koch, no action will meet with the approval of all. For my part I long for a businesslike administration of the library: a condition of things existing where the librarian is prepared to give definite information. . . . It is a disagreeable task to me I assure you, and I know it is to you.

When each member of the Board is notified by letter as to the conditions, let them express themselves fully as to our proposed action relative to Professor Koch, so that the responsibility will not rest alone with us.[29]

Upon receipt of Regent Clements' letter, President Hutchins wired each of the regents, in an attempt to set the regular regents' meeting ahead a week, to July 15. Conflicting engagements on the part of some of the regents made this impossible, so instead a meeting of the deans of the different schools and colleges, the regents' and faculty library committees, Regent Clements, and Albert A. Kahn, architect of the new library building, was called for July 15.

As the drama rose to a climax, Theodore Koch, still completely oblivious of the axe that was about to fall, prepared a communication to be submitted at the regular regents' meeting on July 22. Dated the day before Clements' special meeting on the library – to which Koch had not been invited – it read,

88

I hand you herewith a first draft of some 'Notes on recent University Library buildings with special reference to the library problem at the University of Michigan.' If it meets with your approval, I should like to continue these studies and present later an amplification containing special sections on reading rooms, work rooms, stacks, periodical rooms, public catalog rooms, seminars – similar to the section on the catalog rooms. In order to do this, I should feel it necessary to make trips to such libraries as I have not yet seen, notably Harvard and Brown. I therefore ask that I may do this at the expense of the University.[30]

On Saturday afternoon, July 17, Theodore Koch was summoned to President Hutchins' office. At the end of the interview, Koch was informed that his services were no longer needed. Later in the day Regent Clements wrote Hutchins,

I feel profoundly that we are taking the right course, and that we are making no mistake in ridding ourselves of the services of Mr. Koch. As to administration, he is a self confessed delinquent. To allow him even upon promises to continue would be a mistake, because he does not know what good administration is.[31]

At the regents' meeting, the following action was taken.

On motion of Regent Clements the following resolution was adopted – Resolved, that Librarian Theodore W. Koch be given leave of absence for the year 1915–16 with full salary.

On motion of Regent Clements the following resolution was taken. Resolved, that William W. Bishop be appointed Librarian of the University at a salary of $4,000. per annum, with the rank of full professor, to take office September 1, or as soon as possible.[32]

William Warner Bishop entered upon his duties as University Librarian in the fall of 1915 and served with distinction until his retirement in 1941. From the record, there is no doubt that Bishop was a far abler librarian than his predecessor, but he began his new position with a great advantage that Koch had lacked: the backing of the chairman of the Regents' Library Committee. In everything that Bishop tried to do, William L. Clements gave him full support.

It is interesting to speculate how successful Theodore W. Koch might have been as University Librarian had Clements encouraged him in the same fashion. Koch was appointed University Librarian at Northwestern University, Evanston, Illinois, in 1919, remaining in this position until his death in 1941. Of his career there, one of his former colleagues at The University of Michigan Library, Francis L. D. Goodrich, wrote,

When he went there he found a mediocre library attempting to serve a rapidly developing University. He left it a distinguished collection, housed in an unusually beautiful and commodious building, and administered by a competent staff, serving the needs of a large and exacting body of faculty and students.[33]

NOTES

1   Jenks to Hutchins, January 8, 1914, Hutchins Papers.

2   Hutchins to H. A. Garfield, President of Williams College, Williamstown, Mass., November 22, 1915, Hutchins Papers.

3   Hutchins to H. A. Garfield, December 6, 1915, Hutchins Papers.

4   WC to Hubbard, July 27, 1914, Hubbard Papers, MHC.

5   Koch to WC, April 14, 1915, Koch Papers.

6   WC to Hutchins, April 24, 1915, Hutchins Papers.

7   Hutchins to Demmon, May 1, 1914, Hutchins Papers.

8   WC to Hutchins, November 19, 1914, Hutchins Papers.

9   WC to Demmon, December 28, 1914, Demmon Papers.

10   WC to Hutchins, January 29, 1915, Hutchins Papers.

11   Koch to WC, February 13, 1915, Koch Papers.

12   WC to Koch, February 16, 1915, Koch Papers.

13   Hutchins to Koch, April 6, 1915, Hutchins Papers.

14   WC to Hutchins, April 24, 1915, Hutchins Papers.

15   Hutchins to WC, April 26, 1915, Hutchins Papers.

16   Bishop, 'Some recollections,' pp. 185–91.

17   Koch to WC, May 21, 1915, Koch Papers.

18   WC to Sawyer, May 25, 1915, Sawyer Papers.

19   Sawyer to Koch, March 1, 1915, Sawyer Papers.

20   Koch to Sawyer, July 19, 1915, Koch Papers.

21   Sawyer to Koch, July 20, 1915, Sawyer Papers.

22   WC to Beal, May 25, 1915, Beal Papers.

23   Hutchins to WC, June 10, 1915, Hutchins Papers.

24   WC to Hutchins, June 15, 1915, Hutchins Papers.

25   WC to Hutchins, June 18, 1915, Hutchins Papers.

26   Bishop, 'Some Recollections,' pp. 185–86.

27   WC to Hutchins, June 28, 1915, Hutchins Papers.

28   Hutchins to WC, June 30, 1915, Hutchins Papers.

29   WC to Hutchins, July 2, 1915, Hutchins Papers.

30   Koch to the Regents, July 14, 1915, Koch Papers.

31   WC to Hutchins, July 17, 1915, Hutchins Papers.

32   *Regents' Proceedings*, 1914–17, pp. 226–27. Not everyone on The University of Michigan campus agreed with the regents in the dismissal of Theodore Koch. Koch must have been gratified by a four-page expression of 'deep regret at your prospective departure, and . . . high appreciation of your work for this community' which was signed by fifty-three of The University of Michigan faculty members and given to him on his leaving Ann Arbor (Original copy of this document, undated, in Northwestern University Library Archives, Evanston, Illinois. Copy in Koch Papers, MHC).

33   Francis L. D. Goodrich, 'Theodore Wesley Koch, 1871–1941,' *College and Research Libraries*, III (December, 1941), 69.

IV

GROWTH OF THE COLLECTION, 1915–1920

The period following the appearance of Clements' 1914 check-list of his library was one of further collection building. Despite a business depression which almost immediately followed the declaration of war in 1914 by the major European powers, Clements continued to buy rarities as opportunities afforded. However, an offer by Henry N. Stevens of London that August of the rare and important Sir Francis Drake *The World Encompassed* (1628) for £105 brought much hesitation and soul-searching on Clements' part. He consulted his mentor and confidante Lathrop Harper, wondering whether he should take the book in view of the fact that the business recession had sharply curtailed his funds for book buying. Harper advised against it, suggesting the possibility that there might be something wrong with the portrait in the Stevens copy of the Drake. Further correspondence with Stevens led to his sending the Drake for Clements' inspection and to the conclusion that the question of the correctness of the inscription on the portrait – whether Latin or English – was an insoluble one. Clements' rather grudging agreement to keep the volume at this point belies his evident later pride in his new accession as a high spot in his collection.

The Lumberman's State Bank, Bay City, and the Bay County Savings Bank were consolidated on December 31, 1914, to form the Bay County Savings Bank, with William L. Clements as president. At the same time, Clements took over the presidency of the First National Bank. These new appointments not only added to his responsibilities, but they meant sharply increased financial obligations at a time when his other business interests were suffering the effects of the depression.

Under the circumstances, Henry N. Stevens' suggestion, on receipt of a copy of the 1914 library checklist, that Clements might be interested in expanding his collection to include maps was probably ill-timed. Clements considered the idea, going so fas as to have Stevens send him a list of the maps in his stock, but by the end of the year he had made up his mind not to buy. The offer of George Gardyner's *A Description of the New World* (1651) for $750 by Dr. Rosenbach of Philadelphia in April, 1915, overcame Clements' financial scruples. Gardyner's *Description*, the first book in English to describe New York, was added to the collection on May 1.

Clements' 1914 checklist of his collection had shown only one of the Jesuit Relations, Barthelmy Vimont's *Relation de ce qui s'est Passe en la Nouvelle France e's Annes 1643 & 1644* (Paris, Cramoisy, 1645), part of the Newbold Edgar collection purchased from Harper in 1912. Clements was well aware of the importance of the Jesuits to any serious collection of Americana. In his own monograph describing his collection, he said,

In gathering these little volumes containing the annual reports of the missionaries in America, it is fortunate, and an unusual condition, that here both the historian's and the collector's ambitions

harmonize. Both are intensely interested in securing the complete file for a long series of years. Historically and geographically, for a study of the period and region, they are of the greatest importance. For the collector of rare books and for the bibliographer, the search is one of engrossing interest, but disappointment is certain, for there is nowhere a complete collection of these Jesuit tracts in any single library.[1]

Late in 1914, Robert H. Dodd, an old and highly respected New York dealer in Americana, began negotiating with Clements to induce him to expand his Jesuit collection. Clements' correspondence with Dodd and other dealers as collections of Jesuit Relations and individual desiderata came on the market bulked large in importance over the next several years. Not long before he gave his collection to The University of Michigan, he wrote to J. C. McCoy of New York City, a fellow collector of Jesuit Relations, summarizing his problems and frustrations.

I rather made a mess of my collection in this direction by starting, through the advice of Mr. Dodd, some . . . years ago in trying to form at this time a worth while collection. With some eight years collecting from sales I got about 24 Relations; then, the De Puy and a little later the Edgar Relations came in [sic – on the] market, which, of course, duplicated all I had and might have added many more. After some indecision I paid a large price for the Relations in the Edgar lot which were not included in my lot . . . .

I believe it to be an extreme bibliographical mania, although I have done it, to attempt to get all of the different issues of the different editions, where in many cases the different issues of the same edition vary only in a few words or pagination. In the beginning I did not start out to do this, one Relation for the particular year was satisfactory, but with the acquirement of the Edgar lot, those early rules were cast aside. Now I seem to be in for securing every issue of every edition.

However, as Clements noted in the same letter, the bibliographical intricacies of the Jesuit Relations were as nothing compared to those confronting the De Bry collector.

When you come to De Bry, which bibliographically is infinitely more complicated than the Jesuit Relations, the same question of issues from the different editions immediately turns up. Every one of the large libraries and collectors, so far as I know, have wasted, as I look at it, an immense amount of money to satisfy bibliographical whim. De Bry is not of paramount importance historically, it is a plaything for collectors and a very expensive one.[2]

Plaything the de Bry *Voyages* may have been; expensive they certainly were, but Clements found in his pursuit of elusive variants of them a source of continued fascination to the end of his life.

It was as a by-product to Clements' search for a reasonably complete set of the Jesuit Relations that he began his large-scale collecting of De Bry. In March, 1916, he wrote Henry Stevens, inquiring whether he had a set of the Jesuits to offer him, and at the same time made a casual inquiry about De Bry. He had come to the right man, for Henry N. Stevens, with a background of forty years' study of the subject, was without doubt the greatest living bibliographical authority on the De Bry *Voyages*. Stevens in 1923 wrote an essay with the alliterative title, 'The De Bry Collector's Painful Peregrination along the Pleasant Pathway to Perfection; a Pertinent Preamble by a Bibliographic

Bibliopolist,' which he intended as an introduction to a proposed definitive bibliography of all known issues of the *Voyages*. The bibliography was never completed, but Stevens' brief essay remains as a lucid explanation of some of the problems and pitfalls awaiting the unwary collector. Published over a period of fifty-five years, from 1590 to 1644, a 'straight' set of De Bry in single editions consists of the following parts:

America series in Latin	13
India series in Latin	13
America series in German	14
India series in German	14
America Part I in English	1
America Part I in French	1
The 'Elenchus' in Latin	1
	———
	57 parts

But by the time the De Bry collector has arrived at the proud and happy stage of having secured a complete straight set, his interest has doubtless become thoroughly aroused, and then he begins to realise that he has so far barely touched the fringe of the subject, and is only at the commencement of his real quest. He finds he has merely laid the foundations, as it were, on which to build the superstruction [sic] of a really fine collection of De Bry. It suddenly dawns on him that he has caught the De Bry fever and that his 'appetite had grown by what it had fed on' and become insatiable. Having crossed the Rubicon he must needs go on and endeavour to add to his Collection every other known edition. With renewed hopes and with his ambition fired anew he again sets out in search of the 35 or 40 additional parts which constitute the Second and Third editions .... Should the collector be lucky enough to secure

*all these, he has still to acquire the numerous variations and differ-
ent issues of certain editions . . .*

*Almost every writer who has touched on the subject of De Bry
has commented on the extreme difficulty, not to say impossibility,
of making up a complete set. . . . In 1881 my father wrote . . .
'The purchaser of this remarkably fine and sound set will have laid
a solid foundation for a long life of brilliant bibliographical
quiddling about the never ending variations, a solace for old age
that was unknown to either Cicero or Cato.'*[3]

Whether Stevens regarded William Clements, whose only
substantial purchase from him up to this time had been the
Drake *World Encompassed* early in 1915, as a fit candidate for
'a long life of brilliant bibliographical quiddling about the never
ending variations,' or whether he viewed him at that moment as
merely another well-heeled fly to be enticed into his spider-
parlor, it is hard to say. In answer to Clements' query, Stevens
reported that he had on hand a set of the De Bry *American
Voyages*, parts one through nine, first series, all first editions,
'elegantly bound . . . blue morocco super extra.'[4] On this modest
base Clements and Stevens 'laid the foundations . . . on which to
build the superstructure of a really fine collection,' which, when
Clements presented his library to The University of Michigan in
1923, had grown to be one of the two or three finest and most
complete De Bry collections in the country. With 175 variants
today, it is the fifth best collection in the world.

But after his initial purchase from Stevens, Clements' first
venture into the bibliographical arena of the De Bry collector
was met with quick disappointment. In July, 1916, Stevens sent
Clements a catalog of the 'Remarkable Collection of Americana
selected from the Library of Mr. S. R. Christie-Miller of Britwell
Court, Burnham, Bucks, which is coming up for sale on August

15–17.' The Britwell Court, or Christie-Miller Americana collection, included a handsomely bound set of the De Bry *Voyages*
in 103 parts including a complete set of the Latin and German
versions in fifty-four parts. Clements asked Stevens as his agent
at the sale to bid £1800 for the set, which as he noted to William
Warner Bishop 'far exceeds prices paid for any set of De Bry in
the past. I am inclined to believe that it is a more complete lot
than is given in Church – it is certainly far better than Huth and
contains eleven more rare volumes.'[5] However, to Clements'
dismay, on the very morning of the sale the whole collection was
withdrawn from public auction, having been sold *en bloc* by
private treaty to George D. Smith acting for Henry E. Huntington. Stevens was as much annoyed as was Clements, for he and
his partner, Robert Stiles, 'had put in several weeks of work over
this sale, and had examined, collated, and valued every lot.'[6]

Aware that Huntington would incorporate only the Britwell
De Bry issues lacking in his own set, Clements wrote to George
D. Smith,

*Referring to the Christie-Miller 'Americana' which you purchased
en bloc, I should like very much to have an opportunity to inspect
these books after they arrive in New York, and if you dispose of
them in small lots, to receive your prices.*[7]

Clements knew Henry E. Huntington only from seeing him at
sales. He held him considerably in awe, knowing full well that
in any battle of the auction room, his relatively modest financial
resources would be no match for his rival's. This fact was a
matter of frustration and anguish on several occasions to Clements, as he saw once-in-a-lifetime acquisitions go to Huntington. A visit to Huntington's private library in New York City
was a privilege granted to few people. Clements was therefore

98

delighted to accept an invitation early in November to inspect the Christie-Miller collection there.

Huntington's library made a tremendous impression upon Clements. He of course had seized this opportunity to examine some of Huntington's famed Americana, noting that 'everything is so congested in this library that it is almost impossible to get a fair idea of it.'[8] But despite the crowded quarters, he found the collection

so extensive, covering such a wide scope, that no one mind can grasp the whole proposition. The Church Library, tucked in one corner, important as it is, is there but an incident.[9]

In the course of the morning Clements met Huntington's librarian, the bibliographer George Watson Cole, and learned that his surmise about the Christie-Miller De Bry had been correct; Cole was collating it with a view to incorporating the best of it in the Huntington collection. There was no chance, for this reason, for a private sale of the Christie-Miller De Bry. However, Huntington did agree to sell Clements, through Harper, six other titles, duplicates from his collection, before they were put on public auction. These were *A Relation of Maryland* (1635), $2,100; John Child's *New-Englands Jonas Cast up at London* (1647), $750; Lord Thomas West De La Warr's *Relation* (1611), $900; Great Britain's Council for Virginia, *A Declaration of the State of the Colonie* (1620), $750; Increase Mather's *A Brief History of the War with the Indians in New-England* (1676), $300; and *A Brief Description of the Province of Carolina* (1666), $1250. All were Christie-Miller copies from the Britwell Court Library.

Clements returned to New York again to inspect the Huntington Library duplicates to be sold January 25 and 26 and to enjoy 'a historical set-to' with his friends Clarence E. Brigham of the

American Antiquarian Society, Worthington C. Ford of the Massachusetts Historical Society, and Dr. John W. Jordan. His fears that Huntington would break up the Britwell De Bry were well grounded. Huntington kept the best copies of duplicates from his latest acquisition, throwing unwanted duplicates from both the Church and Christie-Miller collections on the auction block. Harper served as Clements' agent at the sale but succeeded in getting him only ten parts of the De Bry, including some Church De Bry, for $1,320.

George D. Smith bid on his own account against Harper for many of the Huntington duplicates, especially those he knew Clements wanted. Clements began negotiations with Smith in March for the De Bry that Smith had obtained at the sale. Smith, well aware that he was dealing with the only other bidder for the Huntington duplicate De Bry, refused to sell separately any of the seventy volumes he had secured.

Clements' problems were multiplied by the fact that at the time of the Huntington sale, he had contracted to purchase 104 volumes of De Bry from Stevens' stock, for £1700. Stevens, realizing that Clements, if he purchased the large lot of De Bry from Smith, would add many duplicates to his collection, advised against further negotiations with Smith. Weighing Stevens' possibly self-interested advice against his own burning desire to obtain the rarities in Smith's possession, Clements finally closed with him on March 15, 1918, noting that this purchase, with what he already owned, gave him 'the entire Huntington De Bry except no. 38, 42, and 100 in the catalogue.'[10]

The question of uniform binding for the entire set and the problem of dealing with duplicates now needed to be solved. The volumes that Stevens had sold him from stock the previous year had been unbound and badly in need of restoration. As Stevens had described them,

*I don't know whether you have ever seen any De Bry in the original
state in which it generally comes down to us. It is usually in a very
inferior and unattractive condition. The paper is very soft and is
generally more or less foxed or brown stained, so that cleaning
and sizing are almost always absolutely necessary. Very few parts
come without some defect in the plates, such as a bad impression,
or a crooked imposition in the text, or torn or defective maps, &c.
It is only by combining two or more copies, changing various
leaves, and cleaning and sizing the whole that a good perfect copy
can be obtained.[11]*

Stevens had the restoration of Clements' De Bry well in hand,
but wartime shortages of proper skins for binding made the
final steps temporarily impossible. Therefore the Stevens set
had not been delivered.

Clements favored the retention of the beautifully bound
Christie-Miller set just obtained from Smith whenever these
volumes duplicated the Stevens stock. Stevens agreed that this
was wise and suggested that the Stevens lot not be bound in
leather until all the volumes could be collated and compared to
choose the best copies. By that time, leather shortages might be
at an end and the job could be completed. But in the meantime,
Stevens suggested that their original contract, which included
the cost of refurbishing and binding in fine morocco leather, be
altered, and the amount Stevens had allowed for binding should
be eliminated. If this could be arranged, the Stevens volumes
could be delivered to Clements, and Stevens could receive his
money. He suggested that Clements should pay £1180 instead
of £1500, plus the cost for putting the copies into boards, ready
for the final leather casing. The two men agreed in the end on a
price of £1400, to include binding the lot in paper-covered
boards with leather lettering pieces, 'and with the further under-

standing that you [Stevens] will collate the 104 parts sent and supply the individual copies with proper notes.'[12]

Clements' set of De Bry, extensive though it was, still lacked the rare Elenchus volume, which included titles, prefaces, and tables of contents from the fifty-six other volumes in the set, thus forming a kind of index. In his struggle for this final, elusive capstone for his collection he found himself matched once again against Henry E. Huntington and as always in such a contest, Clements resigned himself to defeat.

The library of Frederic R. Halsey came up for sale in 1915. Strong in English literature as well as in Americana, the Halsey collection appealed to Clements not only for his own collection, but also as an opportunity for Professor Demmon to increase the strength of the new rare book collection at the University Library. Clements arranged through Robert Dodd for Demmon and himself to see the Halsey library, and this they did, traveling to New York City for the purpose on June 23.

The star item in Halsey's library, from Clements' point of view, was a fine set of De Bry formerly owned by Brayton Ives, including the rare Elenchus. Harper visited Clements during August, and they discussed the possibility of Clements' acquiring the Americana portion of the Halsey collection *en bloc*. But before Clements could begin his negotiations, Henry E. Huntington purchased the entire collection, both English literature and Americana, even though few things in the Halsey collection were new to his library.

A notice followed shortly in the *New York Times* stating that George D. Smith was to sell the duplicates from the Halsey Library. This, of course, could not be done until George Watson Cole, Huntington's librarian, had collated the collection and compared points with Huntington's own copies. When this had been completed. Clements was able to obtain the part of the

Halsey collection that had excited him on his visit to the Halsey Library: the Brayton Ives-Halsey De Bry, including the Elenchus volume.

Certainly the most interesting volume of the De Bry *Voyages* is the folio Hariot's *Virginia*, the first title in the *Grands Voyages*, published in Frankfurt in 1590, and the only one of the series to be issued in Latin, German, French, and English. Unlike the quarto Hariot, the De Bry folio Hariot was issued with copious illustrations. Of John White, the illustrator, Randolph Adams said,

John White was the first artist of English America to give us any graphic representations of America which are worth considering ... [he] was the 'camera man' of the first English colony in the confines of what is now the United States. His pictures are astonishingly good, both as art, and as reports on what he saw. ... No one in New England ever did anything comparable to this work in the first 'Virginia' colony – until the last hundred years. In other words, these pictures are not only intrinsically meritorious, but they come pretty near being unique for the colonial period.[13]

White, who was with the Roanoke expedition in 1585, painted sixty-nine pictures of plants and animals in the New World, together with a number of pictures of Indians illustrating aspects of their life and culture. De Bry used White's Indian pictures to illustrate the 1590 folio edition of Hariot's *Virginia*. It was a happy choice, and it was reprinted many times between 1590 and 1620. The Clements Library has seventeen editions of the De Bry Hariot in the four languages in which it was issued.

The Latin and German editions of the De Bry Hariot are relatively easy to procure, but Clements was not able to obtain a copy of the French until April, 1919, when George D. Smith offered it to him plus the Beckford-Hamilton Palace-Halsey-

Huntington copy of Fracan Montalboddo's *Paesi Novamente Retrouati et Novo Mondo da Alberico Vesputio Florentino Intitulato* (1507) for $5,000. The Montalboddo was the first issue of the first edition of the second printed collection of voyages, including accounts of Cadamosto, Vasco da Gama, Cabral, Columbus, Pinzon, Corte Real, and Vespucius. Clements considered it a work of highest importance;

The first edition, now of the utmost rarity, was succeeded by many later ones, so that this work became one of the most important foundations upon which was built the structure of general information.[14]

The chance to obtain both the French translation of the De Bry Hariot and the Montalboddo was not one to be passed up. But nonetheless Clements and Smith engaged in their customary bargaining, with Clements finally having the last word with a firm offer of $4500.

Once Clements had the French De Bry Hariot, his collection lacked only one significant rarity, the English edition, the scarcest of the four. His chance came with the sale of the books of Lord Taunton (1798–1869) at Sotheby's on December 2, 1920. Stevens wrote before the sale, urging Clements to place a bid on the De Bry Hariot, stating that 'no perfect copy has come into the market in modern times (except the Christie-Miller copy sold en bloc) [to Huntington].'[15] On the day of the sale Stevens, having had no word from Clements, cabled for instructions. Clements replied, 'Bid English Hariot £1500.'[16]

Stevens' partner, Robert Stiles, wrote shortly after the sale, reporting the result.

Before the sale we did not have the smallest hope of securing the book at this price, but the uncertainties of auction sales are pro-

verbial, and no one was better pleased than we were when it was quite unexpectedly knocked down to us at exactly your mark £1500. We had Quaritch beaten at £1400 and then Sabin bid £1450 to which we replied with £1500 and got it . . . .

We retained the book till today as Mr. Stevens wished to study it carefully and compare it with the famous copy in the Grenville Library, British Museum. Yours makes the fifth copy he has seen, viz. the Bodleian and another copy at Oxford, the Christie-Miller copy which went to America when G. D. Smith bought the Miller collection en bloc, and the Grenville copy. You will be pleased to hear that yours is incomparably the best of the five. . . . Your copy is sound and crisp throughout. The only defect (if defect it be) is that the Adam and Eve plate has been extended about half an inch at the bottom and that some tiny wormholes have been mended in the head line & fore margin &c probably at the time the book was rebound, perhaps about 1850.[17]

Stevens wrote shortly after Clements had received the volume.

As regards the quarto Hariot [1588] compared with the De Bry folio [1590], it is difficult to say which is the rarer of the two or the more desirable. On the whole we think the De Bry is to be preferred for the interest of the pictures, the beautiful typography, and the quaint English diction and spelling. It is given to very few men to possess them both, as in your case.[18]

A second collection of narratives of voyages, Levinus Hulsius' *Sammlung von sechs und zwanzig Schiffahrten in verschiedene fremde Lande* . . . (1598–1660), rivals De Bry in importance for the Americana collector, and, as Henry N. Stevens remarked, is equal to De Bry in bibliographical problems. The Hulsius *Sammlung* consists of twenty-six German and two Latin volumes, small quarto, unillustrated. In contrast to the large De Bry volumes, they are pocket-sized. A reasonably complete set of Hulsius is more difficult to find than a comparably complete set of De Bry, since seventeenth-century readers tended to wear out and discard the small Hulsius volumes but to preserve the handsomely illustrated folio De Bry *Voyages*. And yet for historical importance, Hulsius is probably more valuable for, unlike De Bry, Levinus Hulsius included only unpublished narratives.

Clements began his collection of Hulsius at about the time he started collecting De Bry, and again Stevens provided the nucleus of the collection. In October, 1916, Stevens wrote Clements, telling him that the Henry Huth Hulsius was being sold privately by the Huth family. The Huth set was an exceptionally fine one, a complete set, all first editions, bound in crushed crimson morocco. Stevens suggested that he should begin negotiations with the family promptly. He said,

I should open the ball at say £350 and rise if necessary to your limit. If you approve this idea, kindly cable the one word 'Proceed.'[19]

The transaction was almost too easy; Clements cabled as instructed, and on November 15, Stevens replied that he had secured Hulsius for £350.

Clements was justifiably proud of his latest acquisition, but evidently had second thoughts about the amount he had spent during the course of the year – approximately $16,000 – for additions to his collection. Speaking of the Huth Hulsius, he said to Clarence Brigham,

Someone told me the other day that such books put your collection

'on the map,' but I am sure if I keep on at this rate, I will be off the map, with the chances of the library remaining.[20]

But his misgivings were only temporary. No respectable collector of Americana would be content with a single set of Hulsius, even one which included all the first editions as did the Huth Hulsius; almost immediately Stevens offered twelve variant issues, which Clements ordered in December, 1916. The following January Stevens turned up four more volumes. The sixteen variants, handsomely bound in the best French levant morocco, were sent to Clements in June.

At the same time, Clements began correspondence with Brentano's in New York City concerning the Guggenheim Hulsius, then up for sale. Despite the fact that this set duplicated the Huth Hulsius in part, Clements agreed in February to take the set for $450. Hulsius and its bibliographical intricacies fascinated Clements; as he wrote Harper,

If a person wants to spend a rainy Sunday and forget everything else, let him take up the variations of Hulsius, as outlined in the Lenox bulletin or in Church, comparing their collations with the actual copies, and I assure you he will be occupied throughout that rainy Sunday.[21]

The Charles Leonard Frost Robinson sale was held at Anderson Galleries on April 30, 1917, in the same month that the United States declared war and three months after the Huntington duplicate sale at which Clements had fared so badly. Clements was interested in a number of items in the Robinson sale catalog. With Harper as his agent, Clements obtained eight items, including the first book relating to the Virginia and Carolina back country, the Huth copy of John Lederer's *Discoveries* (1672), for $742.50.

Before he left New York City, Clements visited George D. Smith, hoping to obtain the Christie-Miller-Huntington duplicate sale De Bry for which Smith had outbid Harper in January. Smith was not willing to part with it on terms agreeable to Clements, but while he was there Smith sold him three other important pieces of Americana. These were the rare and important first Eliot tract, *New England's First Fruits* (1643), John Winthrop's *The Humble Request of His Majesty's Loyal Subjects* (1630), and the Church copy of Edward Winslow's *Good Newes from New England* (1624).

To Clarence Brigham Clements complained, 'These are certainly rarities which I should have gotten at the [Huntington] sale instead of paying more for them at this time,'[22] but in a letter written that same day to Harper he seems to have felt that he had driven a good bargain. Of the transaction, he said,

When I was there . . . he [Smith] made me a proposition upon . . . the books . . . the total of which was over $1,000 more than he paid for them at the sale. I cut off $500 and made him an offer for the lot, which he rejected, and I supposed the matter was closed. Shortly after my return to Bay City I found the books here, with the bill made out at my proposition. My proposition [$5,000 for the three books] was but little more than he paid for them at the sale.[23]

Clements acquired one of the most significant items in his library on December 13, 1918, when Dr. Rosenbach sold him James Rosier's *True Relation of . . . the Discovery of the Land of Virginia* (1605), billing him $6,000. With this purchase, Clements had acquired the second of 'the Verie Two Eyes of New-England Historie,' so called, the other 'eye' being John Breretons' *A Briefe and True Relation of the Discoverie of the*

108

North Part of Virginia (1602). These two books are first-hand accounts of the first two expeditions to New England in 1602 and 1605. As Clements himself said, Brereton and Rosier, being 'of the greatest historical importance and well-nigh priceless to the book-collector, are rarely to be met with side by side.'[24] And probably Clements in 1918 would not have given much for his chances to acquire the companion to Rosier. He owed his acquisition of the coveted Brereton to an almost sentimental gesture on the part of the not often sentimental Dr. Rosenbach, when the Brereton came up for auction at the Alfred T. White Nugget sale in New York, February 6, 1920. Harper, who served as Clements' agent at the sale, told the story.

Dr. Rosenbach and GDS ran it [the Brereton] up to $4000 and it stood with the Doctor at that figure. I added $50. and got it. The Doctor would have given a good deal more, but he understood that you wanted it to go with his Rosier, so dropped out. This is certainly a fine book. It is equally as rare as the Rosier, and worth as much money. In addition it is the very first thing in English on New England .... It is a good large copy with the side notes untouched.[25]

Clements' collecting activities accelerated through the war years; in 1916 he said to Clarence Brighem,

All of my leisure time has been spent in investigation and collecting Americana .... I have added considerably to my collection since I saw you last summer and have other acquisitions in prospect.

In 1918, as the war drew to a climax, he wrote again,

I am adding to my Americana as fast as opportunity offers. I do not know what I would do if I did not have this interest.[26]

The year 1919 saw an expenditure of close to $60,000, with approximately $25,000 going to George D. Smith alone. Half this sum was accounted for in one major transaction involving only three books. Late in October, 1919, Clements purchased from Smith for $13,000 the Bridgewater copy of Hakluyt's *Principal Navigations* (1599–1600), the Christie-Miller copy of John Smith's *Description of New England* (1616), and the Christie-Miller copy of John Smith's *True Relation of . . . Virginia* (1608).

The three volumes were neither the most important nor the most expensive that Clements had added to his collection in the years since his 1914 checklist, but were acquired at a significant point in the fulfilllment of Clements' long-held dream: the dream of giving his collection of Americana to The University of Michigan. At this point his library totalled approximately 10,000 volumes. Clements had invested more than $400,000 in it in the years since its inception in 1903. At the September 26, 1919, Regents' meeting, Clements had informally offered his collection to the University. And now, for the first time, Clements felt free to talk openly about his plans. In writing to Smith about the Hakluyt and the two John Smiths, he said,

In the matter of the purchase of Smith's New England, Smith's True Relations, and the Bridgewater Hakluyt with the Molyneaux map, I have considered the matter very carefully and the books are of great rarity, and I would prize them very highly as additions to my library. The defects in the copies of the two Smith books might interfere with the commercial value as compared with perfect copies, but I am not proposing to sell them again.

As I have intimated, these books will be given later to the University of Michigan.[27]

NOTES

1   Clements, *The William L. Clements Library of Americana at the University of Michigan* (Ann Arbor: The University, 1923), p. 85.

2   WC to J. C. McCoy, November 28, 1921, Clements Papers.

3   Stevens, 'The De Bry Collector's Paineful Peregrination ...' MS copy in WLCL, Clements Papers, 2d alphabet. Also in *Bibliographical Essays, a Tribute to Wilberforce Eames* (Cambridge: Harvard University Press, 1924), pp. 269–276.

4   Stevens to WC, April 3, 1916, Clements Papers.

5   WC to Bishop, August 9, 1916, Bishop Papers.

6   Stevens to WC, August 22, 1916, Clements Papers.

7   WC to Smith, September 8, 1916, Clements Papers.

8   WC to Clarence E. Brigham, November 20, 1916, Clements Papers.

9   WC to George Parker Winship, November 20, 1916, Clements Papers.

10   WC to Stevens, March 15, 1918, Clements Papers.

11   Stevens to WC, April 23, 1918, Clements Papers.

12   WC to Stevens, September 18, 1918. It was Stevens' life–long ambition to complete the De Bry bibliography, with financial aid either from Clements personally or from Clements Library funds. As late as 1929, the year before Stevens' death, the Clements Library Committee of Management was still debating the possibility of financing this project (Randolph G. Adams to William Smith Mason, October 22, 1929, MHC #19.)

13   Adams to M. J. Walsh, Goodspeed's Bookstore, June 16, 1936, MHC #13.

14   Clements, *William L. Clements Library*, p. 22.

15   Stevens to WC, November 2, 1920, Clements Papers.

16   Stevens to WC, December 2, 1920; WC to Stevens, December 2, 1920, Clements Papers.

17   Stiles to WC, December 7, 1920, Clements Papers.

18   Stevens to WC, January 14, 1921, Clements Papers. George Watson Cole in 1928 cited the following locations for the 1590 English Hariot: British Museum, Bodleian Library, John Carter Brown Library, New York Public Library, Harvard University Library, William L. Clements Library, and Huntington Library. Several copies at that time, according to Cole, were unaccounted for (Cole to R. G. Adams, August 8, 1928, MHC #14.)

19   Stevens to WC, October 10, 1916, Clements Papers.

20   WC to Brigham, December 27, 1916, Clements Papers.

21   WC to Harper, March 13, 1917, Clements Papers.

22   WC to Brigham, May 16, 1917, Clements Papers.

23   WC to Harper, May 16, 1917, Clements Papers. Smith invoice, May 10, 1917, Clements Papers: The three books listed for $5,000.

24   Clements, *The William L. Clements Library*, p. 111.

25   Harper to WC, February 8, 1920, Clements Papers. Harper invoice February 9, 1920 lists price of Brereton as $4,455 (with Harper's 10 % commission). Harper also got Clements John Smith's *Advertisements for the Unexperienced Planters of New England or Anywhere* (London, J. Haviland, 1631) at the White sale for $1,575 (invoice of February 9, 1920).

26   WC to Brigham, October 26, 1916; April 24, 1918; Clements Papers.

27   WC to Smith, October 31, 1919, Clements Papers.

V

STRATEGIC PLANNING 1915-1919

In December, 1915, William L. Clements wrote to Herbert Putnam of the Library of Congress,

I cannot refrain from mentioning at this time how thankful I am that the University has secured the services of Mr. Bishop. As Chairman of the Library Committee and with the very important work ahead in designing a new library meeting the uses of a large University, I felt myself quite unequal to the task and I felt too that the old Librarian was more unequal to the occasion than any man I knew of and I had to perform the most disagreeable task of getting him out of the way. My predecessors on this Committee had known of his deficiencies and when the President put me on the Committee, I believe he thought that the belligerent act would be performed by me.

The preliminary part of the work has been nearly solved by Mr. Bishop. A great University Library Building has been designed, and in this design, the library uses for University work have been carefully considered by an examination of the principal libraries

throughout the country. I believe we shall have the best University Library in the United States when it is completed, and I cannot tell you what a relief it is to discuss library questions with a man like Mr. Bishop.[1]

Clements seems to have confided his dream of giving his library to The University of Michigan to Bishop early in their acquaintance, along with his doubts and fears as to whether his books would be accepted on Clements' terms. Clements loved his books. He valued them not only as sources of information but as objects of beauty, the rare artifacts of previous eras, still bearing about them the subtle influence of those who had used them in centuries past. Persons who did not share this feeling, those for whom a facsimile or a reprint of a sixteenth-century classic would serve as well, were anathema to Clements. According to Bishop, one of these individuals happened unfortunately to be 'a distinguished historian, long a professor at Michigan.' Not too long before Bishop arrived in Ann Arbor, this person had informed Clements emphatically 'that five dollars was enough to pay for any old book.' The professor's remark hurt; indeed the opinion of the 'distinguished historian' on this matter was taken so seriously that Bishop says that Clements at this point nearly gave up his idea of presenting his library to the University. As Bishop sized up the situation, Clements

was extremely sensitive to the criticism of men whom he regarded as experts, never dreaming that he had become far more expert in his own field than they.[2]

It is likely that the 'distinguished historian' was Claude Halstead Van Tyne, Professor and Head of the Department of History from 1911 until his death in 1930. A widely known scholar,

114

writer, and authority on the American Revolution, Van Tyne knew the depth and quality of Clements' Americana collection; he and his wife had been to Bay City to see the library on at least one occasion. But Van Tyne saw the books simply as sources of information, of value as potential research resources. As such, the books that Clements had collected at so much labor and expense were of little value in Van Tyne's eyes, because many of them had been reprinted and had long been known to scholars. Clements was aware that Van Tyne's opinion would carry weight with the regents when the time came for Clements to present his proposition to them. So it would seem that Clements deliberately set about wooing his favor and support.

A request of the History Department submitted to the Board of Regents at the May 21, 1915, meeting seemed a good opportunity for Clements to make himself useful to Van Tyne. The minutes read:

A communication from the Department of History urging the purchase of files of certain Charleston, S. C., newspapers, was on motion of Regent Bulkley, referred to the Budget Committee.[3]

Three days later, Regent Clements wrote Van Tyne,

I hope there will be found a way whereby you can secure as you desired the Charleston newspapers. Referred as it was to the Budget Committee, I think if the Library Committee will shift some of the funds which will not be needed in the near future for this purpose, the purchase can be made.[4]

Included in the same letter was a casually phrased offer, the first of a number of similar offers, to buy books for Van Tyne's use.

Another meeting of the Board of Regents was held two weeks later, at which time

On motion of Regent Hubbard, the question of the purchase of newspapers, referred at the May meeting to the Budget Committee, was referred to Regent Clements and Professor Van Tyne, with power to make this purchase at a cost not to exceed $2,000.[5]

No further action on the Charleston newspaper matter seems to have been taken during the year. But Clements continued to solicit Van Tyne's interest. In late August, 1915, he issued a four-page addendum to his 1914 checklist of Americana. One of the first persons to receive a copy was Claude Van Tyne. Van Tyne was evidently more interested, for the time being at least, in assuring himself that the new University Library building would include comfortable working quarters for him. Knowing that Regent Clements was actively concerned with plans for the new building, he wrote to inquire about the matter. After the January, 1916, regents' meeting Clements wrote,

In regard to the Library, with the construction of both wings, which will ultimately be used for stacks, I think every working Professor will have ample opportunity if he merits it, to have a quiet place to work in close proximity to the book stacks. The Board decided at the last meeting to consummate the entire Library plan, thereby giving much additional space in the future ... I know this will please you, and I had it in mind when I presented the plan to the Board.

In the same letter, he said,

I am sending you herewith under separate cover a catalog designated as 'Noteworthy Americana,' to be sold February 3rd and

116

4th. [George Washington Greene and others. Books, Broadsides, Prints, Americana, to be sold by American Art Association, New York, February 3-4, 1916]. None of the items in this lot are excessively rare, but quite a number of them seem to be important. I am going to bid on some of the items and if you have time to look over this catalog and return it to me before the 3rd, with items which you think will be of interest, I will send in bids.[6]

Van Tyne responded, and Clements acted on his requests, securing nine items, including a number of early newspapers.

At about this time the matter of the Charleston newspapers came up again, when history Professor Ulrich B. Phillips received a communication from the Charleston, South Carolina, Chamber of Commerce, owner of the papers, stating that 'sometime ago an upset price of $3,000 was placed on the books and the proposition is still outstanding.'[7] This price being half again more than the amount budgeted by the regents the previous June, Van Tyne wrote for advice to Regent Clements. Clements' reply is significant in that it is the first written statement of his plan to involve the University in building to strength in the area of American history, with the ultimate goal for him – not stated at this time – of using this strong general collection as a base for his own specialized library. Referring to the Charleston newspapers, he said,

I do not know just how badly you want these papers. If we secured them it would be the beginning of a new era in our Library in collecting old newspapers, very important historically. The collection would be a fragment and would need a great many additions to be of great value or use. The University has never, I believe, spent any money in rarities pertaining to history or any other line, possibly because they haven't had the money, but principally, I be-

117

lieve, because such matters have not been forcibly presented to the Board of Regents.

The proposed purchase of these old papers brings up for consideration and decision the lines in which the University Library shall work. I believe every library the size of Michigan should have a specialty or specialties .... Whether one of these specialties with Michigan be in American History ... or any other subject, I think they would have something which altogether would be of great use to the University and give the Library renown. Even all large libraries cannot specialize in American newspapers or almanacs, or in Americana, but I for one am in favor of the broadest consideration given our Library matters for a determination of what its future lines of work shall be. ... If it is determined that American history shall be one of the lines of development, then I am in favor of securing the Charleston papers at any reasonable price.[8]

In the next weeks, Clements reached several conclusions as to what should be done about the Charleston newspapers. He seems also to have evolved a strategy to force the regents to accept his collection of Americana on his own terms. He did not tell his plans to Van Tyne at this time, but simply said,

I hope to be able to take the initiative myself in American history matters. I have been thinking over the Charleston paper proposition and I am going to make them an offer of $2500.00 for the lot on my own account. ... I am anxious to secure them for the University. ... They will be valuable working additions to the Library of American History.

I have written Mr. Bishop today, stating that I was writing you about these matters and I also wrote him about the photostat copies of historical matters published by the American Antiquarian

118

Society, Carter Brown Library, and the Massachusetts Historical Society.[9]

On the surface, Clements was simply stating that, rather than try to increase the regents' appropriation of $2,000 for the Charleston newspapers, he would buy the papers himself. He would also pay for the photostat colonial newspapers and other material available through the New England libraries mentioned in his letter to Van Tyne, although he meant to work through Librarian Bishop. However, these items, along with the sundry pieces of Americana purchased at auction by Clements for Van Tyne, were not to be given to the University. For the present at least they were to remain the property of William L. Clements, with the understanding that eventually they might be given to the University. A resolution proposed by Regent Bulkley and passed at the March 1, 1916, regents' meeting confirmed this arrangement.

It would seem that Clements at this point had made several decisions in respect to the gift of his collection to the University. The basic problem to be solved was not merely one of persuading the Board of Regents, most of whom were hard-headed businessmen with no special predilection for rare books or for rare book collectors, to accept his collection as a gift to the University. As a condition for acceptance, he wanted the Board to agree to something never before done at Michigan: to maintain and support the growth of his collection by regular annual appropriations from the University's operating budget, in perpetuity. For this reason, the gift must be presented to the board in such a fashion that its value to the University and to the History Department for historical research would be immediately apparent. Therefore, he had deliberately added to his collection major items personally selected by the History Department and known to be useful to them. More rare and wanted items were added from time to time as Clements skilfully continued his campaign to educate the members of the History Department in the value of the Clements collection as a unique source for historical research.

Clements' plan of purchasing outright, and thus controlling, desirable acquisitions for the use of the Department of History ran afoul of a minor snag at the same regents' meeting which spelled out his custody of purchases made on behalf of the Department. The regents moved to increase their earlier appropriation for the purchase of the Charleston newspaper $500, to a total of $2500, thus removing the matter from Clements' hands, as far as financial control was concerned. At Clements' suggestion, William Warner Bishop visited Charleston, inspected the papers, and suggested that the University let its offer of $2500 stand. After further negotiations, the University acquired the desired files.

The opportunity to acquire a major collection of early American newspapers presented itself in the summer of 1916, when Clements learned that the American Antiquarian Society, Worcester, Massachusetts, was thinking of selling its extensive files of duplicates. He made a trip to Worcester during the first part of June to talk with the director, Clarence E. Brigham. This was the first time that Clements had seen the American Antiquarian Society and he was much impressed with the building. When he returned home he wrote Brigham asking for pictures of the reading room and for floor plans of the building, which he considered ' a design well adapted for advanced work in the study of history at any University.'[10] It may well be that this visit planted the seed of Clements' later decision to house his collection in a separate building. Negotiations with Brigham over the American Antiquarian Society's newspaper duplicate collection were not to be concluded until July, 1918, when approximately 3,000 volumes of eighteenth-century and early nineteenth-century American newspapers were added to the Clements library at a price of $7,000.

Meanwhile Clements began to accumulate photostat files of American newspapers so rare that he could never hope to acquire the originals. In early November, 1916, on the same trip that brought him to Huntington's library in New York, he visited the John Carter Brown Library in Providence to arrange for the photostat reproduction of the rare *Newport Mercury*. Through Bishop he ordered from the Massachusetts Historical Society in Boston photostat copies of the *Boston Newsletter*, 1704-1754. These were shipped to the University Library in installments as photostating was completed. They were bound by the University bindery and sent to Bay City between December, 1916, and July, 1919, where presumably anyone desiring to use them had to go. Clements of course paid for them.

The agreement between Bishop and Clements that the former would order in the University Library's name material such as the facsimile newspapers sets and other items of interest to the History Department, to be paid for by and to remain the property of William L. Clements, seems to have continued for a number of years. Bishop also watched for collections and individual pieces of Americana, which he regularly reported to Clements as possibilities for purchase. In March, 1917, he noted that the William Beer Collection was being offered by the Manhattan Distributing Corporation, Chicago, for $15,000. The Corporation had sent Bishop the card catalog of the collection for his inspection. He reported that it contained a few very fine pieces of Americana but that the bulk of the collection consisted of items of only moderate rarity, with many duplicates of books already in Clements' library. For this reason he thought that if

Clements were interested in the collection, he should offer less than $15,000 for it; he felt that the Corporation would probably accept a smaller sum. Legal problems involving the Beer collection caused the matter to hang fire until Clements lost interest and refused to make an offer. But in the first flush of his enthusiasm in March, 1917, he had been seriously interested in buying it. The letter he wrote to Bishop at that time is a significant statement of his thinking in regard to his plans for his own collection.

I have been thinking more about the Beer Collection of Americana as described by you in our recent interview. I will submit this matter to the Board of Regents in two ways, if you think best, and either way will be satisfactory to me . . . .

First, that we purchase the library jointly, that is, the University and myself, and the University can take such parts of this library as they desire and which relate to a period later than my general collection. . . .

Second, I would take the library entire, myself, if there will be facilities offered for careful examination and favorable terms of payment can be made. Either plan will be agreeable to me, and if the History Department is not enthusiastic and the Board does not want to spend any money at this particular time, then the second plan can be carried out.

In the whole matter of purchasing books of the kind we have been interested in, you will realize that back of all of it is my intention to negotiate the best bargain possible with the Board of Regents when I come to it. . . . If I had an entire proposition, including my own library, to turn over, . . . I should ask for a substantial sum for maintenance each year and for future additions. This, between us, will be my plan.[11]

NOTES

1   WC to Putnam, December 9, 1915, Clements Papers.
2   Bishop, 'Some Recollections of William Lawrence Clements,' p. 188.
3   *Regents' Proceedings*, 1914–1917, pp. 171–172.
4   WC to Van Tyne, May 24, 1915, Van Tyne Papers, MHC. Clements got eight items in the sale, through Stevens & Brown, London. These included four lots of pamphlets pertaining to the American Revolution, the *American Gazetteer* (5 v., 1741–62), Sheffield's *Commerce of the United States* (4 v., 1778–84), Postlethwayte's *Universal Dictionary* (3 v., 1756), and Jeffery's *American Atlas* (1776). Which if any of these were items ordered for Van Tyne's use it is impossible to say (Stevens & Brown invoice, June 24, 1915, Clements Papers.)
5   *Regents' Proceedings*, 1914–1917, p. 183.
6   WC to Van Tyne, January 26, 1916, Van Tyne Papers, MHC.
7   Charleston, S. C., Chamber of Commerce to U.B. Phillips, January 29, 1916, Van Tyne Papers, MHC.
8   WC to Van Tyne, February 4, 1916, Van Tyne Papers, MHC.
9   WC to Van Tyne, February 4, 1916, Van Tyne Papers, MHC.
10 WC to Brigham, June 20, 1916, Clements Papers.
11 WC to Bishop, March 23, 1917, Bishop Papers.

VI

THE WAR YEARS, 1917–1918

Clements started the year 1917 with a major bibliographical project, possibly inspired by his election to membership in the American Antiquarian Society the preceding year. In November, 1916, Clements visited Clarence E. Brigham at the Society headquarters in Worcester. While he was there, Brigham showed him the journal of Major Robert Rogers, kept while he had the command of Fort Michillimackinac on the mainland near the island of Mackinac in Lake Huron, between September 21, 1766, and July 3, 1767. Clements had a strong interest in the history of the Great Lakes region and a fairly good collection of source books on the subject. The idea of editing the Rogers manuscript for possible publication caught his fancy, and he offered to have photostats made of it, in order that he might 'work out a true understanding of the subject.'[1] Brigham agreed to his proposition. By the last of December he had sent Clements the photostats.

But what started out as a rather routine editing project took an unexpected twist with the sudden appearance of Miss Mary

Cochrane Rogers of Boston, great-great-granddaughter and self-appointed biographer of the redoubtable Major Robert Rogers. Miss Rogers started the year 1917 by writing an indignant letter to one William Lawrence Clements, a gentleman whose honesty of purpose she had little reason to trust, it would seem. 'I was surprised,' huffed Miss Rogers,

to learn that you have a photostat reproduction of the records [of Major Rogers] as I had made application for them early in the summer for my book which is nearly ready for the press . . . I wish to be the first to bring out my great, great grandfathers' unpublished journal . . . which I consider very valuable. . . . As I made application first for the copy I feel that through me they should first see light. I have worked a long time on my book and my grandfather who was the family oracle gave me much material.[2]

Clements replied politely and promptly to Miss Rogers, assuring her that the Rogers journal was for his own use, 'and not for publication or comment by me, excepting through [Brigham's] permission.'[3] But he wrote Brigham the same day:

I am in receipt of a rather belligerent letter from Miss Mary Cochrane Rogers, who repeatedly informs me that she is the great, great granddaughter of Major Robert Rogers of great fame. This letter is written to inform me that it would be inexpedient for me to publish or in any way comment upon the photostat manuscript copy of the Report which was sent to me recently . . . .

If I knew you slightly better I would be inclined to believe that her letter was directed to me by you as a practical joke. I might add, too, that Rogers' great, great granddaughter has inherited, I am sure, the tragical characteristics of Rogers, if I can judge.[4]

Miss Rogers, having fired the first volley of grapeshot at Clements and not in the least mollified by his attempt at conciliation, advanced next upon the bastions of the American Antiquarian Society headquarters itself. Brigham reported the encounter. She had

riled nearly all of my assistants with misstatements and faultfinding ... I only wish that I had been in the Library at the time of her visit, as I should like to have seen the exhibition which she gave of some of the worst characteristics of her noted ancestor.[5]

However, something must have been said by someone on the American Antiquarian staff to squelch Miss Rogers, for the time being at least. She subsided for the rest of the year, leaving the field to the enemy. Clements was to hear from her again.

Clements met Brigham in New York City later in January, at the time of the Huntington duplicate sale. At this time they reached an agreement whereby Clements would edit the Rogers manuscript and write an introduction which would serve as a paper to be given at a meeting of the American Antiquarian Society. Clements set to work with enthusiasm and by the next time he wrote Brigham he had formed a definite opinion of his hero. 'Rogers,' he declared, 'was a mercenary, treacherous individual.' Noting Rogers' disappearance after his court-martial and acquittal in 1768, he quipped that 'possibly he was lost in the Cocoanut Grove [a Boston nightclub evidently well known to Clements and Brigham]; at any rate I can find no trace of him after 1778.'

Major Robert Rogers and his escapades went into temporary eclipse, as other concerns claimed Clements' attention. In March he reported to Brigham that he had decided to photostat a third file of early American newspapers, continuing the project he had

126

started earlier in the year with the *Newport Mercury* and the *Boston Newsletter* for research needs of the Department of History. Some time ago, he told Brigham, he had been appointed a member of the Michigan Historical Commission, and it was the suggestion of the Commission that he reproduce the *Detroit Gazette* from 1818 to 1831. Brigham's enthusiastic endorsement was that this project would give Clements access to 'a mine of little known western history',[7] and it probably encouraged him to persevere even after he discovered that neither the Detroit Public Library nor the Burton Historical Collection in Detroit had complete files of the *Gazette*; he was forced to seek scattered issues in the Wisconsin Historical Society, the Lenox Library, the Buffalo Historical Society, and the American Antiquarian Society to complete the run of the newspaper.

Clements' election to a second term as regent on April 2, 1917, antedated the entry of the United States into the first World War by only four days. In comparison with the national turmoil, other matters seemed of secondary importance. Perhaps this feeling prompted Clements to write Bishop,

I thank you for your kind words about my re-election to the Regency. I certainly do not expect, at this time, to serve my full term. The [University] Library and its development greatly interest me and I should like to see the building completed and some other plans consummated before I retire.[8]

Although the United States did not officially enter the War until April 6, 1917, the nation had felt the impact of the struggle for survival in Europe many months before. Trans-Atlantic shipping was uncertain; when Clements tried to send Stevens in London the ten parts of the De Bry which Harper had secured for him at the Huntington Duplicate Sale on January 24, he discovered

127

that the United States Government no longer insured overseas mail shipments. The alternative, American Express insurance for his package, amounted to $300, which he considered prohibitively expensive, so he decided simply to hold the De Bry until conditions improved. Beginning March 1, 1917, Stevens began sending duplicate copies of letters to Clements in separate mails. He asked Clements to do the same, because of the possibility that ships carrying mail might never reach port.

Further letters from Stevens told of the impact of the war on the British in 1917. By mid-March, Stevens' son, Henry Stevens, Jr., was called up to make munitions; by the end of May, the firm's last male assistant was gone, leaving Robert Stiles and Henry N. Stevens to care for the business alone, assisted only by two lady clerks. But the worst was yet to come; in June, Stevens broke his leg in a bicycle accident and was laid up at home for five weeks, leaving Robert Stiles, who was elderly and far from well, to manage the firm alone.

Even before the official declaration of war, Clements had taken his stand on the side of the Allies. But with the enlistment of his youngest son, James Renville Clements, a freshman at Harvard University, in the Aviation Corps, the war became a matter of intense personal anxiety. Clements made a trip to Boston to visit James before he entered training at Marblehead, Massachusetts, about the end of April.

To George Parker Winship, Clements confessed his concern for his son's safety. He said little about his personal affairs to other people. But he demonstrated his support of the war effort by serving as chairman of the Liberty Loan Campaign in Bay County, a position that occupied much of his time and energy during the remaining months of the war, almost to the exclusion of more congenial activities. As he said of his bibliographical project started at the beginning of the year,

128

Our friend Major Rogers is simply sleeping for a short time after a temporary resurrection. Some day he will shine forth in all his glory again by the publication of an article which will confirm the opinion that he was a constant rascal. It is pretty hard in these days, with exciting war news and other things, to settle down to even a little work on such a poor subject.[9]

A fishing trip to Canada with William Warner Bishop at the end of August, 1917, served as a pleasant interlude to the worry of war news. Bishop began urging him to come with him several weeks in advance. Clements was intrigued by the prospect. 'I will try very, very hard to go,' he answered.[10] Bishop explained that they would stay with a guide, Theo. Oakes, and eat at his house. 'My idea,' said Bishop,

would be to go into camp at once, remaining at Killarney only so long as is necessary to 'outfit.' You would not need to bring anything beyond your fishing tackle and some old clothes. It will probably be cold at night, so you should bring winter sleeping garments, including a nightcap or some kind of a cap you can wear at night . . . The country is very mountainous and beautiful. The pine has not been cut off, and it looks practically as it did when the first Jesuits went through the Killarney Channel in 1668. If you prefer we can go eastward to the old Voyageur Channel, through which all the fur trade from the Upper Lakes to Ottawa and Montreal went from the time of LaSalle until fifty years ago.[11]

Clements joined Bishop for four days of fishing, thoroughly enjoying the experience.

Meanwhile, despite shortages of materials and workmen, work on the new University Library building continued. The old rotunda and reading room had been vacated in June, with the new stack wing being used for administrative offices and reading rooms while the remainder of the building was under construction. Bishop reported on October 1 that the library would be ready to open, despite cramped quarters for both library staff and readers in the stacks, with the opening of the fall semester at the University.

By March, 1918, construction was far enough advanced that Bishop felt the time had come to make definite allocation of space and facilities for Clements' collection of Americana, when Clements should decide the time was right for offering it to the University. He wrote:

As the new building shows up more and more from week to week, various departments are beginning to talk about the possible use of the rooms in the West Bookstack, which are now occupied by the Library as reading rooms, and which will be vacated on our taking possession of the new building . . . .

In particular, the second floor, now used for the Graduate Reading Room, has been arranged so that it can be made into a room for the exhibition, storage, and consultation of rare and valuable material. It can be connected with our present Reserved Rooms by a very short staircase. The light is admirable for exhibition and for study. The room is directly connected with the main floor of the Library, and it should make an ideal place for the quiet study of our book treasures under supervision . . . .

Of course, I have had in mind that one of the solutions of the proper housing and care of your own extremely valuable collection of books, when you are ready to have it come here, might lie in the use of this room, and if necessary, the one below it, for that purpose . . . . If, when you come to make a decision, we have the second floor room already devoted to rare books and other similar material, it may be feasible so to arrange this room, the present

130

Reserved Book Room, and perhaps the room below as to afford adequate and convenient quarters for your collection in the immediate vicinity of the rest of the Library, and at the same time, sufficiently separated from it to be marked off definitely and effectually.[12]

It would seem from Bishop's letter that he was unaware of Clements' misgivings, which dated from the administration of Bishop's predecessor, concerning the wisdom of housing his collection in the University Library building under the control of the University Librarian. In view of the close relationship between the two men, this seems strange. One explanation may be that Bishop, who favored housing and administering the collection as a separate unit in the University Library, may have felt that his judgment, which Clements valued, would ultimately prevail, and therefore he proceeded with his plans accordingly. Another more probable explanation is that Clements, although he had been investigating alternative solutions to the question of administration and housing for his collection for more than a year, had not definitely made up his mind in 1918 as to the best procedure.

Clements might well have hesitated as to the wisdom of giving Isaac N. Demmon, whom he had installed as first custodian of the Rare Book Section in 1915, control over his books. Friction between Demmon and members of the library staff did not end with Koch's removal. In October, 1916, Clements had written Bishop,

Certainly something should be done in the Rare Book Section . . . . Professor Demmon intimated that there was opposition by Mr. Goodrich [Assistant Librarian] to the Rare Book Section, and there was opposition from other quarters, on account of the diffi-

culty in getting books now stored there . . . . The whole administration of the rare book collection has been so undecided that it is anything but satisfactory . . . .

So much might be done in this section with the proper person at the head of it. There should be no friction with a reasonable person at the head of this department.[13]

Almost immediately thereafter Clements wrote again to Bishop, telling him that he was going east to visit several libraries and asking him for a letter of introduction to Andrew Keogh, the new librarian of Yale University Library. Almost as an afterthought he asked if Bishop knew the name of the custodian of the Elizabethan Club Library on the Yale campus.

And so, early in November, 1916, Clements started a trip that took him to the John Carter Brown Library in Providence, Harvard Library, the American Antiquarian Society, Yale University and the Elizabethan Club Library, and finally to New York where he made the visit to Henry E. Huntington's library which had impressed him so much. His trip to the Brown Library, of course, was not his first, and the main reason for his stops in Cambridge and Worcester seems to have been for friendly visits with Winship and Brigham. But the trip to Yale, where he met Andrew Keogh and visited the Elizabethan Club Library, was his first.

The Elizabethan Club Library was a collection of rare sixteenth and seventeenth-century English books given by Alexander Smith Cochran (1874-1929) in 1911, because of the inspiration he had gained from undergraduate classes at Yale under William Lyon Phelps and because of his belief that undergraduates should be encouraged to talk about, love, and collect fine books. The collection was given not to Yale University, but to the students. It had its own separate building and was administered by a board controlled by the Student Government of Yale University. When Clements visited the Elizabethan Club in 1916 it was one of the most exciting new ideas for the furthering of undergraduate culture and education in the United States, and it seems to have fired his imagination in regard to his own collection. In 1919, when he was ready to lay his proposition for the donation of his collection before the regents, he singled out this library and the John Carter Brown Library as specific models 'for the operation of a library of American History for the use of Advanced Students at Michigan and for scholars of history.'[14]

It is possible that on his return Clements discussed his misgivings about housing his collection in the University Library and his tentative ideas on separate administration and housing with President Hutchins. But there is no evidence that he elaborated on his visits to anyone else, including William Warner Bishop. And it seems likely that the events of the year 1917 drove further planning out of his mind. At any rate, he took no further steps toward the implementation of his plans for his collection until the summer of 1919, shortly before he presented his proposal to the regents. Meanwhile, Bishop continued to plan for the housing of the Clements collection in the University Library.

The crises of the war years, although they had sent Clements' Revolutionary friend Major Robert Rogers into temporary hibernation, were not enough to silence him – nor his determined descendant, Mary Cochrane Rogers – for long. Although he was bothered with eye trouble, Clements had resumed his study of Rogers and his times by the fall of 1917. Miss Rogers had also been at work. In January, 1918, Clements received an announcement; the results of her labors were about to come forth in a book entitled *Rogers' Rock, Lake George, March 13, 1758. A Battle Fought on Snow Shoes*, now ready for distribution 'in a limited edition.' Evidently fearing that her first announcement had gone astray, Miss Rogers sent Clements a second notice of her publication in March, with the added information that it was available at $2.00 in paper covers and $2.25 bound in boards. Being sure that Clements would not want to miss such an opportunity to add a rare item to his collection, she wrote again the next week, informing him that she was reserving a copy of her book, bound in boards, for him. Another copy of the announcement followed in two days. At this point, Clements capitulated before her onslaught. He sent in his check for $2.25 and, we presume, received a copy of the book in return.

It may be that Miss Rogers' persistent reminders triggered Clements' recollection of his promise to edit Rogers' journal and to write an introduction to it for presentation at a meeting of the American Antiquarian Society. Toward the end of April, he penciled a note to Waldo Lincoln, president of the Society, stating that he was at work annotating the journal, 'showing still further the checkered career of Rogers and local Indian conditions at the time.'[15]

Events related to the war, as it turned out, indirectly prevented Clements from filling his October engagement to give his paper. Tension in the United States and on The University of Michigan campus mounted, as a wave of anti-German hysteria swept the country. Professor Van Tyne, by this time on a three-months' leave of absence from the University to tour the country and give speeches for the National Security League, was one of the most ardent patriots on campus, giving a good deal of effort to sniffing out possible pro-German members of the faculty. In the fall of 1917, he had wanted to know what action the regents meant to take in the case of Assistant Professor Carl E. Eggert, a member of the highly suspect German Department. Regent Clements answered,

In the matter of Eggert ... I cannot see that anything can be done, except through the Executive Committee until the next meeting of the Board, which I believe is on the 18th of October .... We don't want any Pro-Germans or even Pacifists around the University.[16]

In February, 1918, R. M. McElroy, president of the National Security League for which Van Tyne was working, asked the Board of Regents to make an official enquiry into the loyalty of all University employees.[17] This the regents ignored. But they were unable to ignore individual complaints and accusations. In April, Clements wrote Bishop,

The Regents' meeting was most unsatisfactory. Nearly all the time was taken up with debates upon Pro-German professors and none of the matters that I had hoped to present to the Board were presented.[18]

The witch hunt spread from the German Department to the Architectural Department. Van Tyne again wrote Clements, this time in support of Sydney Fiske Kimball, Assistant Professor of Fine Arts, recently discharged by the regents. Those were troubled times. Well might Clements say during that black April of his Americana collection, 'I do not know what I would do if I did not have this interest.'[19] His books in the great library at Bay City were an anchor for storms and a retreat in times of sorrow.

The month of August drew on, hot and humid as only summers in the Midwest can be. Mrs. Clements had gone to Hyannisport, and Clements was alone in the big house in Bay City. Mr. and Mrs. Harper stopped briefly on their way to Chicago but did not stay long. A second invitation to accompany William Warner

Bishop on a fishing trip to Canada served as a welcome break from hot weather and the tensions of national and University affairs. Clements had been uncertain until almost the last moment as to whether he could go. But Bishop left on August 24, and Clements joined him a little later at Killarney, Ontario. Again they enlisted the services of Theo. Oakes as their guide, and the use of his boat gave them more mobility than they had had the year before. However, almost constant rain dampened their enjoyment of the trip. Clements was on his way home again by Sunday, September 1. He described the trip to Junius Beal:

I had a good time fishing with Bishop for he is an excellent companion in camp, and with the almost continually rainy days, anybody's patience was sorely tried. He is still in camp waiting for the sky to clear. Verily he has the patience of a setting hen.[20]

Bishop stuck it out another week, hoping for a break in the weather, and then in disgust broke camp and came home early.

A meeting with Clarence E. Brigham in New York City on July 7, 1918, had concluded the negotiations for the sale of the American Antiquarian Society's duplicate newspapers. The papers were sorted and ready for delivery by September 26. Clements had business in Washington that week, so he was able to make a quick trip to Worcester to check on their packing and condition. By October 4, Brigham had six crates of early nineteenth-century newspapers on their way to the University Library.

If the usual procedure had been followed, the newspapers should have been unpacked and checked by the University Library staff and then rerouted to Clements' library in Bay City. But Bishop had been asked by the American Library Associa-

136

tion to take charge of Student Army Training Corps Library coordination at the Washington headquarters, and, having obtained a leave of absence for the fall semester, he left shortly after the newspapers arrived. They remained crated until he returned about the end of the year.

Despite wartime disruptions of normal routines, Clements persevered in his study of the Robert Rogers journal, and by the first part of October had his paper ready for presentation at the October 16 meeting of the American Antiquarian Society. He was looking forward to the meeting with a good deal of pleasant anticipation, particularly in view of the fact that he had just received a cordial personal letter from Worthington C. Ford, Librarian of the Massachusetts Historical Society in Boston, inviting him to Boston following the Worcester meeting, to dine with him and attend a meeting of the Club of Odd Volumes that evening.

Clements was elated at the invitation, for Ford, a well-known authority on manuscript materials of American history, was an austere individual whose formal manner had discouraged any personal contact from Clements. He wrote to Bishop in some excitement:

I hardly believe it will be possible for me to attend the next meeting of the Board on the 16th, inasmuch as I have the greatest desire to attend a meeting of the American Antiquarian Society at Worcester to be held on the 16th, and further from the fact that I have received a special invitation from Mr. [Waldo] Lincoln [President of the American Antiquarian Society] and also an invitation to attend a meeting of the Club of Odd Volumes . . . from Mr. Ford of the Massachusetts Historical Society.[21]

But before the end of the week, disaster struck the nation in the shape of a virulent epidemic of influenza that swept from coast to coast, causing thousands of deaths, and by the second week in October practically closing The University of Michigan. And before the end of that week, Clements received news from Washington that his own son, James Renville Clements, assigned to overseas duty in France, was one of those dead of influenza.[22]

Clements, always reticent about his personal affairs, told few people outside his most intimate circle of friends of his tragic loss. The turmoil on the University campus, with the Michigan Union converted into a hospital and with daily student deaths, was enough in itself to prevent him from going east for the meeting in Worcester on the 16th. To Brigham he wrote,

Conditions in Michigan are quite alarming. I have just had a telephone message from Ann Arbor reporting eight deaths among the students yesterday from the prevailing influenza, and there are about 400 cases in the hospital. The President has called a special meeting for Thursday next, and in talking with him over the phone, it seems imperative that I must attend that meeting. [It was cancelled for lack of a quorum.]

I am sorely disappointed, for it now seems probable that I will not be in Worcester for the meeting on the 16th. . . . I am sending you herewith Rogers' Journal together with a preface.[23]

And to Ford he said simply,

In view of the very serious situation in Michigan due to the prevailing epidemic and further to the fact that the President of the University of Michigan has called a special meeting of the Regents for Thursday next . . . it now seems impossible for me to attend the meeting at Worcester on Wednesday, and to accept your invitation for the evening. I am very much disappointed.[24]

138

Of the personal tragedy that affected him so deeply, he said little. He wrote to his friend Lathrop C. Harper about a week later, telling him what had happened. Harper replied immediately.

I cannot express the very great shock it was to receive your letter telling the sad news of the death of your son James in Paris.

It is very hard. You have freely sacrificed so much of your time and effort – and now this, which only time can alleviate but never quite heal.

My mind goes back to the morning I met James on 5th Ave. He stopped me. I should never have known him, he had developed so and looked every inch a soldier. I felt you ought to be very proud of him, as I think I told you.

There is not much I can write that will be of any avail. Last night Mrs. Harper and I spoke of nothing else.[25]

Clements revealed some of the depth of his feeling in answer to a letter of condolence from Shirley W. Smith, Secretary of the University.

Your very kind and thoughtful letter I have received. It is indeed very hard for me to reconcile myself to the loss of my dear boy, in whom I had reposed many of my future plans, and I realize, more than ever before, that human wishes, plans and expectations are after all, like everything that we mortals propose. Sorrows are given to us singly, else we could not endure them, but I feel this one to be the greatest one ever given to me, but I shall try hard to reconcile myself to the situation, and I am sure the bereavement teaches me to be more faithful to the living.[26]

He appreciated also letters from officials at Harvard University, wanting a photograph of James and the details of his service, so that his name might be entered on Harvard's Roll of Honor. Clements told President Hutchins of the Harvard action, suggesting that Michigan ought to do the same for University students who died in the service of their country. As he said,

There is much to all the above, even though it be a form, for it shows an interest of the University in its students, and I assure you all has been gratifying to me, for that is about all I have in remembrance.[27]

As for the meeting Clements had missed, his paper was given in his absence by Professor Archer B. Hulbert and later published in the *Proceedings* of the American Antiquarian Society for October, 1918. Brigham reported that Miss Rogers, persistent to the end, had turned up again, wanting to attend the meeting. But, said Brigham, 'I told her she would have to read the Journal in print.'[28]

The month of November found the influenza epidemic still raging. Clements wrote to Bishop, by now at work in Washington on the American Library Association's project for installing libraries in Student Army Training Corps centers on campuses throughout the country.

Ann Arbor is a pretty sorry place at this time and conditions are not mending very rapidly, although I think there is somewhat of an improvement.[29]

And then at last, on November 9, came the word that everyone had been waiting for, the news of the abdication of the Kaiser and the collapse of the German war effort. The Armistice two days later brought joy and relief. The war was won; Wilson and the Allies had fought the last battle, and had made the world

140

safe for democracy in this war to end all future wars. Within two weeks the Students Army and Navy Training Corps units on The University of Michigan campus were disbanded. The influenza epidemic began to subside, the University moved rapidly back to normal.

In England, Henry N. Stevens reported optimistically on the return of his staff. Henry Stevens, Jr., would be back from his job in the munitions factory in a week. By great luck one of his catalogers had been shot in the leg just before the Armistice was declared, and, being wounded, he was likely to be mustered out early. But both the lady stenographers who had loyally held the fort while the men were away at war were ill with the influenza; Stevens was forced to write his letter to Clements by hand.

But for William Clements the Armistice had come too late. And as faculty and students began to come back to the Michigan campus, he must have thought many times of James Renville Clements, who would not return.[30]

NOTES

1   WC to Brigham, November 28, 1916, Clements Papers.

2   Rogers to WC, January 1, 1917, Clements Papers.

3   WC to Rogers, January 4, 1917, Clements Papers.

4   WC to Brigham, January 4, 1917, Clements Papers.

5   Brigham to WC, January 10, 1917, Clements Papers.

6   WC to Brigham, February 16, 1917, Clements Papers.

7   Brigham to WC, April 4, 1917, Clements Papers.

8   WC to Bishop, April 10, 1917, Bishop Papers. Obviously Clements did not hold to this decision. He was elected to a third term in 1925, serving until December, 1933, a total of twenty-four years on the Board of Regents.

9   WC to Brigham, June 11, 1917, Clements Papers. On October 26, Clements wrote to Harper, 'The facts are I have been simply swamped with Liberty Loan matters for I was Chairman of the comittee in this county. We have raised in Bay County approximately $ 2,750,000, an over subscription of $250,000. There are only two or three counties in the state that have done this' (Clements Papers).

10   WC to Bishop, August 8, 1917, Bishop Papers.

11   Bishop to WC, August 10, 1917, Bishop Papers.

12   Bishop to WC, March 14, 1918, Bishop Papers.

13   WC to Bishop, October 26, 1916, Bishop Papers.

14   WC to Ford, August 14, 1919, Clements Papers.

15   WC to Lincoln, April 24, 1918, Clements Papers.

16   WC to Van Tyne, September 22, 1917, Van Tyne Papers, MHC. Professor Hobbs was also actively concerned against Eggert and others.

17   Howard H. Peckham, *The Making of The University of Michigan, 1817–1967* (Ann Arbor: University of Michigan Press, 1967), p. 132.

18   WC to Bishop, April 8, 1918, Bishop Papers.

19   WC to Waldo Lincoln, April 24, 1918, Clements Papers.

20   WC to Beal, September 4, 1918, Beal Papers.

21   WC to Bishop, October 7, 1918, Bishop Papers.

22   James Renville Clements died October 8, 1918. Clements' daughter, Mrs. Betty Clements Finkenstaedt, recalled her brother's death and the events surrounding it as follows: 'My brother, James, was the adored member of the family and tho' he was six years younger than I, we were very close. I was in N.Y. studying to be a nurse's aide in the service when he sailed in July 1918 – the first navy fliers, who were eventually to go to Dunkirk. He died very suddenly in Paris en route. My other brother, Wallace, was in service, stationed in Washington [D.C.]. He was notified first and came right to Bay City to tell my parents. I was in Bay City, expecting to leave for France, when the word came. We were all so crushed that I was persuaded to stay at home, where I helped to run a hospital' (Mrs. Finkenstaedt to Margaret Maxwell, April 19, 1971).

23   WC to Brigham, October 12, 1918, Clements Papers.

24   WC to Ford, October 12, 1918, Clements Papers.

25   Harper to WC, October 25, 1918, Clements Papers.

26   WC to Smith, October 22, 1918, Smith Papers.

27 WC to Hutchins, November 13, 1918, Hutchins Papers. Clements and James Davidson of Bay City gave an airport to the city, named in memory of James Renville Clements, in 1919.

28 Brigham to WC, November 4, 1918, Clements Papers.

29 WC to Bishop, November 2, 1918, Bishop Papers.

30 The sustained sense of loss which Clements felt may perhaps be guessed by a letter which he wrote to Shirley W. Smith, Secretary of the University, on July 26, 1920, nearly two years after the death of his son. He said to Smith:

'I have not received much consolation from anything I have yet heard or read. The problem is so immense that my poor understanding is simply bewildered and establishes nothing.

'A rainy day – a Sunday – a few weeks ago I took up a volume of Montaigne's Essays. In it are his views on life and death, a glorification for the latter – a view quite unusual for a Frenchman – a wonderful bit of philosophy and composition – only one worthwhile translation, by John Florio. Read the essay – the exact title I cannot remember.

'Well! I don't take the same interest in life and in action I used to. I feel this is *wrong*. Surely a death is a most common and uneventful happening, but what it means, we are all in doubt' (Smith Papers).

THE PRINTED CATALOG

In the period between the end of 1916 and February 1920, the month in which the regents formally accepted the Clements collection of Americana and his conditions for its maintenance, Clements tried for a third time to make a full printed catalog of his collection. The inspiration for this catalog, unlike the first, came not from a desire to emulate the printed catalogs of the Church, the John Carter Brown, and other great collections of Americana, but seems to have been part of a strategy to impress the regents with the importance of his collection, so that when he presented his proposition to them, they would accept his conditions. Early in 1919, after two years of frustration, problems, and trials, he wrote to William Warner Bishop, who seems to have had his full confidence in this matter, and spelled out his specific reasons for again attempting the Herculean task of catalog making.

An impression upon the proper persons can be made only by having the proper publications issued in the shape of a catalogue, and then, competent persons passing on the catalog in their [the regents'] presence as to values for study work, and for the reputation of the University.[1]

And thus Clements again determined to attempt a catalog. This time he decided to seek the advice of an expert. In December, 1916, he wrote George Parker Winship, by now the Widener Collection Librarian at Harvard University,

I cannot make up my mind how to proceed with my catalogue of Americana. I have neither the time to do it myself nor a librarian to do it for me [Miss Brown, who made the 1914 checklist of his library, had left because of eye trouble].[2]

In February, Clements made a trip to Cambridge to consult Winship. The day after the visit, Winship sent Clements a long letter including four typewritten pages of sample entries for cataloging rare books. Also included were Winship's 'Rules' which he suggested Clements might follow for his catalog.

The first three or more words to be copied exactly as on the original title page. As much else, and only so much, as gives definite information of interest; this to be copied literally, but without taking account of omissions. Imprint to give only place, shortest form of printer's name, sufficient for identification, and date in arabic figures regardless of form on title. My feeling is becoming strong that the best way to give the size is to give the height of the copy described in millimeters. This is a good test of condition, useful for comparison and one quickly learns to read the figures for approximate size at least as well as '4to' or 'Folio'. Collation in the shortest possible form consistent with exactness. I would give signatures only when necessary to explain curious pagination or to prove completeness.

Of the principles which should govern the making of a bibliographical catalog of the type proposed by Clements, Winship said,

My whole theory is that unless one is producing a real bibliography – with a big B – a Catalogue ought to be interesting. No amount of appearances of infinite learning and scholarship and that sort of thing can compensate for dullness.[3]

Clements took the problem of finding a suitable librarian to make the catalog of his collection to Bishop. In April, Bishop wrote Clements,

While in New York recently I made inquiries at the New York Public Library about the possibility of securing someone to work temporarily on the cataloging of your books. . . . I am enclosing a letter from Mr. [Azariah] Root, who is acting as principal of the Library School this year. I should judge from what he tells me in this letter, and from what I learned about Miss Clizbee in New York, that she would do the work acceptably. You will note however, that she would not be available until the fall.[4]

This did not seem to Clements a major obstacle, since he had made arrangements to close his house for part of the summer and to take a cottage at Pointe-aux-Barques on Saginaw Bay. In May he visited Miss Clizbee in New York and engaged her to begin work for him in October.

In May also, Clements wrote President Hutchins, suggesting that George Parker Winship be given an honorary degree at the next commencement. Characterizing Winship as 'a man who, with Mr. Wilberforce Eames of the New York Public Library, is the greatest bibliographer in this country,' he said that he felt 'it

146

would be an honor to the University to give Mr. Winship a degree.[5] Hutchins responded with enthusiasm, and Winship received the honorary degree of Doctor of Letters on June 28, 1917. This together with Clements' invitation to Winship to visit him in Bay City after Commencement seems to have cemented the growing friendship between the two men.

Miss Azalea Clizbee arrived in Bay City on October 1, and set to work on the catalog of Clements' library. By her own account, at least, Miss Clizbee had 'had a great deal of experience in cataloging.'[6] She was firm in her convictions as to the kind of catalog that Clements must have. Without doubt her ideas reflected her recent training at the New York Public Library School; she determined to apply the full gamut of Library of Congress rules and practices and to catalog and classify the collection accordingly. Her library catalog was to be based as far as possible upon Library of Congress printed cards, and Clements was induced to order the requisite sets of cards for the full panoply of main entries, added entries, and subject cards for as many of his books as the Library of Congress had cataloged. That this ran counter to Winship's notions seems to have fazed Miss Clizbee not one whit, and that her concept bore little relationship to the printed catalog that Clements had in mind for his own purposes seems to have bothered her even less. Clements wrote to Bishop at the end of November, enclosing two catalog entries 'showing the manner in which Miss Clizbee proposes to make the entries . . . I would be very glad to have your criticism upon them.' Another letter to Bishop followed in December, expressing his perplexity. 'I am fearful,' said Clements, 'that Miss Clizbee will not be heavy enough to do anything more than the card catalogue. In this I am greatly disappointed. The work drags on very, very slowly.'[7] Following this cryptic comment, Miss Clizbee seems to have disappeared from the scene. Clements was again without a cataloger, and his proposed catalog was no further along than it had been the year previous.

A painful work it is, I'll assure you, and more than difficult, wherein what toyle hath been taken, as no man thinketh, so no man believeth, but he hath made the triall.

Clements no doubt had many occasions to reflect ruefully upon Anthony à Wood's words which he had himself, via Joseph Sabin, quoted three years before at the completion of his 1914 checklist. Was he never to complete the full bibliographical catalog which would prove to the regents, to scholars, to the whole world, that he had gathered a collection of books worthy not only of academic recognition by The University of Michigan but also of continued financial support by the University?

Clements may have been discouraged, but he was still determined. He soon renewed his search for a proper person to make the catalog. And this time, evidently by April, 1918, he found a young woman who was to prove intelligent, accurate, methodical, sensitive to his ideals for his library – and one who was to enjoy her work so thoroughly that she remained for more than three years before matrimony called and she left Bay City. This was Esther Loud, daughter of George A. Loud, Member of Congress from Oscoda, Michigan, from 1903 to 1913 and from 1915 to 1917, a lumberman, and the vice-president and general manager of the Au Sable and Northwestern Railroad.

Miss Loud does not seem to have taken up her duties immediately; the arrangement was made that she should first attend Bishop's summer course in Library Science. She was a good student; Bishop, knowing she was to work with Clements' collection, gave her special attention and he spoke highly of her.

148

There is no evidence that Esther Loud began her duties as librarian as soon as she had completed her summer courses. Clements was too preoccupied with other crises to devote much thought to his catalog at the time, and it may well be that she started work in the library early in 1919. Her first assignment was the printed catalog of Clements' library. To assist her with the mechanical details of proper bibliographical description, Clements solicited further advice from both Bishop and Winship on proper spacing and punctuation of entries, and Miss Loud accepted their suggestions. Indeed, she proceeded joyfully to the task at hand. As she said to her mentor of the previous summer, 'I often think, Mr. Bishop, of what you said last summer about finding work that one could do con amore. This is certainly that kind of work.'[8]

In March, Clements had two sample entries set in type and run off in proof for Bishop's and Winship's comments. Although Miss Loud had stated that the historical notes 'which Mr. Clements intends making the distinctive feature of the catalog, are being left until later on,' one of the sample entries, that for Silas Dean's 1784 *Address to the United States*, did include a fairly extensive note of this type.[9] The general format was patterned on Winship's cataloging rules of February, 1917, with the author's name followed by a brief title, the place of publication, the printer, and the date in arabic numerals. Collation was given in pages rather than signatures, with size in centimeters. The typography, however, was clumsy: it underwent considerable modification by the end of the year, when another group of entries was run off in proof. Clements acknowledged his indebtedness for this preliminary draft to Winship's ideas, saying,

I have adopted nearly all your suggestions as to abbreviations.

One of these days I will send you a sample sheet to show what your influence has been on a Western book collector in the Catalogue Department.[10]

Progress came to a temporary halt as Clements, on doctor's orders, left in March for a month's rest at Hot Springs, Virginia. Esther Loud was also with the Clements family at this time.

Clements chafed at his enforced idleness at Hot Springs. It was a bad time to be away from Michigan; there were a number of significant issues in which he had a personal interest. President Hutchins, well past retirement age, had asked that a successor be found for him. Regent Clements had been named to the search committee. One of the candidates was James Rowland Angell (son of former President James B. Angell), Dean at the University of Chicago. Following the regents' meeting of March 12, Angell had been visited by President Hutchins and Regent Gore and asked if he would accept the presidency of the University. Hutchins wrote to Clements, telling him that, although Angell had asked for ten days to think the matter over before replying, he thought the answer would be yes.[11]

Furthermore, Clements, absent from Bay City, was not able to direct the final weeks of a bond campaign for a new Carnegie Library, due to come up for vote on April 7. Henry B. Smith, James E. Davidson, C. R. Wells, and Clements had agreed to give the city a site for the new library if the bond issue passed. Clements had engaged Albert Kahn to prepare drawings for the proposed library. The building designed by Kahn was simple, graceful, and functional – perhaps too much so for its time, since in the end the plans were not used, and the standard Carnegie structure of the period was erected.

Before Clements left for Hot Springs, he asked Bishop to speak at Bay City in favor of the bond issue. This Bishop did,

150

throwing the weight of his influence as president of the American Library Association behind the proposal. Happily, the bond issue did pass. Clements not only confirmed his intention of giving the site for the building but coupled this generous gesture with one of rather startling munificence, an offer to support the building of an auditorium.

The week following the passage of the bond issue, Clements prepared to leave Hot Springs for the Johns Hopkins Hospital in Baltimore. He wrote confidentially to Shirley W. Smith, Secretary of the University.

I am leaving here tonight for Washington and Baltimore. I have been unable to get into Johns Hopkins Hospital until this time where I am going for what doctors call a minor operation (it appears to me major) which fact I have not stated broadcast. In consequence I hardly expect to get home before about the first week in May.

I have had a delightful time here – never had anything like it before and I feel like a new man – all in preparation for Baltimore ....Yes,I pause and think frequently, as I never thought before in my life, and then wonder what our lives mean.[12]

But much to Clements' relief, medical opinion at Johns Hopkins Hospital was that he did not need the operation. He left very shortly for home, reaching Bay City on April 27.

Bishop, in the East during the first part of April, visited Worthington C. Ford at the Massachusetts Historical Society. While Clements was still at Hot Springs, Bishop reported an offer from Ford of a large number of duplicate early American newspapers belonging to the Society. By the time Clements returned to Michigan, Bishop, who favored acquisition of the papers, had them at the University Library for Clements' inspection and decision. Clements took all the newspapers not duplicated in his collection. The transaction was completed by the end of June, with Clements paying $3,739.75 for 1730 newspapers, thus strengthening his rapidly growing collection in this area.

On the same trip East, Bishop had learned of another project which Ford and Wilberforce Eames of the New York Public Library were starting. As consultant for the John Carter Brown Library, Ford had become aware of a number of important early publications in Americana not held by the John Carter Brown Library, and of such rarity that they were unlikely ever to come onto the market. This, of course, was a problem common to all the major research libraries. He and Eames were planning to photostat this material, making it available at least in facsimile for scholars using the two libraries. Bishop had suggested to Ford that Clements might be interested in joining them, and that, in light of some of the rare items in Clements' collection, it might be to Eames' and Ford's advantage to include him.

Clements, as it happened, had only recently completed arrangements with Dr. Rosenbach to photostat the Christie-Miller copy of Walter Bigges' *A Summarie and True Discourse of Sir Francis Drakes West Indian Voyage* (London, 1589), which Rosenbach had acquired for $10,000 at the Huntington duplicate sale. Rosenbach, of course, was interested in selling the *Summarie* to Clements. Why he decided to allow Clements to photostat it instead remains an unanswered question. But as a result of Rosenbach's generous impulse, Clements had an extremely attractive item to offer Ford as his opening gambit for inclusion of the Clements collection in the photostat project. Early in May he sent a copy to Ford, which Ford acknowledged promptly, suggesting not only that Clements join the group but that it be expanded to include Henry E. Huntington also.

152

By mid-June the cooperating libraries included the New York Public Library, John Carter Brown Library, the Massachusetts Historical Society, the American Antiquarian Society, the Newberry Library, the State Historical Society of Wisconsin, the Library of Congress, Yale University Library, and the two private libraries of Henry E. Huntington and William L. Clements. The first issue from the Photostat Americana series, 'made under the combination of the leading American libraries to reproduce by photostat rare items of early Americana,' was the 1493 Paris edition of the Columbus letter, from the John Carter Brown Library. This appeared in August, 1919.

Clements' relief from the difficulties which had threatened an operation in mid-April was, unfortunately, short-lived. Rather unexpectedly in May he went to the Cowie Hospital in Ann Arbor for two minor operations. He was back in Bay City on June 3, with plans no more strenuous than for rest and recovery at Hyannisport on Cape Cod during July and August.

However, the regents had other ideas. In the matter of finding a successor for President Hutchins, negotiations with James R. Angell had been terminated, and no one else was immediately in view. President Hutchins reluctantly agreed to remain in office until June 30, 1920, but the task of finding the man to take his place was still urgent. At the regents' meeting of June 13, Regents Leland, Hubbard, Murfin, Gore, Beal, and Clements were appointed to a committee to find a new president.

Despite this added responsibility, Clements seems to have enjoyed a leisurely summer at Hyannisport, postponing until fall any serious efforts to solve the presidential problem. He kept up by correspondence with the summer book auctions in London. Harper had sailed on June 24 for the Huth sale, part seven, to be held on July 8. Clements had asked him to bid on a rare issue of Vespucci at the sale but had little hope of getting it.

His pessimism was well founded; Harper managed to acquire only one item for him, Melchisedech Thevenot's *Recueil de Voyages* (1681), the first published account of the Mississippi River, for which Clements paid $170. The Sir Thomas Phillips sale had been held at Sotheby's two weeks earlier. With Henry N. Stevens as his agent, Clements fared somewhat better, managing to obtain four items totalling £83/4/4.

But Clements, devoting himself conscientiously to regaining his strength after his operation, seems to have taken less than his usual interest in affairs in London. He wrote to Bishop,

My visit here has been without any events of interest. I went fishing one day; went out about six miles and anchored the boat. A good catch of 'black-fish,' big fellows, some twenty of them weighing from three to twelve pds. each, but I was very, very sick. I cannot endure with composure the motion of a boat anchored and in a choppy sea. 'Two days to recover – like bass fishing better,' as Jingle would say. Motoring and wading is [sic] my supporting pasttimes.

Almost as an afterthought, he closed with the comment,

I have had a very good letter from Mr. Ford and I hope to have a visit with him before I return.[13]

Ford met Clements on August 1 in Providence, probably to talk over problems of the John Carter Brown Library, for which Ford was consultant, and of Clements' own library. It seems likely that Clements, who had enormous respect for Ford's erudition, told Ford of his rapidly developing plans for his own collection. Only the final preliminaries remained to be taken care of before he would make his proposition to the regents. And

154

these plans involved Ford's cooperation. About the middle of August he wrote to Ford.

It may be that during the latter part of September I shall bring on from Michigan Mr. Bishop and Professor Van Tyne. . . . The purpose of this visit is to determine in some way a plan for the operation of a library of American History for the use of advanced students at Michigan, and for scholars of history, possibly of use in the same way that the John Carter Brown Library is used, but it is the purpose to investigate both the plan at Providence and the plan of the Elizabethan Club at Yale.[14]

The day to which Clements had devoted his months and years of careful planning, the day he referred to as the 'culmination of all my doings,'[15] was nearly at hand.

NOTES

1   WC to Bishop, January 17, 1919, Bishop Papers.
2   WC to Winship, December 29, 1916, Clements Papers.
3   Winship to WC, February 20, 1917, Clements Papers.
4   Bishop to WC, April 18, 1917, Bishop Papers.
5   WC to Hutchins, May 16, 1917, Hutchins Papers.
6   WC to Stevens, October 1, 1917, Clements Papers.
7   WC to Bishop, November 28, 1917; December 18, 1917, Bishop Papers.
8   Loud to Bishop, March 6, 1919, Bishop Papers.
9   Proof sheet is to be found in Bishop Papers, with Esther Loud's letter of March 6, 1919. A copy is also in the Clements Library in file marked 'Clements' (locked file case).
10   WC to Winship, March 7, 1919, Clements Papers.
11   Hutchins to WC, March 17, 1919, Hutchins Papers. Angell and the Regents could not agree on conditions on which he would accept the presidency, and negotations were terminated. Angell went to Yale as president in 1921 (Peckham, *The Making of the University of Michigan*, p. 136).

12   WC to Smith, April 16, 1919, Smith Papers.
13   WC to Bishop, July 29, 1919, Bishop Papers.
14   WC to Ford, August 14, 1919, Clements Papers.
15   WC to Brigham, March 9, 1920, Clements Papers.

'THE CULMINATION OF ALL MY DOINGS'

I believe we have considered the John Carter Brown and the Elizabethan Club of Yale as two distinct plans for the use of a library of books such as my own, and it was my intention to ask you and Professor Van Tyne to make a trip to Providence and New Haven with me for the purpose of looking over these two libraries and reporting on the best plan for us to use, both for the present and the future. . . . The only thing that prevents me from putting any plan which we might decide upon in concrete form and submitting it to the Regents is the outrageous cost of building at this time.

Thus wrote William L. Clements from his Bay City home to William Warner Bishop. It was August 14, 1919, and Clements had broken his vacation at Hyannisport with a brief trip to Michigan, primarily to attend the regents' meeting on August 6. Plans were shaping up for the gift of his library. Colonial newspapers, which he had been accumulating since 1916 primarily for the use of the History Department, bulked large in his collection, both in Bay City and in storage in the University Library. The very day of the regents' meeting, the first of some 2,000 volumes of American Antiquarian Society duplicate newspapers, purchased the summer before, were sent to the University Library from the bindery, to join Clements' other newspapers in the storage area. Of these newspapers, Clements again warned Bishop,

At the present time and in fact until the Board of Regents and myself come to some agreement, it is not my intention to intermingle in any way my collection with the University collection of papers, and [they] must not be placed in the University stacks until such an agreement is reached.[1]

About the middle of August, Clements returned to Cape Cod to complete his vacation. Just before his return to Michigan, he had lunched in Boston with his friend George Parker Winship and had gone with him to his Charles River farm. Clements found both Mr. and Mrs. Winship such delightful company that he wrote before he returned to Massachusetts, inviting them to go with him – somewhere; they would settle the details later when he got back from Michigan. Winship responded with enthusiasm, and during the first week in September, Clements and George and Claire Winship motored to the White Mountains of New Hampshire for a ten-day vacation. They spent about half their time at the Mount Washington House. Clements reported,

The hotel there is certainly the best I have ever stopped at. The prime requisite of a good table was amply provided for. Mr. and Mrs. Winship were delightful companions, and I thoroughly enjoyed the week's outing, and, at the same time, I tried to saturate myself with the bibliographical information exploded in the air.[2]

158

After his return to Cape Cod, Clements made plans for the visit to the John Carter Brown and Elizabethan Club Libraries which he had mentioned to Bishop and Van Tyne in August. Worthington C. Ford planned to be in Providence to answer questions about the Carter Brown Library. Unfortunately he was prevented by illness from leaving Boston. This evidently caused Clements to alter his plan of having Bishop and Van Tyne join him at that time on his inspection tour. Instead, he went alone, motoring from Hyannisport to Providence, on the afternoon of September 17.

Clements returned to Michigan shortly thereafter, and began his preparations for the regents' meeting, scheduled for September 26. He had decided to approach the regents informally, tell them about his proposal, and gauge their reactions before he made a formal statement of his intentions. He talked to President Hutchins early in the week and was assured of his support. At the regents' meeting, he made his announcement. The minutes read:

Regent Clements made a statement outlining possible additions or adjuncts to the Library Building and the book collection of the University, and suggested the great desirability of a trip by the Regents to visit eastern libraries. ... On motion of Regent Murfin it was voted that the entire Board, including the President, ... should make the proposed trip, and that Professor Van Tyne ... and Librarian Bishop should be members of the party.[3]

October 18 was picked for the start of the expedition.

Clements was cautiously optimistic over the success of his opening gambit. He wrote to Ford, whom he expected to support him as an expert witness in favor of his proposition when the party reached Boston. He told him,

The whole trip is preliminary to a proposition which I shall make to the Board if matters work out as I expect, for the presentation of a building and library of Americana at the University of Michigan.

I am very anxious to have them examine the Carter Brown Library at Providence, which, after all, is the greatest library of its kind in the country, and in many ways is my ideal.[4]

To Bishop, Clements confided a few of the doubts and misgivings which still lingered in his mind as to the wisdom of taking the entire Board of Regents, rather than a select committee. As for the proposed itinerary for the group, he suggested that

arrangements can be made through Mr. Winship or the General Librarian at Harvard for inspection of all they have. I believe too that Mr. Ford will be of great use to us, for he has definite ideas on the use and foundation of special libraries, like the Carter Brown, in fact, both Mr. Winship and Mr. Ford I know have ideas which are quite different, and I think we would be interested in hearing both of them in Boston; then we would visit the Harvard Libraries, and possibly the Massachusetts Historical Society ....

In Providence, we have, of course, the greatest example of a special library in the John Carter Brown, and it is there that I expect to impress the Board the most. ...

In New Haven, you can best arrange the plan through Mr. Keogh, Librarian at Yale, and I think we should meet with Professor [William Lyon] Phelps in connection with the Elizabethan Club Library.

Mr. Winship thought the Hispanic Society building and library was a model in New York, and we could visit that and the New York Historical Society.[5]

Clements left before the rest of the committee, traveling

first to Worcester, where he attended the annual meeting of the American Antiquarian Society on October 15. On October 19, he joined the members of The University of Michigan Committee. The group was met in Boston by Worthington C. Ford, who not only gave them an extensive tour of the Massachusetts Historical Society, but hosted a luncheon for them at the Union Club. Winship took over in Cambridge, showing them the treasures of the Widener Library and inviting them to dinner at the Club of Odd Volumes. On October 21, following a tour of Yale libraries, they were invited by Librarian Andrew Keogh to dine at the Graduates' Club, and to meet President Hadley, Secretary Stokes, and Mr. Barr of the University. They visited the John Carter Brown Library in Providence on the same day. They then left for New York City, where Harper had obtained permission for them to visit the Hispanic Society Library. After a visit to the Grolier Club Library, the University Committee left for home.

Regental reaction to the trip seems to have been mixed. As Bishop remembered it, 'It was a pretty stiff dose for some of the Regents. I recall Regent Murfin's remark that he had not had to meet so many – – highbrows in a dog's age.' But nonetheless, Bishop felt that it 'did much to pave the way for an understanding of the functions and possibilities of such a library as this.'[6]

Worthington C. Ford summed up the visit and his assessment of Clements' own library problems in a succinct letter:

You saw in and around Boston the three kinds of institutions possible. In the Historical Society you have a productive Society rather than a collecting one. We are more anxious to use historical material or to place it at the command of historical students and other libraries than to possess it ourselves. In the Widener Library you saw a book museum, for I cannot imagine any conduct of it which will raise it above the level of a curiosity. You and I will get just as much amusement and knowledge from an edition which costs a dollar as from one which costs five thousand dollars, the text being exactly the same. In the John Carter Brown you had a historical library, a fine collection only waiting to be exploited by trained intelligence united with an instinct for historical research and appreciation of its rarities. [The JCB was currently without a director, and remained so until Lawrence Wroth joined the staff in 1923. Ford served as consultant during the interim period.] That [library] can be made highly productive and in quite another sense from the productivity of the Historical Society. But while it remains without a head the publication of the catalogue must represent its positive contribution to the furtherance of historical studies, and that alone is sufficient to bring reputation to the Library and its management.

You have a problem which will combine features of all three institutions. You have the beginnings of a collection more than sufficient to constitute a laboratory. You have enough to make it one of the show pieces among western libraries, which brings it in a line with museum collections, and there is the possibility of training workers who may go out to other libraries and prove fruitful. No school for such workers now exists, and there I feel is the great opportunity which you have of instituting the great Library of Americana in the West, united to a positive school both of American history and American bibliography. I am only telling you what you already know, but I cannot refrain from again showing how interesting the proposition seems to me in the future.[7]

Clements considered the letter to be of such importance that he had it photostated and distributed to each member of the party which had made the trip east. To Bishop he said,

This letter is full of meat, and offers food for a good deal of reflection.

162

I believe Mr. Ford has expressed, quite impartially, the conclusions that we ourselves may have reached.

No library such as we have in mind, unless it is properly exploited, will produce results commensurate with the outlay necessary for its maintenance. We must not go into the proposition unless we are sure that it will be exploited, and that it will make Michigan the historical headquarters for advanced study of American History in the West.[8]

Bishop, meanwhile, had set down his own impressions of the trip.

The question of a separate building does not seem to me fundamental; the matter of adequate support does. I started on the trip open to conviction on that topic, but inclining to what you very properly characterized as the librarian's point of view in the conference at the Elizabethan Club. I have felt all along that Mr. Kahn could make two floors of the west wing [of the University Library] a beautiful, safe and practical home for the collection, and that without marring the building or injuring its development. And I hoped that the sum which would go into a building might be applied to the increase of the collection or to its endowment.

As a result of the trip I am not so sure. In fact, I can see advantages in securing and keeping support which outweigh more obvious benefits in convenience and use which inclined me to my first view. And there are patent aids to conservation in a separate structure in which a separate and distinct treatment can easily and properly be enforced. As Librarian of the University I can devise ways and means for working successfully either solution of the problem. The separate building – near at hand – is probably, I believe, the better device.[9]

Aside from the question of proper housing, Bishop felt that there were a few necessary conditions to be satisfied if Clements' library proposition were to be a success. Bishop summarized these in an addenda to the same letter, headed 'Summary of impressions of trip, Special Library of American History in a University.' As 'Absolutely Necessary Conditions,' he listed '(1) Safety from fire, theft, careless handling, misuse, neglect and decay. . . . (2) Support for maintenance, increase, publications, as well as adequate and beautiful housing.' Under the heading 'Desirable Conditions' he noted 'Close relation (physical and administrative) with General Library and with History Department of University. Permission to add other gifts in same field – but with distinctive marking.' These conditions were followed by a few 'notes,' among which were cited,

Safety from neglect and decay depends on appropriations from Regents (annual) resulting from a contract to maintain the library in an adequate fashion, and also on personnel of administration . . . . Support to be adequate must include salaries, funds for purchase, funds for publication and for taking part in cooperative enterprises, as well as heat, light and cleaning, and repairs. The minimum at the present time is $25,000 per year.
Housing is the chief difficulty. If separate from the General Library building, it should be as near it as the future development of the Library and the Campus will permit, and there should be a tunnel connection . . . .

Housing involves also a vault for great rarities, ventilated cases proof against dust and the sneakthief, reading room for work under supervision, offices and working rooms for small staff, stacks for ordinary books and newspapers . . . exhibit space where visitors will not disturb persons using the collections, rooms for photoduplication, possibly small class-rooms and office for Head of History Department. (I am not very sure of the wisdom of this. W.W.B.).

. . . As to administration, I feel that it cannot safely be divorced from that of the General Library, and suggest that later the Librarian be made Director of the University Libraries, with responsible heads of the different collections under his direction.[10]

The October and November meetings of the Board of Regents passed without further discussion of Clements' proposal. But Clements was not willing to let the matter lie dormant. He spoke informally to his two book-loving friends, Regents Beal and Hubbard, and asked them if they would exert a little friendly pressure on the other members of the board. Hubbard responded quickly. To Beal he wrote,

I had a hint that Clements expects us to take some action on his proposition and think we'd better 'get busy' so that he can have the proposition to offer at the next meeting. We should approve of a separate building, say near the back of the lot in which the Prest's [sic] house stands, but leaving enough ground on the street for a large building which he may have to erect there some day. We should appropriate enough money to pay a custodian, who would be under the general oversight of the Librarian, and the other necessary help could come from the general library. I should also like to see an annual appropriation, which might be utilized, in part, at least, in publishing facsimiles of the rarer books. Will you consult with Sawyer, Murfin, and Leland? We ought not to lose any time for something might happen to make us lose the fight.[11]

Regent Beal sent identical letters to Murfin, Sawyer, and Leland, urging action on Clements' offer at the next regents' meeting:

Regarding the suggestion of Regent William L. Clements to present his Library of Americana to the University, and the con-

clusions arrived at from our eastern trip to the special libraries, it seems to me that some action should be taken by our Board looking to a proper understanding of the arrangements deemed advisable for its best uses, purposes and administration.

After hearing what was said about the Clements Library by Mr. Worthington Ford, Mr. Coolidge, Dean Briggs, Mr. Brigham, Mr. Winship, and Mr. Keogh, we get a clear idea of the value of this library and of its standing among the best book men of the country, as they all agreed this would put Michigan among the first three libraries of the continent in the sources of American History, thus affording great help to that department of the University. It is something that cannot come again to Michigan, nor to any other university.

At our next meeting it should be brought up and have a determination of several fundamental questions, such as, Shall we house it in the new Library Building or in a separate building? If it is to be kept by itself, Mr. Clements has offered to build the building, and it seems as though that is the best thing to do.

Next, we should decide on its administration to get the most good out of it. This will require an able man like Mr. Ford and some assistants who shall be able to assist him and Mr. Bishop in our Library School training librarians. I understand the Carter Brown has $20,000 appropriated for it annually, which amount covers everything.

I would be pleased to have your views on these and any other things pertaining to this which may occur to you, so that we can all agree on what should be made into a resolution before the meeting, as we can discuss it freer this way.

In considering it I wish you would reread that interesting letter Mr. Worthington Ford wrote Mr. Clements, and which he sent each member, about the proper exploiting of such a collection.[12]

166

Other important business, however, intervened to occupy the regents at the December 19 meeting. The arduous search for a president to succeed Harry B. Hutchins was at an end. The regents unanimously elected Marion LeRoy Burton, president of the University of Minnesota, as the fifth president of The University of Michigan, to take office on July 1, 1920. Clements, probably wisely, did not attempt to have his proposition included on the agenda.

The following week, Bishop had an unexpected letter from Clements' son, Wallace Clements, stating,

Father has asked me to write you and advise that he is confined to his bed and that under the doctor's orders he will not be able to leave it for a week or ten days.[13]

The illness, which Clements referred to as 'a severe attack of indigestion,'[14] could hardly have struck at a more unfortunate moment. Along with his overriding and continued concern for the regents' decision in regard to his library proposition, he had been asked to speak at two important functions. Early in the month, Azariah S. Root had invited him to address the midwinter meeting of the Bibliographical Society of America to be held January 1 at the Hotel LaSalle in Chicago. His assigned topic was 'Some Reminiscences of Book Sales.' Clements had also agreed to speak at the long-awaited dedication of the new General Library building on the Michigan campus, scheduled for January 7, 1920.

The trip to Chicago was clearly an impossibility. Through Wallace, Clements asked Bishop to notify the secretary of the Society of this fact. 'His paper,' added Wallace, 'is partly prepared but is not in such shape that it can be sent on. He is very comfortable and will, no doubt, be perfectly alright [*sic*] in a very short time.'[15]

Bishop had scarcely had time to recover from this news when Wallace wrote again.

While Father feels very well the doctor says he must be quiet and he is still in bed. It is very doubtful whether he will be able to attend the opening of the Library on the 7th of next month.[16]

Bishop's dismay and concern for Clements is evident in his reply:

I thank you for your note of the 27th, and am relieved to hear that your father is at least not suffering.
By the President's direction, I will be prepared to speak at the dedication, on the subject Mr. Clements was to have handled. If, however, he can come down, we shall hope to hear from him. . . . I shall feel that very much of the pleasure of the dedication exercises is gone if your father is forced to be absent. His constant kindness to me during the last four and one half years, and his warm interest in every detail of the library work have endeared him, not only to me but to the entire library staff, and we shall all be greatly distressed at his enforced absence.[17]

Clements had not only agreed to speak at the dedication; he had also volunteered to display some of the more important rarities from his collection in the lobby of the new library building in honor of the occasion. This was the first time that Clements had allowed his books to leave his Bay City library for public viewing. He may have agreed to the exhibition partly to give those regents who had never visited his library a chance to see what he proposed to give the University. While Clements

168

was willing to acquiesce in the doctor's demand that he forego his speech, he was still determined to follow through with the exhibition. As soon as he could get out of bed, he began arranging for the books to be sorted, packed, and sent to Ann Arbor. Esther Loud wrote to Bishop,

This is Mr. Clements' first day downstairs and he and I have spent it selecting the books for your exhibit. There will be sixty five or seventy books. I shall provide labels with short historical sketches. We plan to send the books down in a sealed trunk, by express, and hope to get them off by the end of the week.[18]

Still more welcome news came with Clements' personal assurance to Bishop:

I have so far recovered that I expect to attend the exercises and Regents' meeting next week, but I am going pretty light on work so am going to retire in favor of you or President Hutchins in the speaking programme.[19]

Clements made the trip to Ann Arbor for the library dedication on January 7 and sat with the other dignitaries on the Hill Auditorium stage for the ceremonies. The speakers included William Warner Bishop, who addressed himself to the history of the new library building, the topic that Clements was to have covered. Albert Kahn spoke on the plans for the building, and Richard R. Bowker, then editor of the *Library Journal*, had as his topic 'The Library, Democracy, and Research.' Three thousand persons attended the exercises and viewed the exhibition at the library, which consisted of a collection of illuminated manuscripts belonging to a well-known rare book dealer, Wilfred Voynich, and about seventy-five books chosen from the

169

discovery and colonization period of American history from Clements' library. The most important single item was the 1588 Hariot's *Virginia*. Others from the Bay City library included the Columbus letter of 1493, Eden's *Decades* (1555), Captain John Smith's *True Relation* (1608), Francis Drake's *The World Encompassed* (1628), and Mather's *Magnalia Christi Americana* (1702).

The January meeting of the Board of Regents followed the day after. Although still far from well, Clements was in attendance. With the aid and encouragement of his friend Regent Beal, he again

informally outlined the conditions under which he might tender as a gift to the University his library of Americana with a building for its housing. On motion of Regent Murfin, the President was requested to appoint a committee, of which the President should be the chairman, to discuss the matter with Regent Clements and to make a report to the Board. The President named Regents Beal, Hubbard, and Leland.[20]

To Ford, in a letter written a few days after the meeting, Clements commented on tentative points of agreement which had been reached.

The Board of Regents have agreed to make an annual appropriation of $25,000 for the operation of the library and for accessions, and I have agreed to, first, erect a building of a size approximately that of the Carter Brown and completely equip it; second to give them my library and the newspaper collection, and third, to make additional accessions as may be thought desirable.

All of the above has been tentatively agreed between us, and

I am now 'mulling' over the details which should be embodied in any such important agreement . . . .

I am bound to consider the action of any democratic Board, such as is the Board of Regents controlling the University. One Board cannot control the action of any future Board. A contract made by a present Board unless completely carried out and fulfilled within a reasonable period might not be carried on by a future Board, so the problem of looking after the interests of such a library in case of default for my own interest I must consider carefully. I am inclined to place conditions upon such a default as would allow the library to be taken over by any other reputable Western educational institution who would fulfill the original conditions.[21]

On the same day, he wrote a long letter to his friend Winship:

We had a quiet but interesting time at the opening of the library . . . . Librarian William W. Bishop was Regent Clements. My blood pressure was too high for the Doctor to allow me to say a word.

Mr. Voynich made an exhibit of manuscripts in his usual manner. The manuscripts were beautiful and most attractive to the eye, and had the principal attention of all who visited the building, but no one knew anything about any of them excepting himself, and no one could dispute what he had to say . . . .

That was not so about my own modest exhibit, for I have never been able to 'put anything over' in speaking of any books in my collection – there are too many men who know. I brought to Ann Arbor about seventy five important books in the Discovery of [sic-to?] the Colonial Period, which seemed to attract attention.

I know you will be interested in hearing in general of the situation as to my own proposition at Ann Arbor. I have made it and they have accepted it tentatively, and a Committee has been appointed to jointly formulate with me a general form of agreement and contract . . . . A consideration of it involves:

First. *Whether the Custodian of the Library should be an absolutely independent official, independent of the general librarian, but working in harmony with him and reporting to the Library Committee of the Board of Regents.*

Second. *Whether there should be any mixture of the books now in the University Library with this collection of mine.*

Third. *Whether the general design of the building which I have decided upon is to be of size approximately that of the John Carter Brown.*

Fourth. *How proper protection can be secured for the fulfillment of the condition of an annual appropriation of $ 25,000.00 a year for the operation of the library and accessions to it by the Board of Regents.*

Fifth. *How shall the proper conservation be secured, and by whom shall this library be used.*[22]

And Winship responded:

The position of your custodian depends largely upon the salary he or she is to get. The University Librarian will always scheme to make him a subordinate, and the more important the position is, the more will this be so, for obvious reasons. The Governing Body will probably abet him in this, being business men who recognize the advantages of a systematized organization. I think I know something about the probabilities in the proposed situation, and if I were doing what you are, I should most emphatically create an independent position whose occupant will have an unquestioned primary allegiance to your foundation. I fancy you understand the academic way of doing things well enough to see why this seems to me so important. The independent position will be easier to establish if the title is different from that of the other librarians. . . . An important reason for the independent position seems to me that the independent person will be asked to do things as a favor, and will ordinarily do them gladly, which would tend to become an imposition upon your foundation if required of a subordinate . . . .

As regards books in the general library. . . . There will not be many volumes which are needed for frequent use in both places. The larger, general reference works, biographical dictionaries, and the like, will be used more often in the general library, and your cataloguer may better go there or send for them, than go to the expense of buying (and the greater expense of shelving forever) any of these. In return for this, you will have the special reference works for your special subject, and the general library will apply to you for these on the infrequent occasions when they need them.[23]

As for the size and design of the building, Winship agreed that the John Carter Brown Library was about the right size for convenient administration, although the physical arrangement of the rooms could be improved. As a solution to the problem of insuring the future fulfillment of the contract, Winship echoed Clements' idea that a provision could be made for the collection to leave the state and be given to another institution in case of default.

Winship's suggested solution to Clements' fifth problem should be noted, as it is the first mention of the idea of a Committee of Management, an independent group which today serves as the governing body for the Clements Library. Winship felt that there should be *provision for an advisory committee, which shall present an annual report to be printed by the foundation, coupled with provision for an annual lecture or lectures in the building,*

these lectures to be given by distinguished antiquarians from the east coast or from Great Britain who would also inspect the collection.[24]

Clements also received a long letter from Worthington C. Ford while he was mulling over Winship's advice, but the letters, expressing opposing points of view, proved almost more perplexing than helpful. With the February 20 regents' meeting approaching and with his preliminary statement still unwritten, Clements wrote President Hutchins,

Will you pardon my delay in fulfilling my promise of an outline of a proposed plan for transferring my library to the University, and for constructing a building for same? I have been unable to decide on some of the general features of the program, for indeed it requires a good deal of consideration. During the past two days I have received a long letter from Mr. Ford, and another one from Mr. Winship, two persons whose advice I value very highly. Both of them gave opinions directly opposite, and both have had large experience. For the sake of the University and for myself, I do not want to make any mistakes, hence, I know you will appreciate the fact that much consideration is necessary. I hope to have some kind of a communication ready by the next meeting.[25]

Hutchins replied promptly, and with his usual calm wisdom,

I appreciate that your problem in regard to the library is a difficult one and I think that you should take all of the time that

174

you find it necessary to take in formulating the plan. The fact that the opinions of Mr. Ford and Mr. Winship are directly opposite is certainly an embarassing one. I do not know the men intimately, but from what I saw of them on our trip I judge that Mr. Ford would probably have the broader and safer view.[26]

On February 12, Clements sent a letter, that he called 'an informal expression of what seems desirable,' to President Hutchins, Regent Beal, and Regent Hubbard, for their consideration before the February 20 regents' meeting. Of this letter, he said to Bishop,

It has been rather a difficult matter to come to conclusion, and I am not sure the points brought out in this letter are all entirely proper. They are subject to revision, however.

I wrote some time ago Mr. Ford and Mr. Winship, expressing some general ideas, and their replies were opposite in views so much so, that the letters put me to thinking again, but, I have been influenced all together by Mr. Ford's views, which I regard as sounder and all together better than Mr. Winship's. It is unfortunate that these two men do not work in harmony. Ford appreciates Winship's abilities, but is not at all in sympathy with him, and nothing that Mr. Ford does is well done, as interpreted by Mr. Winship.[27]

Clements included a copy of the letter for Bishop's perusal. Addressed to members of the regents' committee appointed to work out an agreement with him, its stipulations were as follows:

I propose placing upon a high plane for work the Department of American History, at the University of Michigan, that scholars

and students who may be interested in the intense study and investigation of the source books and manuscripts pertaining to the Discovery and Colonization Period: the source books and manuscripts pertaining to the American Revolution, and of later periods of American History, may be furnished with adequate materials for such work. Further, that the highest class of librarians may be developed; that the spirit of investigation and study of history may be submitted, and it is to be hoped may touch the ambition of some undergraduates through a proper exposition of its treasures; that it shall, as it were, in the words of our friend Mr. Worthington C. Ford 'become a drinking fountain, where all students may be led or enticed to come and drink.'

With these purposes in view, I propose to donate to the University of Michigan this library, subject to such use as I may desire to make of it during my life, and to erect and equip a building of size not less than the John Carter Brown Library Building, of Brown University, Providence, R. I. This building shall have exterior facings of Bedford sandstone [The finished building was constructed of limestone], and shall be of fire proof construction throughout. It is proposed that this building shall be placed upon the campus of the University upon a site mutually agreed by the Board of Regents and the donor, and its design, together with its equipment, shall be submitted to the Board for its approval.

The above building will be erected by me at as early a time as is deemed practicable. It is the purpose to proceed as rapidly as possible with the drawings and specifications, and contracts will be let as soon as building conditions are such as to warrant reasonable economy in construction and thoroughness in building operation.

I request that it be my privilege to add to this library, to exchange book material for better, and to exercise such general supervision over accessions which shall be for its increased usefulness and value. With this library there is also included the col-

176

1. Mr. Clements' Library in his home at Bay City

2. *William L. Clements Library at the University of Michigan*

3a. *Main Hall of the Library*

3b. *The Treasure Room for the Rarest Books*

4a. *Director Randolph G. Adams*

4b. *Librarian William W. Bishop*

4c. *President Marion L. Burton*

4d. *Prof. Claude H. Van Tyne*

5. *Entrance to the Treasure Room*

¶ Epistola Christofori Colom: cui etas nostra multum debet: de
Insulis Indie supra Gangem nuper inuentis. Ad quas pergren
das octauo antea mense auspiciis et ere inuictissimorum Fernãdi et
Helisabet Hispaniarum Regum missus fuerat: ad magnificum dñm
Gabrielem Sanchis eorundem serenissimorum Regum Tesaurariũ
missa: quã nobilis ac litteratus vir Leander de Cosco ab Hispa
no idiomate in latinum cõuertit tertio kal's Maii M.cccc.xciii
Pontificatus Alexandri Sexti Anno primo.

Quoniam suscepte prouintie rem perfectam me prosecutum
fuisse gratum tibi fore scio: has constitui exarare: que te
vniuscuiusque rei in hoc nostro itinere geste inuenteque ad
moneant. Tricesimotertio die postquam Gadibus discessi in mare
Indicum perueni: vbi plurimas insulas innumeris habitatas ho
minibus repperi: quarum omnium pro felicissimo Rege nostro
preconio celebrato et verillis extensis contradicente nemine pos
sessionem accepi: primeque earum diui Saluatoris nomen impo
sui: cuius fretus auxilio tam ad hanc: quam ad ceteras alias perue
nimus. Eam vo Indi Guanahanin vocant. Aliarum etiam vnam
quanque nouo nomine nuncupaui: quippe aliam insulam Sancte
Marie Conceptionis. aliam Fernandinam. aliam Hysabellam.
aliam Joanam. et sic de reliquis appellari iussi. Cum primum in
eam insulam quam dudum Joanam vocari dixi appulimus: iu
xta eius littus occidentem versus aliquantulum processi: tamenque
eam magnam nullo reperto fine inueni: vt non insulam: sed conti
nentem Chatai prouinciam esse crediderim: nulla tñ videns op
pida municipiaue in maritimis sita confinibus preter aliquos vi
cos et predia rustica: cum quorum incolis loqui nequibam: quare si
mul ac nos videbant surripiebant fugam. Progrediebar vltra
existimans aliquã me vrbem villasue inuenturum. Denique videns
quod longe admodum progressis nihil noui emergebat: et huiusmodi via
nos ad Septentrionem deferebat: quod ipse fugere exoptabam: terris
etenim regnabat bruma: ad Austrumque erat in voto cõtendere:

*6. First page of the Columbus letter, 1493, relating his discovery of islands
on the far side of the Atlantic.*

A briefe and true re-
port of the new found land of Virginia: of
the commodities there found and to be raysed, as well mar-
chantable, as others for victuall, building and other necessa-
rie vses for those that are and shalbe the planters there, and of the na-
ture and manners of the naturall inhabitants : Discouered by the
English Colony there seated by Sir Richard Greinuile *Knight in the*
yeere 1585. which remained vnder the gouernment of Rafe Lane Esqui-
er, one of her Maiesties Equieres, during the space of twelue monethes ; at
the speciall charge and direction of the Honourable SIR
WALTER RALEIGH Knight, Lord Warden of
the stanneries ; who therein hath beene fauou-
red and authorised by her Maiestie and
her letters patents:

Directed to the Aduenturers, Fauourers,
and Welwillers of the action, for the inhabi-
ting and planting there:

By *Thomas Hariot*; seruant to the abouenamed
Sir Walter, a member of the Colony, and
there imployed in discouering.

Imprinted at London 1588.

7. *Hariot's Virginia, 1588: the first account of the first English colony, on Roanoke Island.*

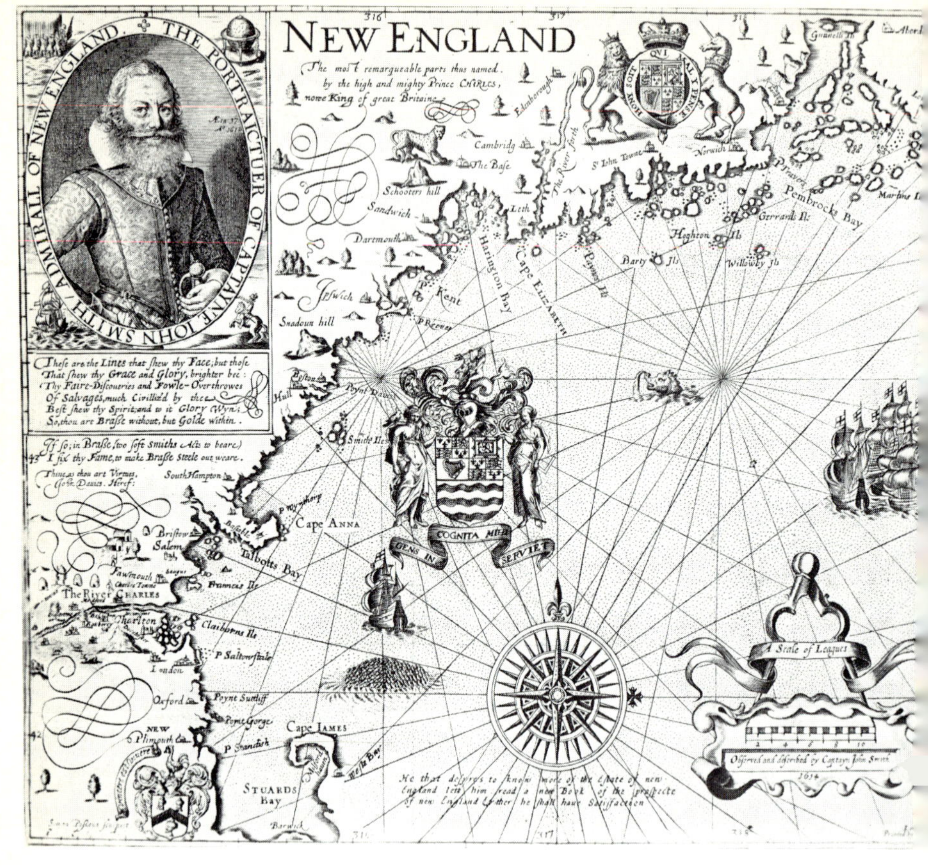

8. *Capt. John Smith's map appears in his Description of New England, 1616, before the region was settled.*

9. *First Bible printed in America, 1663, a translation into an Indian tongue by a missionary, the Rev. John Eliot*

VRYHEDEN

By de Vergaderinghe van de Negenthiene vande Geoctroyeerde West-Indische Compagnie vergunt aen allen den ghenen / die eenighe Colonien in Nieu-Nederlandt sullen planten.

Jn het licht ghegheven

Om bekent te maken wat Profijten ende Voordeelen aldaer in Nieu-Nederlandt, voor de Coloniers ende der selver Patroonen ende Meesters, midtsgaders de Participanten, die de Colonien aldaer planten, zijn becomen.

T' AMSTELREDAM,

Voor Marten Iansz Brandt Boeckvercooper / woonende by de nieuwe Kerck / in de Gereformeerde Catechismus, Anno 1630.

10. *The Dutch West India Company published this work in 1630, the first book entirely about the Dutch settlement in modern New York.*

THE
New-England PSALM-SINGER :
O R,
American CHORISTER.

CONTAINING

A Number of PSALM-TUNES, ANTHEMS AND CANONS.

In Four and Five Parts.

[*Never before Published.*]

Compoſed by WILLIAM BILLINGS,

A Native of BOSTON, in *New-England.*

MATTHEW xxi. 16. — *Out of the Mouth of Babes and Sucklings thou haſt perfected Praiſe.*
JAMES v. 13. ——— *Is any Merry? Let him ſing Pſalms.*

O praiſe the Lord with one Conſent, and in this grand Deſign,
Let Britain and the Colonies, unanimouſly join.

BOSTON : *New-England.* Printed by EDES and GILL.

And to be Sold by them at their Printing-Office in Queen-Street ; by Deacon *Elliot,* under Liberty-Tree ;
by *Joſiah Flagg,* in Fiſh-Street ; by *Gillam Baſs,* the Corner of Ann-Street, and by the Author.

[Price Eight Shillings, L. M.]

11. *Early American composer and singing teacher, William Billings, published*
this book of songs in 1770, with engravings by Paul Revere.

Four Brass Cannon and two Mortars or Cohorns in the [with a Number of small arms] or out Houses of Mr Barrett a little on the other side the Bridge where is also lodged a Quantity of Powder & Ball.

Ten Iron Cannon before the Town = House and two within it which Town = House is in the Center of the Town, The Ammunition for said Guns within the House

Three Guns of 24 Pounders, lodged in the Prison yard with a Quantity of Cartridges and Provision

A Quantity of Provision and Ammunition in other Places, The Principal Deposits are the Houses of Messrs Hubbards, Butler, Jones the Jailor, [near Hubbards] two men of the name of Bond; and particularly at Mr Whitneys who lives near on the Right Hand at the Entrance of the Town, the House plaistered white a small yard in front and a railed fence a large Quantity of Powder and Ball is reported to be deposited in his stores adjoining the House.

A Quantity of Ammunition and Provision together as number of cannon and small arms having been collected at Concord for the avowed purpose of supplying a body of Rebels raised against His Majestys Government, Sir, you will march with the Corps of Grenadiers and Light Infantry put under your Command with the utmost Expedition and Secrecy to Concord, where you will seize and destroy all the Artillery and Ammunition, Provisions, Tents, small Arms, and all other military Stores you can find, you will knock off one Trunnion at least of each of the Iron Guns, and destroy the Carriages and beat in the Muzzles of the Brass ones so as to render them useless. The Powder & flour may be shaken out of the Barrells into the Water, and the heads burst, and the men may put the Balls & Lead into their Pockets throwing them away by Degrees into the Fields Ditches Ponds &c. You have a Plan with on which is marked the Places where the Artillery & Ammunition &c is reported to be lodged, and after destroying the same you will return, and if your Men appear much fatigued you may halt them at Lexington or Cambridge and let them rest in Barns or other out houses, and may hire waggons at Lexington for weak and fatigued Men. If any Body dares to attack oppose you with arms you will warn them to disperse or attack them.

Some men from the Artillery are ordered to attend you and will carry sledge Hammers and other Instruments to destroy the Guns.

12. *The letter that started the Revolution: Gen. Gage's orders, April 18, 1775, in his own hand, sending the British troops to Concord. The orders are preceded by a list of supplies which the rebels had gathered at Concord.*

COMMON SENSE;

ADDRESSED TO THE

INHABITANTS

OF

AMERICA,

On the following interesting

SUBJECTS.

I Of the Origin and Design of Government in general, with concise Remarks on the English Constitution.

II. Of Monarchy and Hereditary Succession.

III. Thoughts on the present State of American Affairs.

IV. Of the present Ability of America, with some miscellaneous Reflections.

Man knows no Master save creating Heaven,
Or those whom choice and common good ordain.

THOMSON.

PHILADELPHIA;

Printed, and Sold, by R. BELL, in Third Street.

MDCCLXXVI.

13. *Tom Paine's Common Sense, first edition, 1776, arguing that independence was inevitable.*

New Windsor May 29th. 1781

Sir,

A day or two ago I requested
Colo. Harrison to apply to you for a pair of
Pincers to fasten the wire of my teeth. — I hope
you furnished him with them — I now wish
you would send me one of your scrapers,
as my teeth stand in need of cleaning, and
I have little prospect of being in Philadelpa.
soon. — It will come very safe by the Post — &
in return, the money shall be sent so soon as
I know the cost of it. —

I am Sir

Yr. very Hble Servt

G Washington

14. *George Washington writes to his dentist, 1781, a letter captured by the British.*

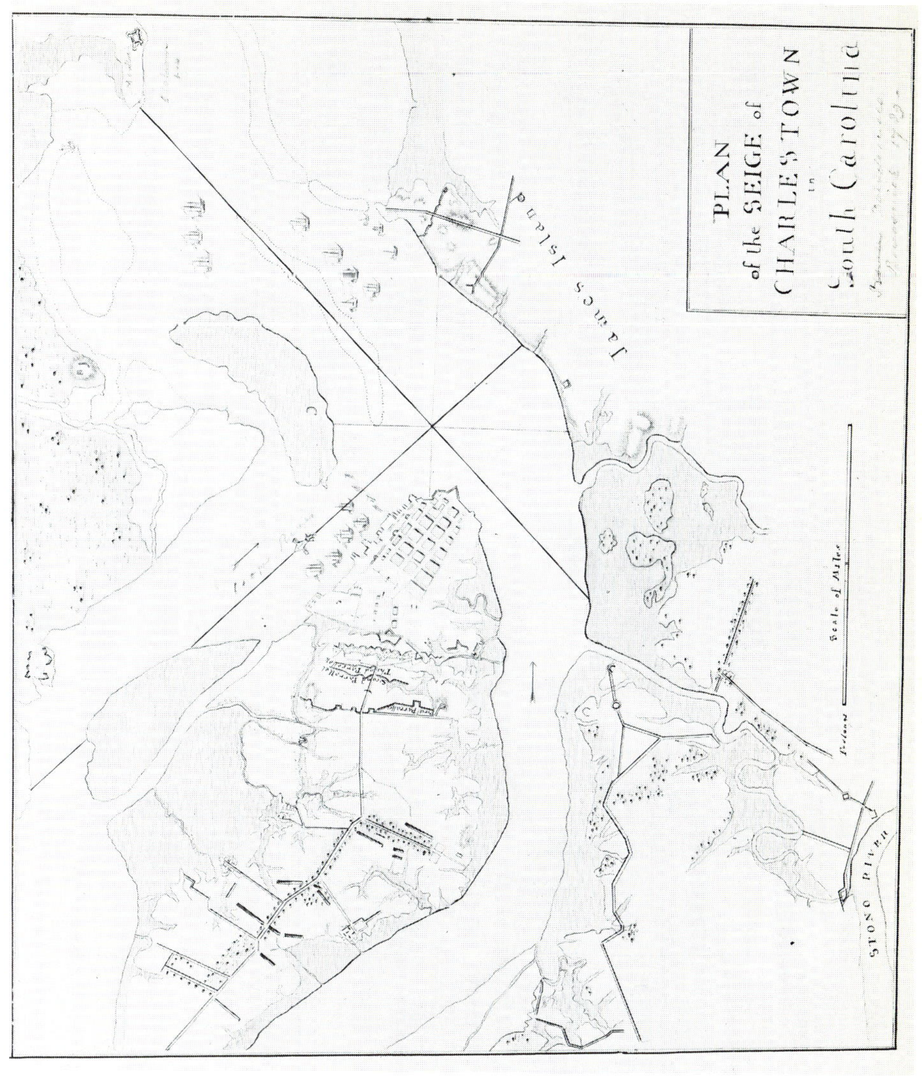

15. *Manuscript map by a British engineer of the siege of Charleston, 1780.
From the Clinton Papers.*

THE

FEDERALIST:

A COLLECTION

OF

ESSAYS,

WRITTEN IN FAVOUR OF THE

NEW CONSTITUTION,

AS AGREED UPON BY THE FEDERAL CONVENTION,
SEPTEMBER 17, 1787.

IN TWO VOLUMES.

VOL. I.

NEW-YORK:

PRINTED AND SOLD BY J. AND A. M'LEAN,
No. 41, HANOVER-SQUARE.
M,DCC,LXXXVIII.

16. *The essays in book form that explained and recommended adoption of the new Constitution, 1788, written by Madison, Hamilton, and Jay.*

lection of American Newspapers covering the Eighteenth and Nineteenth Centuries, housed at present in the general library building of the University, and in my library at Bay City, Michigan. – (A collection numbering from twenty-five hundred to three thousand volumes.)

I suggest the library of books be known as the 'Clements Library of American History.' The newspapers belonging to the library shall belong to the newspaper section, housed in the same building.

I ask in consideration of the fulfillment of the above, the University, through its Board of Regents, to agree:

First.   (a) To receive as its property the library and building above generally described.

(b) To maintain and keep in repair the library of books and manuscripts, the building and its equipment.

(c) To heat and supply it with water, electricity and other necessities.

(d) To keep the building and books therein adequately insured against fire and theft.

Second. To provide a fund of $ 25,000.00 annually for the purpose of:

(a) Paying the salary of a Custodian, who shall be known as the 'Custodian of the Clements Library of American History,' together with such Assistants as may be necessary.

(b) For paying expenses incurred in binding or rebinding or maintaining in repair the books in the collection.

(c) For accessions to the collection with the specific agreement that the sum set aside for accessions shall not be less than three fifths of the total sum appropriated, and that such accessions shall become a part and be de-

Bishop sailed on the S. S. *Homeric* for France on November 11, 1922. They arrived in Paris on November 19, and the following day Bishop went with Champion to Bagneux, a suburb of Paris, to the Vignaud country house. 'His library,' recalled Bishop,

filled three rooms in an old house with a wonderful garden and grove – once part of the country-seat of Cardinal Richelieu. The books were in some cases three rows deep on the shelves, on most shelves two deep. They filled to overflowing two large rooms and one smaller room.[27]

Enlisting the aid of Abel Doysié, whom Bishop had met through Clements' transcription project, Bishop began a detailed examination of the Vignaud library. His conclusion was that the library represented

very fully continental scholarship, particularly French, Italian, and Spanish authorities, and that its purchase will save us ten or fifteen years of work in making the Clements Library productive in scholarly publications; for here are already gathered the critical works which we should at once have to seek out for any man undertaking historical investigation in the discovery and colonization periods.[28]

At the regents' meeting of November 24, President Burton reported a cablegram from Bishop in regard to the Vignaud library. After consideration of the matter,

On motion of Regent Clements, the Board directed that the library be purchased and that a credit of 200,000 fr. be cabled in accordance with Mr. Bishop's recommendations. It was understood that the total cost of the library to the University would not be in excess of $ 21,000. . . . Regent Clements had volunteered

242

to pay one third of the cost of that portion of the library which might be found suitable for incorporation into the Clements Library. Such payment by Regent Clements would presumably reduce the total above mentioned cost by $ 2,000.[29]

Secretary Smith immediately cabled the necessary funds to Bishop who commissioned Champion to take charge of packing, insurance, and shipment of the library; he thereupon left Paris on further University business in the Netherlands and in England. One hundred forty-six cases containing the Vignaud library arrived at the University Library in Ann Arbor on January 22, twelve days after Bishop's return.

Clements considered the Vignaud library chiefly of value as collateral material for his collection. Upon receiving Bishop's first report of titles included in the library, he wrote to President Burton,

As I read over carefully Mr. Bishop's report it would appear that much of what is in this library is as I expected, a most welcome accession to the division of my library which I call 'Books of the Discovery Period.' There is nothing in Mr. Bishop's statement of titles excepting one, which is a great rarity. He states there is in the lot the 'Cosmographiae Introduction' 1507, September edition. This book would have a ready market at a thousand dollars, and I greatly welcome this accession to my own library. As you know, in forming my library as it is I have not gone into books which could be obtained with a fair degree of facility, and I will give one illustration of this policy. Mr. Bishop reports in the geographical section some six or eight different editions of Ptolemy's Geography. There are four editions only which are of great importance – some of great rarity – which the student must use, the editions of 1478, the first printed edition; 1507; 1511 edition with the Ruysch map; and the 1513 with the Waldseemüller map or the Admiral's (Columbus) map. All others are interesting but not necessary.

to house it, be accepted in accordance with its terms, and with the deepest gratitude of this Board.

The resolution was adopted unanimously, Regent Clements not voting.[29]

The *Michigan Alumnus* for March, 1920, carried news of the gift, printing in its entirety Clements' letter to the Board of Regents. The article also included a statement by Clements which gives some idea of the size of the collection at this time.

> *It is impossible in a brief statement to give an adequate account of the Library. It contains:*
>
> A   *Books, maps and charts dating from 1482, pertaining to the discovery and colonization periods of American history. . . . This section of the library has about 2500 entries.*
>
> B   *Books of the later Colonial period. . . . In this section there are about 1,000 entries.*
>
> C   *Pamphlets and books of the Revolution. . . . This section numbers about 2,000 entries.*
>
> D   *Books pertaining to the Confederation and the formation of the Constitution of 1788, and to the history of the United States up to 1830.*
>
> E   *Books which tell of the early settlement and development of the West.*
>
> F   *The newspaper section, to me one of the most interesting of the entire collection. . . . This library of newspapers is now at Ann Arbor in the collating rooms of the University Library. The newspaper section numbers about 3,000 volumes.*

'It is difficult,' concluded the *Alumnus,*

to overestimate the importance of this gift or its significance for *the future of the work in American history in the University. Not only is Regent Clements' collection of extraordinary intrinsic value; it cost him over $ 400,000 and at a conservative estimate is worth much more now; but even more important, it will furnish, by all odds the best facilities in this field anywhere west of the Alleghenies.*[30]

Less than ten years of intensive activity had brought Clements' collection to this point. And now, no matter what the future might hold for him, a lasting monument to his name seemed assured. As he said to Clarence Brigham, 'This is the culmination of all my doings. . . . This does not mean that I am going to give up my library at the present time, but I am going to prepare for its final resting place.'[31]

NOTES

1   WC to Bishop, August 14, 1919, Bishop Papers.

2   WC to Bishop, September 23, 1919, Bishop Papers.

3   *Regents' Proceedings*, 1917–1920, pp. 692–93. The University paid the expenses for the trip.

4   WC to Ford, October 4, 1919, Clements Papers.

5   WC to Bishop, October 1, 1919, Bishop Papers.

6   Bishop, 'Some Recollections of William Lawrence Clements,' p. 190. One of the 'highbrows' to whom Regent Murfin referred would seem to have been Worthington C. Ford. Bishop went on to explain that at Ford's luncheon party at the Union Club, 'Mr. Ford delivered a monologue on source material which perhaps explained Regent Murfin's profane characterization.'

7   Ford to WC, October 24, 1919, Clements Papers.

8   WC to Bishop, November 4, 1919, Bishop Papers.

9   Bishop to WC, October 26, 1919, Bishop Papers.

10   Addenda, Bishop to WC, October 26, 1919, Bishop Papers.

19 WC to Burton, December 16, 1922, Burton Papers. The revised gift agreement, dated December 14, 1922, is included as Appendix A, *Regents Proceedings*, 1920–1923, pp. 692–698.

20 Burton to WC, December 21, 1922, Burton Papers.

21 *Regents' Proceedings*, 1920–1923, December 22, 1922 meeting, p. 687.

22 Champion to Bishop, August 22, 1922, Bishop Papers. Henry Vignaud (1830–1922) 'was born in New Orleans and was a teacher and newspaper editor before the Civil War. He was commissioned a captain in the 6th Louisiana regiment and was taken prisoner when New Orleans was captured in 1862. Escaping, he fled to Paris and never returned to this country. . . . In 1875 he was appointed secretary of the American legation and retained this post until his retirement in 1909. He became interested in Columbus about the time of the 1892 celebration and thereafter devoted himself to research into the life of Columbus and the early explorations of the New World.' (Peckham, *Guide to the Manuscript Collections in the William L. Clements Library*, p. 261.) His library consisted of 17,000 volumes and over 25,000 pamphlets (C. W. Alvord, 'The Shelburne Manuscripts in America,' London University Institute of Historical Research, *Bulletin*, I [February, 1924], 78).

23 Bishop to WC, September 20, 1922, Bishop Papers.

24 WC to Bishop, October 21, 1922, Bishop Papers.

25 Bishop to Burton, December 29, 1922, Report to the regents on his trip, Bishop Papers.

26 WC to Bishop, November 1, 1922, Bishop Papers.

27 Bishop to Burton, December 29, 1922 (Report to regents), Bishop Papers.

28 Bishop to Burton, December 29, 1922 (Report to regents), Bishop Papers.

29 *Regents' Proceedings*, 1920–1923, p. 668.

30 WC to Burton, December 7, 1922, Burton Papers.

31 The first draft of Randolph G. Adams' first annual report of the Clements Library (1923–1924) dated August 26, 1924, states that 5,000 volumes from the Vignaud library had been checked and arranged in order, but 'some thousands of loose maps . . . and pamphlets' were still not accessioned. Many of the pamphlets were merely reviews of books which Vignaud had extracted and had bound. There was also a large quantity of clippings and excerpts from periodicals.

CLEMENTS' SYNOPSIS OF HIS LIBRARY; THE SEARCH FOR THE CUSTODIAN

In December, 1922, with Bishop in France negotiating for the purchase of the Vignaud Library and with the Regents' Executive Committee making final decisions on the revised gift agreement for the Clements Library, Clements wrote George Parker Winship concerning a project he had set for himself, one which was beginning to seem insurmountably difficult of achievement. 'You will remember,' said Clements,

I had some talk with you about a monograph, or something of the kind to be published and distributed by the University at the time of the opening of the library. In a conference, held nearly a year ago, Professor Van Tyne was very emphatic that this could be done in the very best manner by a young man by the name of Arthur Pound, who was a writer for the Atlantic Monthly. His idea was that Pound could write a rather frothy sort of a production, which would give to all people a knowledge in general of what there was in my library. At the time I was not impressed with Van Tyne's idea but little was said, and the matter drifted to supervise the bibliographical work as well as to add the notes above suggested. If it will not be too expensive a plan, I would be very, very glad to have you do it.[1]

Winship's reply was prompt.

There will be no quarrel as to compensation, if you want me to help with your catalogue. I may be able to save something on the printing bills, which are certain to be heavy for work of this character especially if we insist on accuracy in matters of detail. But I have had some experience in this particular line and ought to know how to fix the manuscript so the printer will know what to do. As for the Notes, I will gladly undertake to supply most of them, as I am sure that I know pretty nearly what you want, and where to lay hand on the desired information. I hesitate to say 'all,' for I do not want to promise anything that might require more time for investigation than the results might justify.

The print shop is to have the specimen pages put into type, and I will get the printer to do this at once, so that you and Miss Loud can agree upon the satisfactory form of entry.

My understanding is that you might like to have me:

1 *Help determine the form of entry and appearance of the printed page.*
2 *Supply notes, explaining why each title has a place in a catalogue of Americana.*
3 *Edit the copy so that the printer may return satisfactory proofs.*
4 *Read proof and oversee the work while it is being printed.*[2]

The week of November 10 was a busy one in the Clements household; Clements' daughter Betty was married to Harry S. Finkenstaedt on November 15, 1919, in the library at Garra-

Tigh. When the excitement of the wedding was over, Clements went back to his printed catalog. He wrote to Winship, apologizing for the delay in answering his letter. 'I have been exceedingly busy with a house full of company incident to my daughter's wedding,' he explained. But now that things were back to normal, Miss Loud was continuing her work, which by now amounted to about 600 entries ready to be set in type. Referring again to the annotations, he continued,

At a meeting of the History Department at Ann Arbor the other evening I explained what we were trying to do, and this part of the work met with the heartiest approval. In general no one but collectors or librarians are interested in the bibliographical part, but the historian is interested in what the book stands for and why it is in the catalogue, as you have heretofore stated, so that all together I feel like saying 'On with the dance.'[3]

Winship had the proof sheets for Clements' forty-six entries in the mail to him by December 5, along with a suggestion that Clements get Bishop's criticism of the appearance of the entries. Corrected page proof followed in a few days. Bishop was prompt and generous in his offer of assistance. His only criticism of the page proof was the use of large capitals for the catch words, which he felt 'gives the page a spotted appearance.'[4] He also offered to read proof for the completed catalog.

The effort of preparing the tentative agreement for the February 20 meeting of the board seems to have pushed everything else to the background. It was not until April, while he was vacationing in Hot Springs with Mrs. Clements and Miss Loud, that Clements gave any more thought to the catalog. To Bishop he wrote,

On receipt of Clements' letter, Pound wrote in obvious exasperation to Van Tyne,

All winter I have been trying to spur Regent Clements up to the point where I could begin the articles on the library as planned, but he has never come to bat in a way that would permit me to do so. The enclosed letter is a sample of the delays encountered. On his return from Hot Springs the time will be rather limited to do a good job.[5]

Pound was still in the East in November, but Clements had by this time begun to have serious doubts about his competence to do the writing for him, even if he could schedule it in time for the dedication of the Clements Library. To President Burton he wrote,

The phrase [sic] that the monograph, or whatever you want to call it, should appear in the Atlantic, – thus gaining great publicity from the nature of Mr. Pound's article, which was to be lightly written, – never strongly appealed to me. In fact, whether or not it ever appears in any periodical seems immaterial. I have always had in mind a simple story telling of the formation of the library with more or less detail about the books in it, – what these books stood for and how they could be used by students of history. As I think of it, it should be divided into four parts: (1) Pre-Columbian and Discovery period books; (2) books of the Colonial period; (3) books of the period of the Revolution; (4) Bibliography of American history.

And now to the point. Mr. Pound expects me to make out the lists, tell the important things I know about these books and do all the investigating for him, as preliminary to his entertaining

article. Frankly, I might just as well be as entertaining as possible and put these facts together, as do all of this work for Mr. Pound, so that I am going to suggest that the whole thing be turned over to me.[6]

It was about a month before Clements decided that composition of a full-scale scholarly monograph dealing with his library was not something to be tossed off casually at odd moments. George Parker Winship, who had recently been so helpful in the revision of Clements' gift agreement and who had given freely of his vast bibliographical knowledge in the planning of Clements' library catalogs, might again be willing to help. Desperately, Clements wrote, explaining his predicament,

In a moderate fit of indignation, I told the President and Van Tyne that I never thought much of the plan [Pound's article] in the first place, but that rather than let the whole matter drop I would endeavor to do something myself, and to have it ready for the press not later than February. When I sat down and began to think I fully realized what a mighty big task I had undertaken, especially in connection with the many other things I have to do, but I am in for it and I have started on a reckless career, one of trying to write something. Now, what I am going to do is to send to you, probably about Christmas time – not a Christmas present – a first copy of the first section on the books of the Discovery Period. There will be two other sections, the Colonial and the period of the Revolution. Lord only knows what I will do with them. I want you to look the section over, add, subtract, or tear up the whole book, just as you see fit. I will make this preface, however, that it is not to be a scholar's text book, nor after all, a most ephemeral sort of a production suitable for a school boy. It will be simply a light sort of a production, giving a short list the fall of 1921, after Esther Loud's marriage during the summer.[7] But Miss Stewart did not fall heir to the job that had baffled her predecessors. By September, 1921, Clements had finally given up the idea of printing the full-scale catalog. The new John Carter Brown Library catalog had been issued beginning in 1919, and Worthington C. Ford, as editor, had written to Clements, suggesting that any catalog he might issue would simply duplicate the Brown catalog on a smaller scale. Furthermore, said Ford, such a catalog would go out of date quickly and would be of limited use to collectors and librarians. 'I am still inclined to believe,' said Clements wistfully,

that a catalogue is the only proper accompaniment for a good library, even though it does get out of date. Card catalogues are unsatisfactory ... but there are many things against putting a large amount of money in a library catalogue, I must admit.[8]

Clements made no further attempt to print a catalog, contenting himself from this time on, though unwillingly, with a card catalog of his collection.

The problems of his catalog and the perplexities of his gift agreement did not cause Clements to forget Van Tyne and the History Department. During his brief visit with Worthington C. Ford in Boston the previous summer, Ford had suggested another important source for research on the American Revolution – archival material from the British Museum and the Public Records Office in London. Following his visit with Ford, Clements wrote Van Tyne,

It seems to me that in order to make the historical library at Michigan of greatest importance in your particular line, namely the study of the Revolutionary period of history, if a transcription

could be made of the most important archives in the British Museum and the Public Record Office in London, these transcriptions ... would make a library of greatest importance for the study of this period and would bring students of American History, who are interested in this period, to Michigan. These transcriptions could be done by the photostat, and as soon as a list of documents can be made for transcription, I will take it up with parties in London and have the work done.[9]

A week later, Clements wrote Stevens, asking if he could help.

Stevens was not willing to undertake this research work, but he was too good a businessman not to realize that Clements' newly enlarged frame of reference for his collecting activities meant added sales for him. Since Clements was now interested in Revolutionary material, it just happened that Stevens had at his house in the country 'a large collection of contemporary pamphlets on the subject, including the Stamp Act and events leading up to the war, which we have been accumulating for more than twenty years.' Stevens hoped to sell the collection *en bloc*; he would be glad to send Clements the slip catalog for the pamphlets, letters A through H, which he had completed.[10] Clements, with Van Tyne's encouragement, was indeed interested. He wrote to Stevens, asking for the slip catalog. But the British documents photostating project, partly because of Clements' difficulty in locating an agent in Great Britain, was never carried through.

Clements' serious illness during the Christmas season of 1919, together with the problems of formulating his first tentative gift proposal to the regents, probably served to put Stevens and his Revolutionary pamphlets out of his mind during the next few months. But Stevens, naturally, was not willing to see the matter hang fire indefinitely. In February, 1920, he wrote again, urging proaching completion and the dedication set for June, Clements found much to take his mind from his literary endeavors. A first informal meeting of the Clements Library Committee of Management, authorized by the terms of the revised gift agreement accepted by the regents in December, had been held on January 16, just before Clements left for his New York meeting with Winship. At this meeting, Clements, Van Tyne, and Bishop, meeting with President Burton in his office, had discussed the possible candidates for outside members of the Committee. George Parker Winship seemed an obvious choice for one of the two. Since Clements was to see Winship shortly, it was suggested that he ask for his ideas as to the second member at large. At the regents' meeting held January 26, the members of the Clements Library Committee of Management were officially named: President Marion L. Burton; Regent Clements; William Warner Bishop, University Librarian; Claude H. Van Tyne, the ranking Professor of American History; and the two outside members, George Parker Winship, appointed to a four-year term; and William Smith Mason of Evanston, Illinois, member of the Grolier Club and owner of the principal private collection of Benjamin Franklin material in the United States. Mason was appointed to a two-year term, beginning July, 1923.

But with the formal organization of the Clements Library Committee of Management taken care of, the search for a suitable director grew urgent. President Burton wrote to Clements,

The question of the Custodian is now our most immediate and pressing one. Do you want me to be a little more active in this matter? I have felt that you know so much more about the whole situation than any of us, it was for you practically to decide who should be made custodian . . . . [11]

254

More people than President Burton were concerned over the answer to that question. The ink had hardly dried on Clements' February, 1920, preliminary gift proposal before Professor Van Tyne began eyeing the field for a suitable candidate for custodian – one, not unnaturally, who would share his ideas on the importance of Clements' collection as a tool for teaching and research and, preferably, one who would be guided by Van Tyne in his administrative procedures. In June, 1920, a close friend of Van Tyne's, Waldo Leland of the Department of Historical Research at the Carnegie Institute, Washington, D. C., wrote to him regarding a position he was considering. The John Carter Brown Library had been without a director since Winship's departure for Harvard in 1915. Worthington C. Ford, who had been serving as consultant to the Brown Library since 1919, had indicated, according to Leland, some interest in considering his candidacy for the position. 'In any event,' wrote Leland, 'I can't consider the matter seriously for another year or so because of my obligations to the Carnegie Institution, and I understand that Ford is content to let the place remain open for a while so that he may use the salary for other things.'[12] Van Tyne wrote promptly to Leland, suggesting that he interest himself in the possibility of the directorship of the Clements Library. Leland's answer was equivocal, but it is evident that he considered the idea attractive.

With the start of actual construction of the Clements library building in January, 1922, another candidate put himself forward. J. Christian Bay, head of the John Crerar Library in Chicago, wrote that he would be interested in the position as soon as the building was completed.

Possibly Bay's letter served to remind Clements that it was none too soon to be thinking about the choice of a custodian for his library. Particularly since the gift agreement then in force

Particularly in view of Clements' inadvertent acceptance of Stevens' first offer on the pamphlets, his feelings may be imagined as he answered Ford,

I regarded the prices [on the Revolutionary pamphlets] then unreasonably high, but after all, in getting such a block of them, I thought I was really accomplishing a good deal. The deal is closed between Stevens and myself for pamphlets through the letter H (about one half of the entries he has). I have made no definite arrangement about the balance, probably 650 more, and I certainly do not want to pay any more than is a fair price, and before I make any further arrangements we will talk the matter over, and see what can be done. As you say a strike is the usual way of settling such matters, but not being in a Union, I hardly know how to begin.[13]

Knowing that Stevens would be working ahead on the Revolutionary pamphlet slip catalog and hoping to forestall further high prices, Clements wrote to him,

On this side of the Atlantic I am inclined to think that book prices are not going to be as high the coming year as they have been. That our friend George D. Smith put fictitious values on books there is no question.[14]

But before Clements' letter reached Stevens, Stevens wrote, offering a rarity so enticing that all thought of striking for lower prices seems to have been forgotten. One of the Newbold Edgar books that Harper had sold Clements in 1912 was a copy of John Filson's *The Discovery, Settlement and Present State of Kentucke* (1784). Because the map which goes with this book was published separately, copies of Filson with the map are extraordinarily rare; Clements' otherwise fine copy did not have it. Stevens reported that he had been able to obtain a 'fine, sound, clean, crisp' copy of the map which he would sell Clements for only $2,000. Clements did not capitulate immediately. But a cablegram from Stevens brought him into action:

Before negotiating Filson elsewhere would you care make offer strongly urge desirability perfecting book while opportunity occurs willing if possible meet you cable reply.[15]

Clements evidently considered Stevens' offer for several days before he consulted his mentor Harper. He telegraphed,

Stevens London offers copy of original map going with Filson's Kentucky. First offer which I refused was $2000. He now cables for me to make offer. . . . What offer would you make? I have original text.[16]

Harper made immediate reply, suggesting an offer between £275 and £400. The next day, Clements cabled Stevens, 'Offer £375.' Stevens' acceptance was accompanied by a pained letter reminiscent of the great Dr. Rosenbach.

We need scarcely say that it is not our usual custom to make such a heavy rebate from our original quotations, but the circumstances in this case are quite exceptional, and you must not regard them as a general precedent.[17]

Clements wrote almost apologetically to Worthington Ford about his latest transaction with their mutual friend.

I am still the victim of paying high prices for some things. The

last matter of this kind was an offer from Henry Stevens for a Filson map to go with Filson's Kentucky. He wanted $2,000 for it, but I made him an offer and secured it at $1300. This is a very good western item, particularly for a collector, but I do not feel at all satisfied that I reached bottom when I made my offer. . . . I have a wonderful copy of the text, which belonged to Mr. Edgar of Brooklyn, so I naturally wanted a genuine map.[18]

As for Stevens' Revolutionary pamphlet collection, the transaction was completed in two more installments, an addenda A-M, and pamphlets from I to L, totalling 179 pieces, for $2374,86, and the balance of the collection, 1166 pieces, M-Z, for $12,660. Despite his grumbling over the price of the collection of 1,990 titles, Clements considered it one of the most important parts of his library. He devoted an entire chapter of the synopsis of his library to a description of items contained in it, stating that they were

of all kinds – pro- or anti-colonial or pro-English in sympathy – written in support of or in criticism of the actions of party leaders in Parliament and dealing with the many vital questions of the day. . . . The vast extent of this literature may be appreciated when it is stated that the Library contains at least two thousand titles, written from the English viewpoint of the questions.[19]

The rest of the year 1920 found Clements making further extensive additions to his collection. As he said to Regent Beal, 'I am adding to my library all the time, and it takes about one person to look after accessions alone.'[20] A trip to New York City in August sent him to George D. Smith's shop, curious, no doubt, to see how business was faring now that the master had departed. He described the visit to William Warner Bishop.

194

I called at George D. Smith's while in New York, and on the second story floor was an immense pile of miscellaneous packages, mostly bibliography of all kinds. Their new congested quarters had no room for any of it, and for the first time in my life, I made a gamble on what the pile contained and purchased the whole lot, to be sorted over during Sunday mornings of the coming winter, part of it thrown in the junk pile, some of it added to my library, and some of it put among the duplicates for such disposition as I may see fit later. . . . The above lot, together with a couple of volumes of the Boston Chronicle, 1768 and 1769, and a rare Vespuccius item, which I happened to come across are about all the additions I made last week.[21]

In September, Harper told Clements that Herman LeRoy Edgar had decided to sell his library sometime that fall. 'With the scarcity of money and GDS not on hand to boost things, there may be some chances at this sale,' he remarked optimistically.[22] The sale was held November 22. Clements reported afterward to Worthington Ford,

I attended the Edgar Sale, and did not secure but two or three of the items. It was very evident that high prices were prevented by the absence of many old time buyers, who, perhaps were not in financial shape to take advantage of some prices which were really quite low. . . . The Edgar books were most of them in fine condition, but in considering my own library, I found that I had fully two-thirds of the titles offered. I secured one of the Eliot tracts, the fourth one, leaving me a complete lot of the eleven, excepting one.[23]

A few days after the Edgar sale, Bishop, also in New York City, wrote to President Burton,

Although it is not for publication until Mr. Clements tells about it, I cannot refrain from sending you a word about his purchases in Americana here last week and this. They amount to nearly (or over) $20,000. And they include some very remarkable items which will add great distinction to an already notable collection. Among them are a lot of ms. letters of General Lewis Cass covering fully his treaties with the Indians in 1820, a very full set of correspondence which, as Mr. C. says, ought not to be anywhere but in Michigan. He also purchased a great number of books, many of them Washingtoniana, selecting them from a much larger number offered him. I was fortunate enough to aid in the selection. And to crown all, he got for a large sum the autograph ms. account of Gen. Washington's last illness and death written by his physician and secretary Tobias Lear. This is particularly not for announcement as yet, but Mr. Clements will be glad to have you know of it, I am sure. I wish I could have been with him a little earlier, for my interest merely, to see some of his purchases last week. What a wonderful thing it is to have a man of such discrimination and knowledge behind our library affairs.[24]

Clements was equally mysterious about the transaction. Although he too had been sworn to secrecy, he could not resist dropping a hint to Harper. He said,

From another quarter in New York, a quarter I was particularly asked to say nothing about, I have secured about 300 pieces of Americana, some of considerable rarity, and all of them desirable additions. ... When Mr. Bishop and I were in New York, we carefully inspected them, but for some reason secrecy was enjoined upon us.[25]

The 'quarter' to whom Clements had reference would seem to

196

have been Hector M. Havemeyer, son of William F. Havemeyer, who died in 1913. A member of the Grolier Club, William F. Havemeyer had a fine collection of colonial autographs and manuscripts, particularly strong in Washingtoniana, that presumably was left to his son. Hector sought out a New York dealer with whom Clements had already done a little business, Joseph Sabin, to see if the books and manuscripts could be sold without publicity. Sabin, 'rather famous for these private transactions,'[26] got in touch with Clements and made arrangements for him and Bishop to inspect the collection. The transaction, amounting to roughly $10,000, would have remained a secret except for J. Percy Sabin's statement after his father's death, that the books had come from William F. Havemeyer.

Following the Edgar and Havemeyer purchases, Clements returned to Michigan. He made further additions to his collection, the most notable being the acquisition of the seventeen-volume set of the Edgar Jesuit Relations which Rosenbach, who had obtained them at the Edgar sale the previous November, sold him for $6750. He was also working with his lawyer, James E. Duffy, to draw up a formal gift agreement for consideration of the regents, which would ensure the preservation and growth of his collection after he transferred it to the University.

At the April 29, 1921, meeting of the Board of Regents, more than a year after the regents' agreement to accept Clements' 'preliminary to a formal contract,' Clements presented his first gift agreement. This formal contract embodied most of the stipulations of the preliminary document. Clements agreed to give the University his library,' as listed in the first party's card catalogue thereof.' He also agreed to build a building to house the library on a site yet to be determined on the University campus, 'at a cost not exceeding the sum of $175,000,' with furnishings and equipment provided to the amount of $15,000.

In return, the regents agreed to provide physical maintenance of the building and the collection, and to 'provide a fund of Twenty-five Thousand ($25,000) Dollars annually,' not less than three-fifths of which was to be used for accessions. The remainder was to go for custodial salaries and for 'binding, rebinding, or maintaining in repair the above collection.' As in the preliminary document, the custodian was to

perform his duties as Custodian and Librarian in conjunction with and under the general instruction and supervision of the General Librarian of the University of Michigan, in order to insure harmony in operation with the general library, and to prevent duplication of efforts and purchases of book material.[27]

Clements, however, seems to have had second thoughts regarding the stimulation of *undergraduate* interest in the material of his library. This statement was simply dropped in favor of a general provision for 'exhibitions, conferences, and lectures' to stimulate 'the study of history, bibliography, and cartography.
A final proviso, new to the contract and one evidently originating with Winship, stated that in case of default on the part of the University, the library collection would revert to Clements or his heirs.[28]

The gift agreement was signed and attested on May 5, 1921. Almost immediately thereafter, Clements left with Mrs. Clements for a lengthy vacation in Europe. The trip had been planned ostensibly for a rest, but he confessed to Ford, 'I am sure I could not resist the temptation to visit some of the book stalls' while abroad.[29]

Mrs. Clements had been in New York for about a week, arranging for passports and visas, when Clements arrived on May 9th. They reached Paris on May 20th and because of crowd-

198

ed conditions there, stayed at the American University Union. This proved to be most advantageous. Through the director, Dr. Horatio Krans, Clements was able to gain entrée to the leading French dealers in Americana. Thus he met Charles Chadenet, who, as he told Bishop,

has a wonderful lot of Americana, not all rare, but very extensive. They are peculiar, these book sellers here, but rare as I understand the privilege is, I was admitted to his rare book department.[30]

From Chadenet he purchased about two hundred volumes giving the French side of the American Revolution. Also through his connections at the American University Union he met Edouard Champion of the Librairie Ancienne Honoré Champion. Purchases from Champion, which included an important collection of letters of Pierre Augustin Beaumarchais, totaled 39,448 fr. and were sent directly to the University Library.

While still in Paris, and 'after considerable formality,' Clements managed to obtain access to the Bibliothèque Nationale and the Archives de la Marine. Here he spent several days looking over documentary material pertaining to the American Revolution. Before leaving Paris, Clements made arrangements with Abel Doysié, a Frenchman who had previously been employed in a similar capacity by the Library of Congress and by the Carnegie Institute, to transcribe 2500 pages of material pertaining to the history of the Old Northwest and Great Lakes region, from the records he had inspected. Clements also commissioned Doysié to photostat 150 maps for the Clements Library from the collection in the Bibliothèque Nationale.

One compelling reason for the Clements' visit to Paris was their desire to see their son James' grave at Suresne, outside Paris. They made a pilgrimage to Suresne on Memorial Day, when special services were held for the war dead. Even aside from this, it is evident that Clements thoroughly enjoyed his stay. Quite apart from his book and manuscript browsing and buying he had had a good time. Bookseller Edouard Champion had made the rounds of the 'bons endroits' with him. And, more important bibliographically, he met and dined with the erudite French bibliographer, Seymour de Ricci.

Mr. and Mrs. Clements left for London on June 15. As soon as they arrived, Clements called on Henry N. Stevens. He described Stevens' place of business to Worthington C. Ford.

Stevens has in his building two floors solidly stacked with books, evidently of years' accumulation for I do not believe many of them are rare. His collection of maps, atlases, etc., stored in another room is extensive, and I believe contains much good material, but he does not know himself what is there. At his house he has a room assigned for the library, and in it are the Revolutionary pamphlets. The collection is not nearly of the size I expected to see. I should say it did not exceed over twenty feet of shelving room, and judging from the samples I have received from him from the same lot there is nothing excessively rare left.[31]

Stevens immediately took Clements in tow. On June 16, they attended an auction at Sotheby's, where Stevens secured for Clements a 'beautiful and perfect copy' of George Mourt's *A Relation; or, Journall of the Beginning and Proceeding of the English Plantation Settled at Plimouth in New England* (1622) for £557.10. Clements was particularly elated over this acquisition; he told Bishop, 'This completes my early New England foundation pieces.'[32] But even greater things were in store for Clements in London than the acquisition of Mourt's *Relation*. He wrote in high excitement to Bishop:

200

In London I ran unexpectedly into the sale at Sotheby's of the Earl of Shelburne's letters and papers. You will remember he was Prime Minister during the Revolution until in 1783 he was superseded by Lord North. I spent with Stevens two days looking these over, and if you have a copy of Sotheby's sale catalogue for July 11 (Monday) even this does not convey any adequate idea of the importance of the collection. In the entire lot there are about 220 manuscript volumes, about half of them pertain to the politics of the Revolution, the balance to Canada and India, but to get any I must take the whole lot. They indeed are wonderful material and I shall do my best to get them, but as to who will be my competition I cannot tell. There is a reserve on them of about £2000. They may go as high as £4000, possibly more. I do want them, for my library in Revolutionary material with them would be unsurpassed in the United States. Van Tyne would find a mine of wealth in new and unpublished material in them. I am to be in London at the sale and please pray for me and ask Van Tyne to do likewise.[33]

Having made his inspection of the Shelburne papers, Clements could do nothing but await the day of the auction as patiently as he could.

Meanwhile he and Mrs. Clements were enjoying a two-week motor tour of England and Scotland. Mrs. Clements had sustained a badly sprained ankle a few weeks earlier, but she was now 'able to get about with a cane and walk a little.' Grasmere, in the Lake District, said Clements,

is most beautiful. Wordsworth's house is a few feet from where I am writing and I have thought today of Southey and Coleridge who have made this district so interesting. All England is so full of history, and is so old, that every place has its own interest.[34]

From the Lake District they traveled to Edinburgh, where Clements did a little desultory bookshop browsing, but did not make any significant purchases. By July 7, they were back in London, and Clements settled himself to wait out the time until he would meet Stevens at his office before the Sotheby auction.

On July 11, the Shelburne papers were sold to W. L. Clements for £1400, or £1540 with Stevens' 10 percent agent's fee. It had been almost too easy. As Clements described the event to Ford,

The fact that there were not more American bids, I believe, is accounted for because of the short interval between the issuing of the catalogue and the sale. I was fearful at the time that the Huntington Library would be a bidder, in which event I would of course have had to drop out. Quaritch of London was an under-bidder, but the facts are that London book dealers are overburdened with stock and financial obligations, and this rather saved the day for me from that source.

Well, as a result, I secured them and altogether I believe a prize has been added to the Revolutionary material in this country. If they are well catalogued they would be of great use to historians covering diplomatic conditions of the time.[35]

Clements' last week in Great Britain was full of activity. In London on July 13, he visited Quaritch's and selected forty pamphlets supplementing those he had procured from Stevens, dealing with the American Revolution. He also acquired an unusually perfect copy of the first issue of Captain John Smith's *The Generall Historie of Virginia, New England, and the Summer Isles*, (1624), for £570. This remains one of the most important items in the Clements Library. Of it, Clements said,

202

It is rarely that the 1624 edition can be seen, as here, in its original vellum covers and latchets, with the early states of the maps and plates, and the portrait of the Duchess of Richmond, always desired by collectors.[36]

The next day, Clements paid a last visit to Henry N. Stevens, Son, and Stiles. From Stevens' stock he purchased a copy of Thevet's *La Cosmographie Universelle* (1575), for £45. He also took a 111-volume set of the *Parliamentary Register*, 1774-1813, for £15.

During the Clements' first week in England, Stevens had taken him to Buckingham to visit Stowe House, the ancestral home of George Grenville, British prime minister from 1763 to 1765.[37] Here he and Stevens had inspected the library and some of the furnishings of the house, all to be auctioned in mid-July. The library seems to have been a typical nineteenth-century gentleman's library, containing long runs of a number of British periodicals and Parliamentary histories, in unusually fine condition. Clements was aware that the General Library at The University of Michigan already had these sets, but he decided that if Stevens could get them at a low cost, he would add them as a sort of ready reference section to his library. He left England about July 18, giving Stevens instructions to attend the sale and procure the books if he could at low price. Stevens was most eminently successful; he secured 1,114 volumes, many of them folios, for £167/14. Clements was still in England at the time of the Stowe sale of furnishings, but it would seem that he did not go out again to Stowe. Stevens again served as his agent, procuring for him two workboxes for £15, two walnut book holders for £8, a velvet cover for £21, and an oil painting of the Madonna and Child for £94/10.

Mr. and Mrs. Clements arrived home on July 26. Clements

had enjoyed the entire adventure. As he said to Stevens,

I had as my companions across the Atlantic several very ardent book men and business acquaintances so that the voyage returning did not seem as long as the one going. It certainly is a most enjoyable episode in a man's life to make such a trip, and you should tear yourself away from business and come to the United States.[38]

NOTES

1   WC to Winship, November 4, 1919, Clements Papers.

2   Winship to WC, November 7, 1919, Clements Papers.

3   WC to Winship, November 16, 1919, Clements Papers.

4   Bishop to WC, December 12, 1919, Bishop Papers.

5   WC to Bishop, April 16, 1920, Bishop Papers. The article seems to have disappeared. It may have been the germ of his later synopsis of his library, *The William L. Clements Library of Americana at the University of Michigan* (Ann Arbor: The University, 1923), which he began early in 1923.

6   WC to Bishop, March 4, 1921, Bishop Papers.

7   Elsie Stewart served as Clements' librarian from the fall of 1921 until July, 1923, when in the absence of a custodian she took over the Clements Library in Ann Arbor. After Randolph Adams was hired as the first custodian in October, 1923, Miss Stewart served as assistant custodian. She continued in this position until November, 1924, when she returned to Clements' library in Bay City. She remained with Clements until about 1927.

8   WC to Hubbard, September 6, 1921, Hubbard Papers, MHC. The Clements Library did not have a printed catalog of its entire collection until 1970, when G. K. Hall (Boston) issued the seven-volume *Author/Title Catalog of Americana, 1493–1860 in the William L. Clements Library, University of Michigan, Ann Arbor, Michigan.*

9   WC to Van Tyne, August 14, 1919, Van Tyne Papers, MHC.

10 Stevens to WC, October 11, 1919, Clements Papers. Evidently Clements and Van Tyne were still interested in the idea of photostating

    this material as late as spring 1921, when Van Tyne reported that the Library of Congress had already copied much of the material in the British Museum on American history that he and Clements had been interested in, and that they were working in a similar fashion with documents in the Public Records Office.

11   WC to Bishop, April 5, 1920, Bishop Papers.

12   Ford to WC, May 22, 1920, Clements Papers.

13   WC to Ford, June 3, 1920, Clements Papers.

14   WC to Stevens, August 4, 1920, Clements Papers.

15   Stevens to WC, August 26, 1920, Clements Papers.

16   WC to Harper, August 30, 1920, Clements Papers.

17   Stevens to WC, September 3, 1920, Clements Papers.

18   WC to Ford, September 16, 1920. An interesting sequel to the Filson acquisition followed some time later. As Randolph Adams reported the story to Col. Lawrence Martin of the Library of Congress (January 30, 1930, MHC #19) 'Mr. Clements had a copy of the Filson map, American edition. When he built the library it cost him almost a hundred thousand dollars more than he had figured on. He determined to dispose of what he called his Western Americana, under which came his great collection of Indian Captivities, etc. Mr. Lathrop Harper, I believe it was Mr. Harper, induced him to agree that the Filson map was unimportant because it was western. Therefore Mr. Clements sold it to Mr. Harper [cf. WC to Harper, February 4, 1924; Harper to WC, February 15, 1924, Clements Papers] and Mr. Harper sold it to the John Carter Brown Library. ... If you want to retain my friendship, do not bring this matter up again, as what I should like to say on the subject is not fit for print.'

Randolph Adams did not regain his equanimity until December 1, 1933, at a dinner which Clements gave the Board of Regents in his Bay City home on the occasion of his retirement from the Board. Again, Randolph Adams told the story:

'Such an occasion had to be marked by the announcement of one acquisition – a hard job in these times. Mr. Clements permitted us to buy for the Library here, and announce at the banquet the accession of the newly discovered early variant of the John Filson's map of Kentucky. You may remember the circumstances in which he disposed of his previous copy, which now rests in the JCB, where they persist in exhibiting it with Mr. Clements' book plate. I was glad that we were able to round out his connection with the University by replacing the one item he ever let go, which had created a serious lacuna in our collections. He has often said he thinks that was the only bit of book trading he ever regretted. Well, the damage is repaired now' (RGA to Winship, December 8, 1933, MHC #3)

19   Clements, *The William L. Clements Library of Americana*, p. 203.

20   WC to Beal, August 20, 1920, Beal Papers.

21   WC to Bishop, August 10, 1920, Bishop Papers. The 'rare Vespuccius item' was Montalboddo's *Itinerarium Portugallensium e Lusitania in India et Inde in Occidentum et demum ad Aquilonem* (1508) which he purchased from Harper stock for $400. (Harper invoice, August 12, 1920, Clements Papers.)

22   Harper to WC, September 24, 1920, Clements Papers.

23   WC to Ford, November 29, 1920, Clements Papers. The tract referred to was Winslow's *Glorious Progress of the Gospell* (1649) which Harper procured for $253. (Harper invoice, December 1, 1920, Clements Papers.)

24   Bishop to Burton, November 25, 1920, Bishop Papers.

25   WC to Harper, December 29, 1920, Clements Papers.

26   Douglas G. Parsonage to Margaret Maxwell, April 26, 1971.

27   *Regents' Proceedings*, 1920–23, pp. 174–76.

28   *Regents' Proceedings*, 1920–23.

29   WC to Ford, April 27, 1921, Clements Papers.

30   WC to Bishop, June 12, 1921, Bishop Papers.

31   WC to Ford, September 10, 1921, Clements Papers.

32   WC to Bishop, June 30, 1921, Bishop Papers.

33   *Ibid.*

34   WC to Bishop, June 30, 1921, Bishop Papers.

35   WC to Ford, August 17, 1921, Clements Papers. Clements bought the collection *en bloc*.

36   Clements, *The William L. Clements Library of Americana*, p. 100. An inquiry about the book from Wilberforce Eames in 1926 elicited a little further information on it. Clements said, 'I found this at Quaritch's in 1921, and Mr. Ferguson [of Quaritch's] told me it came from a suburban London library belonging to a school. I have no further information about it than that. He spoke of it as the most beautiful and perfect copy he had ever seen.' (Randolph G. Adams to Eames, February 11, 1926, quoting Clements.)

37   Stowe House, a magnificent neo-classical structure which in its general architectural features bears a striking resemblance to the United States Capitol Building without the dome, was, along with its spacious and elaborate grounds, one of the show places of the eighteenth century.

38   WC to Stevens, August 10, 1921, Clements Papers.

CHAPTER X

'THE PROJECT HAS SET SAIL'

'I arrived home from my trip on Tuesday last [July 26, 1921] and have hardly recovered my equilibrium after about twelve weeks of what might be called 'dissipation.' "[1] So said Clements to William Warner Bishop, who he knew would be interested in his bibliographical wanderings in Europe. But vacation was over, and it was time to continue the project left unfinished at home.

More than a year earlier, indeed almost as soon as the regents had approved the preliminary offer of his library on February 20, 1920, Clements had begun his plans for the building to house it. The first problem had been the choice of a proper site.

When President James B. Angell had retired in June, 1909, the regents had given him permission to occupy the president's house on South University Street for the rest of his life. Harry Burns Hutchins, Angell's successor, had been dean of the Law Department of the University before accepting the presidency; he owned a home in Ann Arbor where he continued to live. After President Angell's death in 1916, the president's house had stood vacant for almost four years when Marion LeRoy Burton was appointed to the presidency by the regents on December 19, 1919. Burton's contract included the use of a residence, with heat, light, water, and janitorial service to be taken care of by the University. Clements as chairman of the Regents' Buildings and Grounds Committee was authorized to look into the condition of the eighty-year old house and to determine what remodeling would be needed to make it comfortable for the new president.

But Clements was perhaps not an entirely disinterested party to the proceedings; he had been eyeing the site of the vacant and decaying president's house as a possibility for his own library building. And, though he valued antiquity in books, not a tremor of hesitation disturbed his equanimity as he contemplated razing the oldest building on the University campus, the sole residence remaining of the four original professors' houses built in 1840. In March, 1920, he approached President Hutchins. Architect Albert Kahn had told him that it would cost over $40,000 merely to make the president's house habitable, and he advised against putting that much money into it. Clements knew of two fine homes for sale in Ann Arbor; he suggested that one of them, the mansion belonging to Chauncy Millen near Hill Street and Washtenaw Avenue, would make a good president's house. 'Further,' continued Clements,

I am not looking at my own interest at all, but of course I would be greatly gratified if the present site of the President's house was selected for my library. In that event, the building would face University Avenue, and would well occupy it. My library building will be approximately seventy feet by one hundred feet, and I trust will be an architectural addition to the campus. This plan should not influence our decision as to remodeling the President's house.[2]

President Hutchins was quick to agree that

it would be unwise to put even $40,000 into the old residence. As you know, I think, I have desired from the first that your library go upon that lot. It is the ideal place for it. I cannot help but feel that in any other location on the campus it might look somewhat crowded. A gift of such importance as yours should have a liberal setting, if possible.[3]

But not all the regents shared his enthusiasm for tearing down the president's house. Clements was vacationing in New York and Hot Springs during the next few weeks and so did not attend the March 26 and April 30 regents' meetings. After the meeting of May 28, he wrote to Albert Kahn,

At the last meeting of the Board of Regents, the Committee, having charge of the location of my library building, made a general survey of the campus, and after such a survey, the general consensus of the opinion seemed to be that the best location of this building was immediately in front of the present old Museum building, which Museum building, you will remember, is about 200' North of the Memorial building, and faces on State Street. The idea of this location was that within the next few years certainly the Museum building would come away, inasmuch as it originally was a very cheap building, is now in bad repair, and as soon as funds are available, a new Museum building will be undoubtedly constructed.

Of course this location is prominent enough, in fact, the most prominent one at this time on the campus, nearly facing, as it will, the new Michigan Union building. I have not as yet had an opportunity to talk with Mr. Bishop about this location, but it is only two or three hundred feet farther away from the location

210

which we looked at when you were last in Ann Arbor.[4]

Three days later Clements sent Kahn some rough sketches of the building which he had worked out in conjunction with Bishop and Van Tyne. 'The general plan of the building,' he said, 'is a combination of the John Carter Brown at Providence, and other features which we saw in several buildings.' The sketches approximated in their basic outlines most of the final plans of the building. As for the exterior, Clements told Kahn that this 'is left entirely with you to make such an architectural monument as you will be proud of.'[5]

The architect chose an Italian Renaissance style for the library. In his travels through Italy he had seen and sketched a casino erected about 1587 on the grounds of the Villa Farnese in Caprarola. To enlarge it, Kahn drew it higher, flattened the roof, lengthened the windows, and rendered the arched entrance more elegant. The interior rooms were to be paneled in English oak above the recessed bookcases. Although Kahn became known as the father of the modern factory and though he did a number of fine residences, he always regarded the Clements Library as his favorite building. The proportions of the main room, with its colorful curved ceiling, across the front of the building are especially pleasing.

The meeting of the regents on June 18 found the question of a suitable site for Clements' library building still unsettled. A new site was proposed, east of University Hall, on the mall running from the University Library to North University Street. After some discussion, the regents referred the problem of location to the Executive Committee, with power to act in consultation with Clements and Kahn. The plans submitted by Kahn were referred to the Buildings and Grounds Committee.

On July 1, 1920, President Hutchins retired, and Marion L.

Burton became the fifth president of The University of Michigan. One of his first letters as president was written to Regent Clements, assuring him of his interest and cooperation in regard to the gift of the Clements Library. Referring to the regents' discussion of June 18, he said,

President Hutchins has informed me that your mind is running quite definitely in the direction of locating the library on the mall close to the new library. With my present understanding of the situation this would seem to me to be a very delightful location. I assume that it is your thought to have it face the mall with the long side visible as one approaches from the south.[6]

Still troubled by the question of a proper location and dissatisfied with the architectural drawings, Clements met with the regents on July 23. A further idea was developed at this meeting, the possibility of an overall plan for campus building development, centering about a mall running directly north from the new University Library. Clements confided his doubts to Bishop after the meeting; he did not think that the regents could fit all of the proposed buildings of the University on either side of a mall, and he was dubious about the proposed location of his building 'upon a line perpendicular to the main axis of the Mall . . . in the rear of University Hall.'[7]

He was even more dubious, however, about the plans for the building itself, as he had told Bishop a week before the regents' meeting. The ever-efficient and well-organized Bishop could usually be counted on to come up with a solution to Clements' problems, and once again he rose to the occasion, with a report which he had just submitted to President Burton. 'I have drawn up a statement of what seemed to me the requirements for a library of Americana attached to the University,' he wrote to Clements.

212

On these there may be some difference of opinion, and I may have omitted something of importance. Still, it seems to me, that if we have the probable size of the collection and the probable use of the collection definitely in mind, the question of the size of rooms and their distribution becomes very easy.[8]

Bishop's statement, entitled 'The Clements Library, a Working-Plan for a Library of Americana in a University,' gives an interesting summary of the makeup of the Clements library at that moment. He enumerated six types of material in the collection:

1   Rarities. *The most valuable portion of the Library consists now of about one thousand volumes – mostly small – of great rarity . . . .*

2   Rariora. *In addition there are a larger number of valuable and rare books not of the first rank. These amount to about two thousand or twenty-five hundred at present . . . .*

3   Reprints. *Further, there is a large collection of later editions of the very valuable books and reprints by printing clubs, and transactions of historical societies . . . . They are part of the working collection . . . .*

4   Bibliographies. *There is already an extensive bibliographical collection, both general and special. This is also part of the working collection, and now numbers about fifteen hundred volumes . . . .*

5   Newspapers. *An extensive collection of American newspapers – about twenty-six hundred volumes – is now part of the collection . . . .*

6   Maps and Atlases. *The collection of maps and atlases is now small – less than five hundred in all . . . .*

As probable users of the collection, Bishop listed the custodian and his staff, the history faculty of the University together with 'a small group of advanced students,' visiting scholars, and casual visitors. With the above collection and users in mind, Bishop suggested that an adequate building should include

1. A vault (or other specially protected room) for about two thousand books. 2. Reasonably secure cases for twenty thousand books of more than ordinary value. 3. Shelving for reprints and historical society publications (six thousand volumes) on open shelves in work rooms. 4. Newspaper shelving (steel) for at least five thousand volumes, 18 by 22 inches and 4 inches thick. 5. Map and atlas cases for three thousand maps and one thousand atlases.

For visitors and library users, the building should provide

1. Adequate office space for the director. 2. Separate reading room for work under supervision. 3. Rooms for the historical faculty and advanced students [offices and seminar rooms]. 4. Working space for the staff, including unpacking, storage, etc. 5. Photostat and photographing rooms. 6. Newspaper consultation room. 7. Hall for visitors and exhibits (perhaps also for occasional lectures), which may contain the rariora *of the collection. 8. Janitor's room.*[9]

Bishop felt confident that his 'working plan' would provide the key to resolving the difficulties Clements faced in deciding on a proper design. The location was, after all, of lesser concern. Clements did not attend the regents' meeting of September 10, and consideration of the location of his library building seems to have been postponed until the following month. At the October 1, 1920, meeting, the regents reached a decision.

On motion of Regent Murfin, the Board voted that the Clements Library building be located upon the east and west axis of the Mall.[10]

214

No further action seems to have been taken during the winter, although Albert Kahn was not happy with the regents' decision. At the April 29, 1921, meeting the regents voted to accept the formal contract for the gift of Clements' library and the building to house it. They also took action to change the location of the building, evidently at Regent Beal's suggestion. Clements wrote to Bishop the week following the meeting to tell him of the change.

In regard to the location, the Board very magnanimously decided to locate this building upon property now owned by the University, namely upon the half block facing South University Avenue and opposite [i.e. next to] the President's house and directly across the street from the Martha Cook building. Mr. Kahn was never satisfied with the interior campus location where he thought the building would be dwarfed and I must say at the bottom of my heart I never did fully like it, so that to me it is a very happy disposition of the whole matter.[11]

The formal contract for his gift had been approved by the regents, and they had at least informally decided on a more desirable location for his building. The interior design had been worked out. As Clements made ready to leave for New York and the Continent in May, 1921, he sent Bishop a set of blueprints taken from the architect's drawings, 'which drawings are the final designs from which [Kahn] is making the detailed and finished prints for the use of the contractors.' Plans had progressed to the point that Clements felt he could be away for three months. No further changes were contemplated; as he told Bishop,

The matter is left entirely in Mr. Kahn's hands and for disposition

as he may see fit. He is authorized to proceed forthwith and do anything he pleases.[12]

After all his earlier anxiety about details of his library building, Clements seems completely to have lost touch with any University action in this regard while he and Mrs. Clements were on their three months' vacation to England and the Continent. A letter from Bishop on August 9, shortly after Clements' July 26th return to Bay City, suggesting some minor changes in the plans, seems to have brought the matter to his attention once again. At the September 30, 1921, meeting of the Board of Regents, President Burton

presented sketches . . . indicating the expected development of the campus in coming years. On motion of Regent Leland, these were approved in so far as they indicated a general locating of the 'humanities' in the south and west portion of the campus . . . and of the 'sciences' in the east and north portions, including the different locations indicated on the plan for buildings designed for . . . the Clements Library.[13]

Final action regarding the Clements Library building was taken during the course of the same meeting, when the regents signified approval of bids for letting the contracts for the building, 'subject to the advice of Regent William L. Clements, and that the Buildings and Grounds Department of the University be authorized to bid on such portions of the general contract as plumbing, heating, wiring, rough mason work, etc.'[14]

Meanwhile, the Shelburne papers and the books from Stowe House began to arrive. Clements wrote to Worthington C. Ford,

Today's freight brought fourteen large boxes of books, most of

216

them, however, except the Shelburne papers, for use in the study rooms located in the gallery of my new building. They will be stored for some time inasmuch as I am only now ready to make contracts for my building. The Architects are at present tabulating bids, and I have profited by awaiting normal building conditions.[15]

But Clements had been overly optimistic in his prediction of normal building conditions. Less than a week later he wrote anxiously to President Burton,

I received a letter from Mr. Kahn this morning stating that the excess costs, due to higher wage scales and expense in living of mechanics at Ann Arbor made an excess cost on my building of $30,000 as compared with Detroit, which is considered the next highest place as to building costs in the state. He is at work revising the specifications somewhat, and I have left it entirely in his hands to make such disposition of the contracts as he thinks best. . . . The building trades at Ann Arbor are like a pack of vultures waiting for the carrion to appear. Certainly if we go ahead with the program we should take steps, with the immense size of it, to correct the situation.[16]

By the end of the month, arrangements were almost complete for letting the contracts. When the final decision was made, the contract did not go to an Ann Arbor firm but to the Owen-Ames-Kimball Company of Grand Rapids. Despite his qualms regarding business conditions, the actual letting of bids and signing with the contractor was a matter of relief and happiness to Clements. To his friend Ford, who had been a source of encouragement and advice from the first, he wrote,

The project therefore has set sail and the landing will be in the far future – long after, I suppose, all of us are gone.[17]

Preliminaries to actual building started promptly after this. At the December 8 regents' meeting,

On motion of Regent Murfin, the Board authorized the expense, estimated at $875, of tearing down such portion of the old Engineering Building, and supplying temporary walls, as required by the placing of the Clements Library. Regent Clements did not vote.[18]

By the end of the month, Bishop wrote to Clements,

The workmen of the Grand Rapids Contractors have made quite a start on tearing down part of the Old Engineering Building, and they are erecting their shops and setting up their boiler, etc., today, despite the cold weather.[19]

Clements' reply, though perhaps half joking, reflects his sense of solemnity at the long-awaited commencement of his great undertaking.

I hope when the first spadeful of excavation proper is made there may be someone standing attention and meditating as to what the outcome of our proposition is to be.[20]

Whether Clements intended his statement to be taken seriously or not, Bishop was on the spot to mark the occasion. He reported,

I think you will be interested to know that the steamshovel is rapidly completing the excavation for your building. By great luck I was present last week when the first shovelful of bricks from the Old Engineering Building was loaded into a truck, so at least

218

there was someone to rejoice over the beginning of the work.[21]

Neither Bishop nor Clements seemed aware that the bricks being dumped into the builder's truck had formed the walls of the last survivor, aside from the president's house, of the four original professor's houses built on the campus in 1840. And if Clements gave any thought to the fact that he had lived for several years as a very small boy in the corresponding house on the northeast corner of the campus square, he never mentioned it. Perhaps the occasion was worth marking for more than one reason.

By January 6, 1922, the excavation was practically complete, and a week later the contractors were pouring the concrete for footings. With work going forward at such a pace, Architect Kahn wanted Clements to decide on proper inscriptions to be carved in the stonework over the windows. Characteristically, Clements asked for advice, first from Worthington Ford, who responded with several suggestions, but said 'it requires what is called the "lapidary mind" to do that sort of thing well.'[22] Clements had also asked Professor Ulrich B. Phillips of the History Department for suggestions, and he came up with one that Clements liked. He wrote to Bishop, seeking his opinion.

Mr. Kahn has been after me for inscriptions to be carved into the stone work over the windows. Professor Phillips has suggested one good inscription it seems to me, which is as follows: 'In darkness dwells the people which knows its annals not.' What can you offer in the way of a suggestion for the three tablets in the loggia? A local library in England had this inscription: 'Here, on the contrary, the dead open the eyes of the living.' I don't like the word 'dead.'[23]

Bishop suggested that Phillips' inscription was probably too

219

long for the use intended, and that 'a quotation from some well known historian or some person connected with the annals of America' should be used instead.[24] Clements, however, decided to use Phillips' epigraph, and another he composed for the second tablet: 'Tradition fades but the written record remains ever fresh.' As for the round panels in the loggia, Clements told Ford,

I think the matter of inscriptions has been overdone in many buildings, and instead of using inscriptions in the loggia the architect is preparing to use in colors the coat of arms of Columbus and Washington with the Michigan arms in the center, so that there will be only two inscriptions under the present plan.[25]

With the matter of the number of inscriptions taken care of and the building taking shape, the regents began to plan for the eventual dedication of the building and for the cornerstone-laying ceremonies. The date for the cornerstone laying was set for March 31, the afternoon of the March regents' meeting, so that the regents could be in attendance. Pleased with the attention the regents were giving his project, Clements wrote President Burton,

I would be very proud of the happening, for it does represent the work of years of accumulation and will represent an opportunity for investigating and study not over-shadowed by any in the middle west.[26]

A few days later, Clements made a few observations on the art of laying cornerstones to his friend Bishop, who had also been asked to participate.

I understand on Friday you are to make a few remarks at the corner-stone laying. The President has written me that you have accepted this duty and that I am expected to lay the stone. My experience in corner-stone laying has been confined to the building of a stone fence. I do not know how to wield gracefully a trowel. I have observed as a boy the cornerstone laying of several churches but my only recollection of them now is that I wondered what would become of the man under the derrick if the derrick broke while he was laying the stone. I am going to leave the whole matter of corner-stone laying to those in Ann Arbor who know about such things, and I will be guided by their instructions. In all seriousness, however, I do think the matter is worthy of a little ceremony, almost like the celebration of a wedding feast.[27]

But Michigan weather, always unpredictable in early spring, did not cooperate on March 31. After their morning meeting, the regents reassembled in University Hall and immediately called a recess to attend the cornerstone-laying ceremony. The trees and ground were glazed with ice, and a cold, penetrating rain made even the short walk from University Hall to the South University site of the building unpleasant. The assembled group stood uncomfortably in the rain to hear Bishop's brief address, which he made even briefer because of the downpour. Then Regent Clements wielded his trowel to seal the cornerstone. In the cornerstone was deposited a parchment which read,

March 31, 1922
This day was laid the corner-stone of the Clements Library of American History; in the presence of the Board of Regents, the faculty and students of The University of Michigan. William Lawrence Clements of Bay City, Michigan, Regent of the University and donor of the building, laid the stone and William

Warner Bishop, Librarian of the University, made the address. This box contains copies of the Regents' Proceedings for February, 1919, April, 1921, and September, 1921, in which appear the terms of Regent Clements's gift of this building to the University of Michigan, the catalogue of the University for the year 1921-1922, a list of the regents of the University, and copies of the Michigan Daily and of the Ann Arbor Times-News.
Officers of the University of Michigan

> MARION LEROY BURTON, *President*
>
> HARRY B. HUTCHINS, *President Emeritus*
>
> SHIRLEY W. SMITH, *Secretary*
>
> J. O. MURFIN
>
> WALTER H. SAWYER
>
> JUNIUS E. BEAL
>
> FRANK B. LELAND
>
> WILLIAM L. CLEMENTS
>
> BENJAMIN S. HANCHETT
> *Regents*[28]

The ceremony was completed. Drenched and chilled, audience and participants scattered. For Clements in particular, it had been a day to remember. His project was now officially launched beyond recall.

NOTES

1   WC to Bishop, July 28, 1921, Bishop Papers.
2   WC to Hutchins, March 5, 1920, Hutchins Papers.
3   Hutchins to WC, March 6, 1920, Hutchins Papers.
4   WC to Kahn, June 1, 1920 (copy in Bishop Papers)
5   WC to Kahn, June 4, 1920 (copy in Bishop Papers).

6   Burton to WC, July 9, 1920, Burton Papers. Copy also in Beal Papers.

7   WC to Bishop, July 16 and 26, 1920, Bishop Papers.

8   Bishop to WC, July 16, 1920, Bishop Papers.

9   Bishop, 'The Clements Library, a Working-Plan ...,' addendum, Bishop to Burton, July 16, 1920, Bishop Papers.

10   *Regents' Proceedings*, 1920–1923, p. 22. This location would have placed the building directly east of the present Angell Hall and south of the Natural Sciences building near the University Library.

11   WC to Bishop, May 6, 1921, Bishop Papers.

12   WC to Bishop, May 6, 1921, Bishop Papers.

13   *Regents' Proceedings*, 1920–1923, p. 279.

14   *Ibid.*, p. 280.

15   WC to Ford, October 4, 1921, Clements Papers.

16   WC to Burton, October 8, 1921, Burton Papers.

17   WC to Ford, November 2, 1921, Clements Papers.

18   *Regents' Proceedings*, 1920–1923, p. 347.

19   Bishop to WC, December 22, 1921, Bishop Papers.

20   WC to Bishop, December 24, 1921, Bishop Papers.

21   Bishop to WC, January 4, 1922, Bishop Papers.

22   Ford to WC, February 4, 1922, Clements Papers.

23   WC to Bishop, February 3, 1922, Bishop Papers.

24   Bishop to WC, February 4, 1922, Bishop Papers.

25   WC to Ford, March 23, 1922, Clements Papers. The coats of arms are not in color and the Washington family is not represented. The stone carver was furnished a book containing the Washington coat of arms; but on the facing page were the arms of the British royal house of Stuart which he copied by mistake! (R. B. Brown, *The Visitor and the Clements Library*, Clements Library Bulletin, LXI [Ann Arbor: Clements Library, 1950], pp. 5–6.)

26   WC to Burton, March 18, 1922, Burton Papers.

27   WC to Bishop, March 24, 1922, Bishop Papers. The trowel in question is preserved in the library.

28   *Regents' Proceedings*, 1920–1923, p. 438. Typescript copy also in Burton Papers.

CHAPTER XI

1922: THE REVISED GIFT AGREEMENT

As construction activity began in the area east of the president's house, public interest in the Clements Library project grew. An article appeared in the *Michigan Alumnus* on December 15, 1921, including floor plans of the proposed building and a short description of the Clements collection. Included were two items that irritated Clements: the enumeration of the cost of the building and of the collection itself.[1] '1922,' resolved Clements, 'is going to be a period for consolidation, not for purchasing. ....I will try and not get in any more mischief until the building period is over.'[2] Like many another New Year's resolution, this one was more honored in the breach than in the commitment, although Clements did hold his total expenditures for his collection down to little more than half of the $ 70,000 he claimed to have spent in 1921.

Clements was in New York City just before the February 24th regents' meeting. At this time he made his most expensive single purchase of the year, a copy of Peter Martyr's *De Orbe Novo Decades* (1516), the first edition of the three *Decades*, from

Harper for $ 1,100. This book Clements considered to be a keystone in his collection; he said of it,

The first historian of America was Peter Martyr.... He knew Columbus, Vespuccius, and many of their contemporaries, and later investigators have found him a truthful recorder and intelligent commentator on events.... He called his book, which was chronologically arranged, the 'Decades'.... To possess on the shelves of this Library, if possible, all the writings of Peter Martyr, in their successive editions, has been an ambition steadily held, and very nearly consummated, during the years that it has accumulated. There is no other author whose works are more essential to a knowledge of the beginnings of New World history.

The earliest edition of the First Decade ... was published at Seville in 1511.... The copy in the Library is in what is probably its original binding, on the sides of which are the arms of the Marquis de Fromista-y-Caracena. This Decade was reprinted at Alcala in 1516, with the addition of the Second and Third Decades, in a volume entitled 'De Orbe Novo Decades,' which is said to be even scarcer than that of 1511.... The library's copy came from the same old library as the first edition.[3]

Clements returned to Michigan in time for the regents' meeting. The following week, he invited President Burton to visit him in Bay City. It would seem that this was President Burton's first opportunity to see Clements' library. He was greatly impressed by what he found there. He wrote to Clements,

I had heard many fine things of your library and I was prepared in my mind for a most excellent collection, but I must concede to you at once that I was simply amazed and overwhelmed by the wealth of your collection and the skill and wisdom with which

225

it has been selected. It seemed to me that I wanted to spend months and years just sitting down and reading the things which you have, and it makes me doubly grateful for the generous action which you have taken in arranging for its ultimate presentation to the University of Michigan.

May I also say that we greatly enjoyed meeting the friends whom you invited to your home. We particularly enjoyed the group Sunday night at dinner and also during the evening. The organ concert was beautiful. . . . I shall not attempt to tell you how much I enjoyed the oil paintings in your home, the beautiful books and the music to which we listened Sunday night.[4]

Contacts Clements had made with book dealers and others in England and on the Continent during the previous summer led to further acquisitions in 1922. In February, 1920, when Clements began his negotiations with Stevens for the Revolutionary pamphlet collection, Stevens had offered him 'a very choice and extensive collection of maps of the Revolution period, say between the Peace of 1763 and the Peace of 1783, including a number of battle plans, which would form a most interesting and valuable historical adjunct to the collection, and serve especially to illustrate the military and naval pamphlets relating to the great struggle.'[5] Clements had not cared to expand his library in the direction of maps at that moment, and the matter was held in abeyance until Clements' visit to England in the summer of 1921. At that time he expressed interest in the map collection, and Stevens promised to send him a slip catalog as soon as the maps could be collated. The slip catalog was not completed and sent to Clements until March, 1922. The 149 maps were divided into three groups: plans of individual actions of the Revolution, maps of the country published while the war was in progress, and maps laid down according to the Treaty of 1783. Said Stevens,

Some of the most important maps under this latter heading were originally prepared in accordance with the terms of the Treaty of Paris of 1763 and had several times reappeared in the intervening twenty years with considerable alterations in each state, although printed from the identical original plates. So impressed are we with the importance from an historical point of view of this cartographical evolution, that we have included in the Collection, where possible, not only the map of purely Revolutionary interest, but also the parent or prototype map and as many of the intervening states as we have been able to find.

Pointing out that this map collection was the result of study and collection by three generations of Stevenses, he offered it at a great bargain, all 149 maps for only $ 6834.50, which with his customary 15 percent discount came to $ 5809.33.[6]

Clements was impressed. He wanted the Stevens Revolutionary map collection, but it would never do to accept Stevens' first offer without bargaining. He answered Stevens' letter rather casually, noting that he himself had 'in absolutely chaotic condition' about two hundred Revolutionary maps and that, since these were not cataloged, they might well duplicate maps in the Stevens collection. 'I am hoping,' said he,

that under all circumstances, the fact that they are going to be kept intact as the Henry N. Stevens Collection of Revolutionary Maps for study purposes at the University of Michigan will permit you to see your way clear to give me the lot for $ 5500. net.[7]

Stevens promptly accepted his offer and forwarded the maps to Bay City.

In March, 1922, Clements wrote to Lord Fitzmaurice of Leigh in Wiltshire, England, a descendant of Shelburne and author of a biography of him, in an effort to acquire a copy of Gainsborough's portrait of Lord Shelburne to go with his Shelburne papers, acquired the summer previous in England. Lord Fitzmaurice referred Clements' request to Lord Kerry, Fitzmaurice's nephew and son of Lord Lansdowne. Kerry generously offered to give Clements a portrait of Shelburne by Laurent Mosnier, a contemporary of Shelburne, then hanging in Lansdowne House. The painting was restored and sent to Clements shortly before the dedication of the library building in 1923. For some years it hung in the Rare Book Room over the fireplace, until it was replaced with the portrait of the donor. It now hangs in the Main Room.

On June 29, 1922, the annual meeting of the Bibliographical Society of America was held in The University of Michigan Library. Bishop, then president of the organization, had arranged a program appropriate to the geographical area of the host library: a survey of material for the study of American history to be found in libraries of the Great Lakes region. He had asked Clements to be one of the speakers.

In April, 1922, Abel Doysié, whom Clements had commissioned in Paris to transcribe documents from the Bibliothèque Nationale and Archives de la Marine pertaining to the Central Northwest, had begun to send Clements the finished transcripts. These transcripts Clements found interesting, and by the first part of June he was embarked on some 'research' on the seige of Detroit in 1763. Whether or not he thought that this research would furnish a basis for his promised paper, it is difficult to surmise. He may even have forgotten that he had promised to appear on the program until a few days before the meeting. When the time came, he seems to have spoken

228

in a very impromptu fashion from notes rather than from a prepared paper.

Clements also misunderstood the scope of his assigned topic,
which was to be a survey of materials for the study of American
history in libraries of the Great Lakes region. Instead, he spoke
on 'Source Books for the History of the Lake Region,' confining
his remarks to materials in his Bay City library. The paper as
later printed in the Bibliographical Society of America *Papers*
seems disorganized and poorly put together; it was criticized
because Clements had ignored 'the much greater amount of
material dealing with the Discovery Period, the Era of Colonization, and the American Revolution.'[8]

Clements, it would seem, had his mind on things other than
the preparation of papers. Details of building construction occupied his attention, and he was beginning to have doubts about
the wisdom of some of the sections in the April, 1921, gift
agreement. He confided his feelings to Worthington C. Ford at
about this same time.

*Final conclusions have not been reached in all matters pertaining
to administration [of the Clements Library] and I am anxious
for mature advice. I am not at all satisfied with some of the conclusions which those interested in Ann Arbor have presented to
me; in fact I am going to make my own plans and ask for a picking
to pieces conference. . . . In all of the above you can render me
valuable assistance.[9]*

Clements' family had gone to Hyannisport for the summer,
but owing to the pressure of business and University affairs he
was not able to get away until the first part of September. He
had intended to talk to both Winship and Ford in Massachusetts, but Ford, who had been ill, was not in Boston. He did

not see Ford, but over a leisurely dinner at the Copley Plaza Hotel, he and Winship discussed in detail problems of the future administration of his library.

Even before Clements had presented the Board of Regents with his tentative proposal for the gift of his library, Winship had urged as part of the administrative structure 'provision for an advisory committee, which shall present an annual report to be printed by the foundation,'[10] something similar to the John Carter Brown Library Committee of Management. This provision had not been included in the formal contract between Clements and the regents. But apparently Clements had been considering this and other ideas Winship had put forth for the administration of the library. When Clements returned home he wrote,

*I think you are entirely correct in the suggestion that there should be a committee or a board of trustees or some similar body to whom the custodian may refer matters, and from whom he may receive advice and positive instructions. This committee or board to be under the general supervision of the Board of Regents . . ..
For harmonious administration in connection with the Department of History, the University Library and the Board of Regents, that if a committee or board of trustees, consisting of five members, were appointed by the Board of Regents, consisting of the head of the Department of American History, the Librarian of the University, one member of the Board of Regents, and two men of recognized standing and ability from diverse parts of the country, were selected, such a plan would lead to efficiency and good results.*[11]

Winship heartily concurred. As for the two outside members of the committee, he suggested that they be appointed for terms

230

of three years, not renewable except after a break. 'If the outsiders get expenses,' he went on,

they should be expected to do something extra while at Ann Arbor. I would not limit this to a public lecture, but provide for various alternatives – a series of conferences with undergraduate or graduate students, a short course of semi-public lectures, etc. . . . . The essential thing is that both the University public and the general Ann Arbor public be impressed with the importance of the Library and its distinguished committee-men.[12]

Clements shared Winship's letter with President Burton, and Burton, said Clements,

agreed to recommend such plans to the Regents, so that I am on the point of submitting to the Board, at its coming meeting next week, the 27th, a revision to my contract, arranging for an Advisory Committee of Management, which Advisory Committee shall consist of five members with the President ex-officio chairman, or in his absence the University Librarian chairman.[13]

At the regents' meeting of October 27, the Board discussed the proposed changes and referred the matter to the Executive Committee, with power to execute. The following week, Clements sent a formal letter enumerating and discussing the changes he wished to have made to President Burton as chairman of the Executive Committee. Before he did this, however, he made sure that Bishop understood and approved of the new plan of administration. As Bishop told Burton,

Mr. Clements talked over this matter with Regent Hubbard and myself last week. He seemed to feel that I would perhaps object

to the creation of a Board of managers. Of course, I told him that my feeling was quite the opposite, and that I thought the setting up of such a Board was a distinct advantage and a very great improvement in the prospects for a good working out of the problems of the operation of both libraries.[14]

But neither Bishop nor the regents seems to have noticed one item that Clements had quietly included – or more accurately, excluded – in the revised contract, probably at Winship's suggestion. Whether Clements had deliberately neglected to enumerate it among the changes listed in his letter to President Burton is open to conjecture. This was the removal of the Clements Library custodian from the jurisdiction of the University Librarian. After President Burton received the revised contract, he carefully compared it with the tentative agreement of February, 1920, and the original contract of May 5, 1921. Obviously puzzled as to Clements' intentions, he wrote to Clements,

I want to say to you that I feel that the new proposal greatly improves the agreement.

In two outstanding respects, it seems to me, there is marked improvement. First, in regard to the actual administration of the Library wherein the Committee of Management is provided for, and secondly, in the very generous way in which you have modified the penalties in case of default. [Clements gave the University two years in case of default before the heirs could take possession of the library. The original agreement called for immediate repossession.] . . . .

I am so pleased with the whole proposal that there is practically nothing more that I care to say. Two relatively unimportant queries have occurred to me and since in your personal letter

of November 1 you have asked me to express myself with frankness, I am not hesitating to do so, although I fear that there is nothing involved in what I am about to bring up and if there is nothing in my suggestions which appeals to you they can be easily forgotten.

My first query or suggestion relates to the exact relationship which under the new proposal will exist between the General Librarian (Mr. Bishop) and the Custodian and Librarian of the Clements Library of American History. Doubtless you have thought this subject over carefully and the new proposed contract represents your thought upon it. I do not mean to be ungracious in speaking of it. . . .

I assume that you are fully conscious of the omission of the following phrase 'under the general instruction and supervision of the General Librarian for the University of Michigan' from the new proposed contract. Was this your deliberate wish? I have no desire whatever to press the matter . . . but I sometimes think that a clear-cut understanding from the beginning as to who is superior and who is subordinate makes for good will and real achievement. As the new contract now stands I should assume that the Custodian of the Clements' Library would not be a subordinate of the General Librarian. Am I right in this assumption?[15]

President Burton wrote Bishop the same day he wrote to Clements.

One phase of the subject which seems to me at least worthy of consideration – both in the original tentative proposal submitted in February, 1920, and in the agreement executed on May 5, 1921, specific provision was made for the Custodian and the Librarian of the Clements Library to work under the supervision of the General Librarian of the University. Personally I still think this provision wise and I hope that we may modify the new contract in this direction.[16]

Bishop's response was immediate and dismayed.

I feel I should put on record my assent to your proposal that the Custodian of the William L. Clements Library should work under the supervision of the Librarian of the University. . . . It seems to me that some method should be found of explicitly stating the relations between the two officers, leaving the matter of general policies and of acquisitions to be decided by the Board of Management, and matters of routine work, of loans from the General Library, etc., etc., to be worked out between the Custodian and the Librarian. So long as I am Librarian, I do not think that there will be any conflict. It is, however, perfectly possible that the Custodian and the Professors of American History may wish books placed in the Clements Library for work being done there, which other people will feel are imperatively needed in their own work in the General Library, or for the work of other courses. In such matters and in all of the routine things which affect the relations of the two organizations, there seems to me no question that the Librarian of the University should have authority.[17]

Evidently President Burton sent Clements a copy of Bishop's letter. The ensuing week, Clements responded with a letter that fully expressed his mistrust of professional librarians in general, and his irritation at Bishop in particular. 'To begin with,' he said,

I am very much surprised at Mr. Bishop's letter dated the 7th of November to you, for it is quite contradictory, it seems, to his expression to me. The evening before the last meeting of the Com-

234

mittee of Five, [a special committee for campus development. Members were President Burton, Secretary Smith, Regent Clements, Architect Kahn, and Professor John Shepard] Regent Hubbard, Bishop and myself had a conference at the Michigan Union, and at that time I had a copy of the revised contract, which I read to both Dr. Hubbard and to him and I left the copy with him, but in a full one hour and a half discussion, in which the plan of management was fully outlined with the independency of the Custodian and Librarian fully brought out to both of these gentlemen, and with a preliminary statement to Mr. Bishop in which I expressed the greatest confidence in him, but with a feeling that for all years to come the independent Librarian and Custodian together with the Committee of Management was the proper thing to have, he expressed himself most emphatically that he agreed with me, as did also Regent Hubbard. In fact Librarian Bishop said he had thought of such a revision and had considered a similar plan. Naturally I was pleased with the re-inforcement of this idea, which was the same as we had discussed in your office some time before, you will remember. . . .

I had two reasons why I thought best to revise the contract; one was the fact that the Custodian might be dominated by the General Librarian (not by Mr. Bishop, surely) and further, that the management plan was very imperfect. In thinking the whole matter over I do not understand how the independency or the dependency of the Custodian crept into the original contract at all. . . .

My reasons for making the Custodian free and independent to a large extent of the General Librarian has come from a long observation of the work of general librarians.

A general librarian looks at library matters in an entirely different angle from the librarian for a library such as mine. The slogan of any great and good general librarian is circulation:

teach the public and users to read and circulate the books available, and so freedom of the stacks to all, even now existent in many public libraries, will be, I believe, a fact in the near future. That is the General Librarian's education today. It was the defence of former librarian Koch, of the University of Michigan library, who loaned freely for use at home to faculty members all books even the folios of Shakespeare, the rarest books the University owns, and only when one of the folios was left on the stairway overnight did the case become a scandal, and the present rare book section of the general library . . . came into being. Pray do not consider this a criticism of Librarian Bishop – certainly he would not tolerate such doings. He is a great librarian and I admire him and support his work, but I am looking into the future. Future librarians at the University of Michigan may not be of the Bishop kind.

Where dependency has taken place, the specific library has either been submerged into the general library or its work seriously curtailed. I could mention several cases of this kind, notably the Lenox Library, which is now a part of the New York Public Library. It is notorious that every student of American history who uses the Lenox division severely criticizes the manner in which the once independent Lenox Library, located on Fifth Avenue, has degenerated into an inefficient division of the New York Public Library. Mr. Lenox was not as wise as John Carter Brown. The John Carter Brown Library remains as the greatest monument of a library on a specific subject in the country because of such independence. There, is proper conservation of books important. . . . It is the crowning glory of Brown University.

The Librarian and Custodian is directly a subordinate to the President and the Board of Regents, and his actions, through the fact that he is not even a member of the Managing Committee, (which Committee reports directly to the President and Board of

Regents) places him as a subordinate to the Managing Committee, and the Managing Committee's chairman is the President, or in his absence, the chairman is the General Librarian. Therefore it would appear to me that even as the plan now is, the Custodian and Librarian is largely under the influence of the General Librarian, if not directly a subordinate . . . .

As I have stated, I am exceedingly sorry that Mr. Bishop did not bring these objections to my attention. I had supposed that he was heartily in accord with all that was suggested.

As a final afterthought, Clements added a handwritten note at the bottom of the letter.

P.S. – Do you believe we could get a Librarian and Custodian with outstanding intelligence, like Ford, Winship, or Eames, if the feature of subordination is so clearly drawn as in the original contract? I fear not, and as I have stated, with the other conditions surrounding him, why 'rub it in.'[18]

The matter of the revised contract was not settled by the November 24 regents' meeting. Anticipating the December 22 meeting, Clements sent Burton two copies of the revised gift agreement, signed by Clements and witnessed and enclosed in a special leather case, for the University officials to sign. 'I am very glad indeed,' noted Clements, 'that there is unanimity of opinion in regard to the position of the Custodian and his relations to the General Librarian.'[19]

Burton's response was deferential and phrased to indicate to the donor that he appreciated the solemnity of the occasion. 'It rather inspires me,' he said, 'to think how in the centuries to come students of American history and others interested in the welfare of this University will study the Agreement which we have been attempting to formulate.'[20]

The regents approved the revised gift agreement the following day. The most important changes in the new agreement were also incorporated into the University By-Laws, with Chapter 8, Section 6, being revised to read:

The William L. Clements Library of American History, as a unit of the University library system, shall be administered by a Committee of Management, and the building in which it is housed, administered in common with other University buildings . . . .

A Custodian-Librarian, appointed by and responsible to the Committee of Management, and approved by the Board of Regents, shall have charge of said library, and act as secretary to said committee. He shall cooperate with the University Librarian, for the common interest of both libraries. He shall promulgate and enforce rules for the conduct of said library when they shall have been enacted by the Committee of Management and approved by the Board of Regents.

In conjunction with said Committee of Management he shall make an annual report to the Board of Regents or to its Library Committee, and do all other acts required of him by said deed of gift.[21]

Bishop had left for France shortly after his letter to President Burton expressing his disagreement with Clements' changes. He was still abroad when the regents approved the revised gift agreement, including the semi-autonomous position of the Clements Librarian. As far as the record shows, he did not know of this decision until he returned to Ann Arbor in January, 1923. To his credit, he seems to have kept any misgivings to himself and to have made up his mind to work with the situation as he found it.

The business that took Bishop abroad so precipitously was of great importance, both for the University Library and for the Clements Library. In August, 1922, Edouard Champion, a French book dealer with whom both Bishop and Clements had done considerable business, wrote to Bishop, saying,

I am on the point (I also wrote to Mr. Clements on this subject) of deciding Mr. Vignaud, well known for his works on Christophe Colomb, to sell his library. He is very old, and ill, but desires to keep his volumes while he is living, he has besides a few volumes which are not yet entirely written [i.e. which he had not completed writing] and for which he wants the others. I think, however, that he would be willing to sell the whole library while still alive, only to be delivered, however, after his death. This library is of great importance and I think it is an occasion of which you should take advantage, as it contains a good number of very rare documents, Mr. Vignaud having for over fifty years, collected books concerning America.

I should like you to send a delegate to visit the library with me. We can speak later of this offer.[22]

But before Bishop received the letter, Henry Vignaud was dead. Bishop lost no time in writing to Clements. Vignaud was well known as a scholar, as well as the longtime secretary of the American Embassy in Paris, and the opportunity of obtaining his library for the University was too good to pass up. 'If you care to follow the matter up from this end,' he said to Clements,

I suggest that Professor A. H. Sanders is leaving to-day for Paris, and although his field of work is classical literature, he is very keen and has good business sense. I should rather take his report than that of a bookseller whom I did not know very well.[23]

With Clements' approval, Professor Sanders was authorized to inspect the Vignaud library and report on its value. As soon as Bishop heard from Sanders, he communicated with Clements. Clements was cautiously interested in the library, but he wrote to Bishop,

I would not hesitate going into the matter if I thought the material was good and of sufficient importance to add to my library. Whilst I have confidence in Sanders, yet unless a person has made a study of books relating to Americana subjects he is likely to make serious mistakes. . . .

From the price I should judge it contains few or no rarities. . . . There are so many things connected with the whole matter and so many mistakes could be made by rushing hastily in, that I have only one suggestion in the matter to make – it must be inspected and carefully examined.

It might be such a valuable accession to the University that I am going to bring the matter up before the Board at the coming meeting.

If therefore, it seems a fair proposition, it might be best to cable Sanders that only with an option extending over thirty days or so, allowing for a journey to Paris and inspection, could the matter be considered. Of course, I am as anxious as anybody can be to improve material for the best of work in my library and this may be a unique opportunity to do so.[24]

Bishop appeared before the regents at their October 27 meeting to discuss the possible purchase. The regents agreed to

the use of the balance remaining in the appropriation made the previous year for a book-buying trip to Europe to meet the ex-

240

penses of a trip to inspect the Vignaud Library and report on the wisdom and desirability of its purchase by the University.[25]

The matter of financing the cost of the library, should purchase be decided upon, was not yet settled. Evidently there was some discussion of using the first year's $ 15,000 accession fund of the Clements Library for this purpose. To this idea, Clements wisely refused to agree. He said to Bishop after the regents' meeting,

In thinking over the whole proposition, it seems to me it would be very unwise to mortgage the funds of my library for even a year with such a purchase, and especially before the Custodian has been appointed. If my advice is followed, this accession fund should be left intact. And in connection with the whole matter, I am ready to suggest that if, in your opinion after investigation and inspection, the library should be purchased both for the use of the General Library of the University and my library, in the portion assigned to my library I would be willing to pay and donate to the University one-third of the cost of such books, provided I could use them for a year or so for study purposes and for making monographs, the balance [of] two-thirds, therefore, would have to be paid by the University either by special appropriation from the Board of Regents, or from the General Library fund – which I assume is not in any shape for such a burden. I will state it clearly that if the material seems desirable, I will gladly pay a third of my part, under the conditions as above named. If circumstances were different and I had not been spending so much money in other directions, I should be glad to assume the whole burden.[26]

Bishop spent the first weekend of November in Bay City checking Clements' holdings in the period before 1700. He and Mrs.

Bishop sailed on the S. S. *Homeric* for France on November 11, 1922. They arrived in Paris on November 19, and the following day Bishop went with Champion to Bagneux, a suburb of Paris, to the Vignaud country house. 'His library,' recalled Bishop,

filled three rooms in an old house with a wonderful garden and grove – once part of the country-seat of Cardinal Richelieu. The books were in some cases three rows deep on the shelves, on most shelves two deep. They filled to overflowing two large rooms and one smaller room.[27]

Enlisting the aid of Abel Doysié, whom Bishop had met through Clements' transcription project, Bishop began a detailed examination of the Vignaud library. His conclusion was that the library represented

very fully continental scholarship, particularly French, Italian, and Spanish authorities, and that its purchase will save us ten or fifteen years of work in making the Clements Library productive in scholarly publications; for here are already gathered the critical works which we should at once have to seek out for any man undertaking historical investigation in the discovery and colonization periods.[28]

At the regents' meeting of November 24, President Burton reported a cablegram from Bishop in regard to the Vignaud library. After consideration of the matter,

On motion of Regent Clements, the Board directed that the library be purchased and that a credit of 200,000 fr. be cabled in accordance with Mr. Bishop's recommendations. It was understood that the total cost of the library to the University would not be in excess of $ 21,000. . . . Regent Clements had volunteered

242

to pay one third of the cost of that portion of the library which might be found suitable for incorporation into the Clements Library. Such payment by Regent Clements would presumably reduce the total above mentioned cost by $ 2,000.[29]

Secretary Smith immediately cabled the necessary funds to Bishop who commissioned Champion to take charge of packing, insurance, and shipment of the library; he thereupon left Paris on further University business in the Netherlands and in England. One hundred forty-six cases containing the Vignaud library arrived at the University Library in Ann Arbor on January 22, twelve days after Bishop's return.

Clements considered the Vignaud library chiefly of value as collateral material for his collection. Upon receiving Bishop's first report of titles included in the library, he wrote to President Burton,

As I read over carefully Mr. Bishop's report it would appear that much of what is in this library is as I expected, a most welcome accession to the division of my library which I call 'Books of the Discovery Period.' There is nothing in Mr. Bishop's statement of titles excepting one, which is a great rarity. He states there is in the lot the 'Cosmographiae Introduction' 1507, September edition. This book would have a ready market at a thousand dollars, and I greatly welcome this accession to my own library. As you know, in forming my library as it is I have not gone into books which could be obtained with a fair degree of facility, and I will give one illustration of this policy. Mr. Bishop reports in the geographical section some six or eight different editions of Ptolemy's Geography. There are four editions only which are of great importance – some of great rarity – which the student must use, the editions of 1478, the first printed edition; 1507; 1511 edition with the Ruysch map; and the 1513 with the Waldseemüller map or the Admiral's (Columbus) map. All others are interesting but not necessary.

The above four are in my library, and none of them are in the Vignaud, probably because they were the most expensive. Put the two collections together, however, and you have a fine lot. There were seventy editions of this book published between 1478 and 1730, the last issue. A somewhat similar statement might be made regarding the Atlases, and I might continue indefinitely, writing about the different items I have examined carefully in Mr. Bishop's list. Taken altogether nothing could be added which would strengthen the collection more than the Vignaud, as I now look at it, and I shall have the greatest enjoyment in selecting those books which will add strength. Combined we shall have the source material which makes any library notorious and the scholars' reprint material for work.[30]

It was some time before Clements had a chance to examine the Americana portion of the Vignaud library. For lack of personnel to deal with them, the 146 boxes containing the library sat for several months in the University Library hall after their arrival. Clements' share of the $ 17,698.95 cost by regental agreement had been set at $ 3,500, based on the expectations that $ 10,500 worth of material would go to the Clements Library. At Bishop's suggestion, this sum was used to pay the salaries of several extra people hired to unpack, sort, and catalog the books. By April, Bishop had the non-Americana boxes opened, and Miss Kathryn Wead was searching and cataloging the material.

Some eighty boxes containing the Americana portion of the library were transferred to the new Clements Library building toward the end of May, to be put on shelving installed in the upper collating and bibliographical room before the mid-June dedication of the library.[31] The work of sorting and cataloging the Vignaud books was not completed for more than a year after the opening of the library in June, 1923.

THE REVISED GIFT AGREEMENT

NOTES

1   'The New Clements Library of Americana,' *Michigan Alumnus*, XXVIII (December 15, 1921), 96–97. Figures given were $175,000 for the building and $400,000 for the collection.
2   WC to Bishop, December 19, 1921, Bishop Papers.
3   Clements, *The William L. Clements Library of Americana*, pp. 22–23.
4   Burton to WC, March 9, 1922, Burton Papers.
5   Stevens to WC, February 3, 1920, Clements Papers.
6   Stevens to WC, March 17, 1922, Clements Papers.
7   WC to Stevens, April 3, 1922, Clements Papers.
8   'Minutes of the meeting, June 29, 1922,' Bibliographical Society of America, *Papers*, XVI (1923), 64.
9   WC to Ford, June 15, 1922, Clements Papers.
10   Winship to WC, January 29, 1920, Clements Papers.
11   WC to Winship, September 25, 1922, Clements Papers.
12   Winship to WC, September 27, 1922, Clements Papers.
13   WC to Winship, October 19, 1922, Clements Papers.
14   Bishop to Burton, November 3, 1922, Bishop Papers.
15   Burton to WC, November 6, 1922, Burton Papers. Winship's statement on this very matter more than two years previous to this time is curiously prophetic of Burton's feeling. 'The position of your custodian depends largely upon the salary he or she is to get. The University Librarian will always scheme to make him a subordinate, and the more important the position is, the more will this be so, for obvious reasons. The Governing Body will probably abet him in this, being business men who recognize the advantages of a systematized organization. ... If I were doing what you are, I should most emphatically create an independent position whose occupant will have an unquestioned primary allegiance to your foundation.' (Winship to WC, January 29, 1920, Clements Papers.)
16   Burton to Bishop, November 6, 1922, Bishop Papers.
17   Bishop to Burton, November 7, 1922, Bishop Papers. It is probable that Clements did not spell out as emphatically as he claimed the change in relationship between the University Librarian and the Clements Librarian. It seems obvious that the change came as a surprise to Bishop.
18   WC to Burton, November 15, 1922, Burton Papers.

19   WC to Burton, December 16, 1922, Burton Papers. The revised gift agreement, dated December 14, 1922, is included as Appendix A, *Regents Proceedings*, 1920–1923, pp. 692–698.

20   Burton to WC, December 21, 1922, Burton Papers.

21   *Regents' Proceedings*, 1920–1923, December 22, 1922 meeting, p. 687.

22   Champion to Bishop, August 22, 1922, Bishop Papers. Henry Vignaud (1830–1922) 'was born in New Orleans and was a teacher and newspaper editor before the Civil War. He was commissioned a captain in the 6th Louisiana regiment and was taken prisoner when New Orleans was captured in 1862. Escaping, he fled to Paris and never returned to this country.... In 1875 he was appointed secretary of the American legation and retained this post until his retirement in 1909. He became interested in Columbus about the time of the 1892 celebration and thereafter devoted himself to research into the life of Columbus and the early explorations of the New World.' (Peckham, *Guide to the Manuscript Collections in the William L. Clements Library*, p. 261.) His library consisted of 17,000 volumes and over 25,000 pamphlets (C. W. Alvord, 'The Shelburne Manuscripts in America,' London University Institute of Historical Research, *Bulletin*, I [February, 1924], 78).

23   Bishop to WC, September 20, 1922, Bishop Papers.

24   WC to Bishop, October 21, 1922, Bishop Papers.

25   Bishop to Burton, December 29, 1922, Report to the regents on his trip, Bishop Papers.

26   WC to Bishop, November 1, 1922, Bishop Papers.

27   Bishop to Burton, December 29, 1922 (Report to regents), Bishop Papers.

28   Bishop to Burton, December 29, 1922 (Report to regents), Bishop Papers.

29   *Regents' Proceedings*, 1920–1923, p. 668.

30   WC to Burton, December 7, 1922, Burton Papers.

31   The first draft of Randolph G. Adams' first annual report of the Clements Library (1923–1924) dated August 26, 1924, states that 5,000 volumes from the Vignaud library had been checked and arranged in order, but 'some thousands of loose maps ... and pamphlets' were still not accessioned. Many of the pamphlets were merely reviews of books which Vignaud had extracted and had bound. There was also a large quantity of clippings and excerpts from periodicals.

CLEMENTS' SYNOPSIS OF HIS LIBRARY; THE SEARCH FOR THE CUSTODIAN

In December, 1922, with Bishop in France negotiating for the purchase of the Vignaud Library and with the Regents' Executive Committee making final decisions on the revised gift agreement for the Clements Library, Clements wrote George Parker Winship concerning a project he had set for himself, one which was beginning to seem insurmountably difficult of achievement. 'You will remember,' said Clements,

I had some talk with you about a monograph, or something of the kind to be published and distributed by the University at the time of the opening of the library. In a conference, held nearly a year ago, Professor Van Tyne was very emphatic that this could be done in the very best manner by a young man by the name of Arthur Pound, who was a writer for the Atlantic Monthly. His idea was that Pound could write a rather frothy sort of a production, which would give to all people a knowledge in general of what there was in my library. At the time I was not impressed with Van Tyne's idea but little was said, and the matter drifted on, and a little later I had a visit from Pound, who is a bright young fellow and writes entertainingly, but I was impressed that what he proposed doing was not what was wanted. To speak frankly, I was dumbfounded and disgusted with the idea he had that he could spend a couple of days in a library, even like mine, grasp its contents and write an article which would command respect. To me it would appear that such an article would be the most ephemeral sort of a production, with no value either for the student or the casual reader. Most of us spend a lifetime in the study of bibliography, and then, unless we are conceited, believe we know but mighty little.[1]

Arthur Pound, a contributing editor to the *Flint Saturday Night*, seems first to have come to Clements' attention through an article on the newly inaugurated President Marion L. Burton. Clements wrote to Pound, complimenting him on the article, and reminded him that they had met at the Convocation Reception at the University that fall. He closed his letter with the courteous hope that he might see him again some time. Pound, sensing a possible story, took Clements' invitation seriously. The next month he wrote to 'Judge Clements,' informing him that since he would be in Bay City to attend a Rotary Club dinner, he would be glad to visit Clements in his home, see his library, and write a feature article on it. Unfortunately, 'Judge Clements' was not at home to receive Pound.

In April, Pound again wrote to 'Judge Clemens,' *[sic]* referring to an article he had recently written on 'the educational phase of the social problem presented by automatic machinery,' for the *Atlantic Monthly Magazine*. 'I have an idea,' said Pound, 'that your library might become material for the same magazine, as well as for publications in the state.'[2] Clements was interested and probably flattered. He invited Pound, together with Pro-

248

fessor Van Tyne, who was a friend of Pound's, to visit him during the last weekend in April. Unfortunately, Van Tyne was unable to come, and the visit was again postponed.

In the fall, when Clements returned from his trip to Europe, he thought again of Pound. He had invited the Michigan Historical Commission, of which he and Van Tyne were both members, to meet at his home on November 11. Probably at Van Tyne's suggestion, he asked Pound to visit him and see his library at the same time. Pound agreed to come.

Following his visit to the Bay City library, Pound wrote to suggest that the article might be expanded to book length and used as a dedication volume for his library, rather than as an ephemeral essay. Clements responded with enthusiasm, suggesting that since Pound lacked expertise in the field of Americana, he would be glad to

select the titles of about say thirty to forty source books of the Discovery Period, write these titles upon cards and state why these books are important, and give other information concerning them which would be of interest. ... An interesting story or narrative could connect all of these books, which writing you could do better than anybody else. As you suggest, such a book would be an exceedingly important and interesting one at the time this library is turned over to the University.[3]

But other matters took Clements' attention and, despite repeated urging from Pound, he did not find the time to get the cards describing his books ready. In April, as he left for a month in Hot Springs, Clements wrote, 'In any event, it does not seem probable that the library will be dedicated until very late next fall or winter, or possibly as late as June 1923, so much work remains to be done here and the building has just been started.'[4]

On receipt of Clements' letter, Pound wrote in obvious exasperation to Van Tyne,

All winter I have been trying to spur Regent Clements up to the point where I could begin the articles on the library as planned, but he has never come to bat in a way that would permit me to do so. The enclosed letter is a sample of the delays encountered. On his return from Hot Springs the time will be rather limited to do a good job.[5]

Pound was still in the East in November, but Clements had by this time begun to have serious doubts about his competence to do the writing for him, even if he could schedule it in time for the dedication of the Clements Library. To President Burton he wrote,

The phrase [sic] that the monograph, or whatever you want to call it, should appear in the Atlantic, – thus gaining great publicity from the nature of Mr. Pound's article, which was to be lightly written, – never strongly appealed to me. In fact, whether or not it ever appears in any periodical seems immaterial. I have always had in mind a simple story telling of the formation of the library with more or less detail about the books in it, – what these books stood for and how they could be used by students of history. As I think of it, it should be divided into four parts: (1) Pre-Columbian and Discovery period books; (2) books of the Colonial period; (3) books of the period of the Revolution; (4) Bibliography of American history.

And now to the point. Mr. Pound expects me to make out the lists, tell the important things I know about these books and do all the investigating for him, as preliminary to his entertaining

250

article. Frankly, I might just as well be as entertaining as possible and put these facts together, as do all of this work for Mr. Pound, so that I am going to suggest that the whole thing be turned over to me.[6]

It was about a month before Clements decided that composition of a full-scale scholarly monograph dealing with his library was not something to be tossed off casually at odd moments. George Parker Winship, who had recently been so helpful in the revision of Clements' gift agreement and who had given freely of his vast bibliographical knowledge in the planning of Clements' library catalogs, might again be willing to help. Desperately, Clements wrote, explaining his predicament,

In a moderate fit of indignation, I told the President and Van Tyne that I never thought much of the plan [Pound's article] in the first place, but that rather than let the whole matter drop I would endeavor to do something myself, and to have it ready for the press not later than February. When I sat down and began to think I fully realized what a mighty big task I had undertaken, especially in connection with the many other things I have to do, but I am in for it and I have started on a reckless career, one of trying to write something. Now, what I am going to do is to send to you, probably about Christmas time – not a Christmas present – a first copy of the first section on the books of the Discovery Period. There will be two other sections, the Colonial and the period of the Revolution. Lord only knows what I will do with them. I want you to look the section over, add, subtract, or tear up the whole book, just as you see fit. I will make this preface, however, that it is not to be a scholar's text book, nor after all, a most ephemeral sort of a production suitable for a school boy. It will be simply a light sort of a production, giving a short list of important books covering important subjects which are in my library.

Can you give a little time to look over such an unsatisfactory sort of work on my part? This will probably be my first and last appearance among the constellations of historical contributors.[7]

A prompt reply from the ever-helpful Winship assured him that 'I am quite at your service in helping to fix up the book about your library. ... It ought above everything to be *your* book. But if there is anything I can do by way of detail, it will be a great pleasure to cooperate.'[8] It would seem that Winship did not get his 'Christmas present' as scheduled. Shortly after the first of the year Clements wrote again.

The first section, the Discovery Period, is pretty well along but I would prefer to hand it to you with all apologies rather than send it by mail, so that surely some time this month ... we will have an opportunity to sit down and pluck it to pieces. It has got to be in the printer's hands not later than March, and two other sections have to be written in the meantime, namely the Colonial and Revolutionary periods – but in these two latter I am not going to enumerate titles as I have tried to do in the first section – there are too many, and the design of the composition must be that of a general survey, it seems to me ... The facts are that I never should have attempted in so short a time to get together anything so pretentious as even this monograph, and I sometimes feel like tearing the whole thing up, but I will at least hold on to it until we talk the matter over.[9]

Winship met Clements in New York City on January 20, and spent several days going over the manuscript with him. He was perfectly candid in his opinion. 'The manuscript,' he said, 'seems

252

to me like a hand full of snow – the makings of a perfectly good snow ball, but needing a lot of handling before it will hit anybody very hard.' It needed revision, and obviously, 'the best [procedure] would be for WLC to work it into shape himself.' But in the interests of time, Winship proposed that it should be 'turned over for revision to a (more or less) professional literary person – such as GPW.' The 'professional literary person' might 'revise the mss . . . drastically, making it a sort of joint production. This might give it a certain professional appearance, but it would be certain to leave it much more commonplace and characterless, with no compensating advantages.' Or, a more satisfactory solution, the revision might involve 'taking out redundant expressions and omitting some of the discussion of historical events that do not directly concern the books – but retaining the present phrasing and form. This is probably the thing to do. It leaves the book essentially WLC's production; his name would appear on the title.' As to a printer for the finished manuscript, Winship suggested that

the alternatives seem to me Ann Arbor, Detroit, or Bay City, or an Eastern press. . . . If it is to be printed with the idea of typographical distinction and is to be issued in June, I think the alternatives are Yale, Harvard, and Updike presses. . . . [Bruce Rogers] is typographical adviser to the Harvard Press, but one has to specify that his services are wanted, and will be paid for, when asking them to do a book. GPW could probably get the book through the press at Cambridge on time but makes no promises.[10]

Following their conference, Winship returned to Boston, taking the first section of Clements' manuscript with him, and Clements, ill with a severe cold, left for Michigan.

Once home again, and with his library building rapidly approaching completion and the dedication set for June, Clements found much to take his mind from his literary endeavors. A first informal meeting of the Clements Library Committee of Management, authorized by the terms of the revised gift agreement accepted by the regents in December, had been held on January 16, just before Clements left for his New York meeting with Winship. At this meeting, Clements, Van Tyne, and Bishop, meeting with President Burton in his office, had discussed the possible candidates for outside members of the Committee. George Parker Winship seemed an obvious choice for one of the two. Since Clements was to see Winship shortly, it was suggested that he ask for his ideas as to the second member at large. At the regents' meeting held January 26, the members of the Clements Library Committee of Management were officially named: President Marion L. Burton; Regent Clements; William Warner Bishop, University Librarian; Claude H. Van Tyne, the ranking Professor of American History; and the two outside members, George Parker Winship, appointed to a four-year term; and William Smith Mason of Evanston, Illinois, member of the Grolier Club and owner of the principal private collection of Benjamin Franklin material in the United States. Mason was appointed to a two-year term, beginning July, 1923.

But with the formal organization of the Clements Library Committee of Management taken care of, the search for a suitable director grew urgent. President Burton wrote to Clements,

The question of the Custodian is now our most immediate and pressing one. Do you want me to be a little more active in this matter? I have felt that you know so much more about the whole situation than any of us, it was for you practically to decide who should be made custodian . . . .[11]

More people than President Burton were concerned over the answer to that question. The ink had hardly dried on Clements' February, 1920, preliminary gift proposal before Professor Van Tyne began eyeing the field for a suitable candidate for custodian – one, not unnaturally, who would share his ideas on the importance of Clements' collection as a tool for teaching and research and, preferably, one who would be guided by Van Tyne in his administrative procedures. In June, 1920, a close friend of Van Tyne's, Waldo Leland of the Department of Historical Research at the Carnegie Institute, Washington, D. C., wrote to him regarding a position he was considering. The John Carter Brown Library had been without a director since Winship's departure for Harvard in 1915. Worthington C. Ford, who had been serving as consultant to the Brown Library since 1919, had indicated, according to Leland, some interest in considering his candidacy for the position. 'In any event,' wrote Leland, 'I can't consider the matter seriously for another year or so because of my obligations to the Carnegie Institution, and I understand that Ford is content to let the place remain open for a while so that he may use the salary for other things.'[12] Van Tyne wrote promptly to Leland, suggesting that he interest himself in the possibility of the directorship of the Clements Library. Leland's answer was equivocal, but it is evident that he considered the idea attractive.

With the start of actual construction of the Clements library building in January, 1922, another candidate put himself forward. J. Christian Bay, head of the John Crerar Library in Chicago, wrote that he would be interested in the position as soon as the building was completed.

Possibly Bay's letter served to remind Clements that it was none too soon to be thinking about the choice of a custodian for his library. Particularly since the gift agreement then in force specified that the Clements custodian was to work under the direction of the University Librarian, Bishop needed to be consulted. Sometime during the month, Clements and Bishop discussed the matter. A month later, Bishop submitted to Clements and to President Burton a list of suitable candidates. Each of the men was rated in comparison with Worthington Ford, Wilberforce Eames, and Reuben G. Thwaites, all recognized authorities in the field of Americana. Listed were Lawrence J. Burpee, Secretary of the Canadian Section, International Joint Commission, Ottawa, Canada; Frederick W. Hodge of the Museum of the American Indian, New York City; John Franklin Jameson, Director of the Department of Historical Research, Carnegie Institution, Washington, D. C.; Waldo G. Leland, staff member in the same department as Jameson; Herman H. B. Meyer, Chief Bibliographer, Library of Congress; Augustus M. Shearer, Librarian of the Grosvenor Library, Buffalo, New York; and George Parker Winship of the Harvard University Library. Noting that each of the men would be willing to leave his present position if he were asked, Bishop recommended Burpee and Meyer as the most highly qualified. In a letter to Clements enclosed with the list, Bishop said,

I feel it very important that the Custodian should be appointed and should be at work before the formal transfer of the Library to the University. I do not know how long before that transfer he should be here, but it would be well if he could assist in the actual removal of the books and in their installation. The progress of the building is such that we can forsee its completion at a date not many months ahead of us, and although you have never told me just when you propose to remove the books to Ann Arbor, I have supposed that you would not delay that much beyond the completion of the new structure.

256

Personally, I do not regard any one of the men whom I have made the subject of this report as the ideal person for the place. We do not seem to have developed anyone since Justin Winsor, with the exception of Worthington Ford, who gives promise of combining Winsor's historical knowledge and bibliographical ability. The bibliographers are not historians, and most of the historians are decidedly not bibliographers. We are, therefore, faced with the dilemma of taking a historian and entrusting him with bibliographical rarities, about which he knows very little or nothing, and trusting to experience to qualify him to take care of them properly, to add to them properly, and to promote their proper use; or else we must take a bibliographer of sorts, used to dealing with book rarities (preferably in the field of Americana), and train him to work with university professors and graduate students to their mutual advantage.

I feel that all the men whom I have mentioned are too old to fill our ideals for the position. We want somebody between thirty-five and forty, who has his big work before him, and who will do it with the material in your Library and in the University Library. A man who without question can understand and value properly the extraordinarily precious material entrusted to him, who knows American history thoroughly, and has the capacity to grow is what I have been looking for – so far without success.[13]

Clements did nothing further in regard to the choice of a custodian until after his return from Hot Springs, about the first of May. He wrote to Bishop,

The matter of custodianship for my library is still hanging over us, and then, too, the plan of operation of the library, the work to be done by the custodians and many other questions must re-

ceive very careful consideration in the near future. I want your advice in all these matters, and in fact, the plan of operation is so important I think we should bring in with us in these considerations one, two, or three of the History Department, so that they, too, may be entirely satisfied in the plan.[14]

Bishop, who strongly favored H. H. B. Meyer of the Library of Congress over the other available candidates for the position, wrote to Clements in July,

To my distress I learned, when I was in Detroit last Friday and Saturday, that the Iowa State College at Ames is making overtures to Mr. Meyer. Now, I do not know that you or President Burton or the history people here will feel that Meyer is the right man for the Custodian of the Clements Library of American History. He is, of all those of whom I have made a note, much the most acceptable to me personally. I know him so thoroughly, and know his worth so well, that I should personally prefer him beyond any of the other men on the list I sent you, despite the fact that he is not a specialist in American history as are all the others. He is par excellence a bibliographer and an administrator.[15]

But Clements was not to be pressured into a decision. He answered,

Referring to yours of the 5th, relating to Mr. Meyer, I am in doubt what to say. You know Mr. Meyer, and I met him only for a short visit, and whilst my impression of him was very favorable, yet the position of a custodian for my Library is so important and affects me so vitally that I would fain not make a quick decision.[16]

Fall came, bringing with it problems attendant on the revision of the gift agreement for the Clements Library. The decision as to a proper custodian was no closer than it had been at the beginning of the year. In November, just as Bishop was about to leave for France to begin negotiation for the Vignaud Library, a new star rose on the horizon. Clements wrote to Bishop,

Perhaps you have noticed a recent publication entitled 'History of the Early Press of Maryland,' by a Mr. Wroth of the Enoch Pratt Library of Baltimore. When I was in New York, I got a copy of it, looked it over carefully and was surprised at the thoroughness with which the subject was treated and the modesty of the writer. Afterward I happened to mention the book to Mr. Winship. He at once said that Mr. Wroth had sprung into notoriety overnight by the publication of this book. He stated that after a careful review he had concluded it was the most scholarly piece of bibliography published in recent years. He stated further that he had never met Mr. Wroth but was going to make a trip to Baltimore to see him. Since that time I have been wondering whether you ever met him and whether he is a good candidate for the work at Ann Arbor ... I would make a trip to Baltimore to meet Mr. Wroth if you think him worthy of consideration. Certainly some active work must be done in this direction for I hesitate about many matters until I know the man with whom we are to work.[17]

Lawrence C. Wroth, the man to whom Clements had reference, was not known to Bishop. J. Franklin Jameson of the Carnegie Institution, however, knew him, and Clements wrote him for an opinion of the young man's capabilities and qualifications. A few weeks later, on receipt of Jameson's letter concerning Wroth, Clements wrote to President Burton,

I am free to say that [his] specializing in Spanish-American history does not appeal to me particularly, although in this I may be prejudiced; but when a man specializes so long in one subject it is difficult to switch from a main line to something with possibly more life in it. The period of the Revolution is better for a man to specialize in if he would desire living principles to work on, not that I undervalue study in the Discovery Period or in Spanish-American history.[18]

With this, Clements seems to have eliminated Wroth as possibility.[19]

Bishop, meanwhile, continued to urge the appointment of a librarian rather than a historian to the Clements Library position. He wrote to President Burton,

I sincerely hope that in the consideration of the various persons for the Custodianship of the Clements Library, we shall not lose sight of the fact that after all it is a library for which we are providing a head. To appoint one whose experience is merely professorial is to throw the burden of the organization of the Clements Library itself, the publication of the catalog, and all its relations with the University Library very much more heavily on my shoulders than would be the case if we appoint a man who understands at first hand the task of library administration. Our professorial friends are inclined to belittle this requirement just because, in my opinion, they have never themselves had any first-hand acquaintance with the work, but have always relied upon the efforts of other people to provide more or less well the means of their researches in libraries.

After all, what we want is some one who can make the library useful to the reader on a high plane, at an early date. I am con-

fident that so to do will require a very much greater amount of library experience and acquaintance with bibliographical methods than may be supposed by my colleagues who are primarily teachers, I am sure that Regent Clements will have the same point of view on reflection, because he knows – as few of us do – the intricacies of historical bibliography.

To this end, I sincerely hope we may bring on here Mr. H. II. B. Meyer, of the Library of Congress, and let the various men whose judgment should influence us meet him.[20]

Meanwhile, a triumvirate from the History Department, Professors Van Tyne, Phillips, and Arthur Lyon Cross, had fixed on their candidate for the position of custodian of the Clements Library. With Waldo Leland out of the running, Professor Verner W. Crane of the Brown University History Department became their choice. Urged by Van Tyne to name Crane as custodian, Clements wrote to President Burton, 'my principal objection to Crane as custodian is that he is primarily a teacher, not a bibliographer, and has not as far as I know a sense of the high aesthetic value of certain materials.'[21]

In moments of discouragement and hesitation, Clements often turned to Bishop, and once again he sought his advice. But Bishop, too, had turned partisan. He used Clements' letter to him as an opening to urge his own candidate. 'One of the reasons why I particularly welcomed the creation of the Board of Management,' said he,

was that I felt that it would materially strengthen the position of the Librarian of the University and the Custodian of the Library in dealing with the natural impulse of the professorial group to consider the Clements Library an adjunct to the Department of American History. I think this impulse can be kept under control, and can be made to yield admirable fruit in the way of productive scholarship, if we can put the right man in as Custodian.

It is because of this particular aspect of the problem that I have been very urgent that we get some one who is both a bibliophile and bibliographer, as well as a librarian, for the custodianship. But it must be somebody who is able to meet scholarly people on their own grounds, one who is worthy of every respect, and who will carry weight by reason of his attainments. Mr. Meyer is such a man, and Mr. Burpee is another.[22]

Meanwhile, members of the History Department, knowing Clements' respect for George Parker Winship's judgment, sought to gain his endorsement for their candidate, Professor Crane. It is evident that Arthur Lyon Cross wrote to Winship in this regard; Winship's answer, however, was an unexpected rebuff:

Your letter states quite clearly that it is written by the spokesman for a group which knows exactly what it wants, and intimates precisely what is wanted of me. The letter would have annoyed me ... if I had not taken for granted a reason for the careful phrasing and diplomatic expressions ... Both Mr. Clements and President Burton value your judgment and criticism, and it looks to me if you were working yourself into a position wherein in this Clements business – they might have to regard your advice as that of a partisan.[23]

Winship, indeed, had tried to keep out of the custodian question from the beginning. His answer, almost a year previous, to a request for advice from Clements had been diplomatically non-committal. He had said, 'the custodian problem is sure to be hard to solve. I'll help anyway I can, though I have a feeling that Bishop doesn't take kindly to my poaching on his pre-

262

serves.'[24] From the record, at any rate, he had confined his further comments to advice on the administrative set-up of the new library and, recently, at Clements' urgent request, to revisions of Clements' monograph on his library. But now, along with a re-draft of Clements' first chapter which he had taken back to Boston with him for revision, he sent his nomination for custodian   Clifford B. Clapp of the Huntington Library.

Meanwhile, Clements, with a desperation born of an approaching deadline, mailed Winship the rest of his manuscript dealing with the Discovery Period, 'just as it came from the scratch book which I use in assembling thought and material', he noted in a covering letter. Rather plaintively he continued, 'Inasmuch as I have spent so much work upon it, I would appreciate it if you would just leave the skeleton of the body which I have written.'[25] But Winship returned scant consolation for all of Clements' industry. By return mail he informed Clements that he had learned from the Harvard University Press that they would not guarantee to have Clements' book out by June 1 unless they had copy by March 15. Regarding the choice of a custodian, he noted, 'I am going to Providence on Wednesday for a committee meeting; I expect to see a man who will tell me what they think there of Professor Crane.'[26]

Clements' feelings on receiving Winship's letter may be imagined. It was utterly out of the question to get the manuscript to the press by March 15. 'If I get to you by March first all of the section of Colonization,' he noted,

that will be about my limit, and the 15th of March or the 20th must be given for the Revolution. My brain does not work rapidly enough to fulfill any such condition as seems to be necessary.

As for the matter of the custodian, Clements continued,

I note that you say you are going to Providence. I wish you would see Crane and tell me what you think of him. He would be eminently satisfactory to Van Tyne, but Bishop says he is not a bibliographer, and he does not care to keep his school of bibliography open evenings to teaching, and then I am fearful, too, that Crane is more of a teacher than he will ever be a book lover or bibliographer.

Relative to Burpee, Bishop thinks Burpee or Meyer of the Congressional Library, Washington, the best men for the work, but the President was not taken with Burpee and I was not taken with Meyer, so we are in the air.[27]

Winship did not see Crane in Providence, but he did talk to Crane's department head, Professor Collier, and with the Brown University comptroller. 'Nothing developed to change may previous opinion that you do not want him,' he wrote Clements, but he made a further suggestion as to a custodian. Said he, 'I hereby and officially call to your notice my old and good friend W. B. Parker. Personally, I recommend him strongly.'[28]

Clements' reply revealed what he had not told either Bishop or Burton, the real reason for his unwillingness to make a decision on the Clements Library custodian. Said he to Winship,

There certainly is a very good field for a man under all conditions at Ann Arbor, and I am free to say, but I say so without qualification, that were the whole matter in your hands I would have no doubt of the outcome. I fully realize the uncertainties on your part of moving from a place and position that is altogether congenial to you, and I have therefore not pressed the matter at all, for I would not want to be responsible for any unhappiness in your career later.[29]

264

Clements was selected chairman of Bay County delegates to the state Republican Convention at Flint on February 21. Since his friend Regent Beal was up for reelection he felt an obligation to support him, despite the fact that he was sorely pressed for time. In odd moments, he finished the section of his manuscript on Virginia and sent it along to Winship. Winship proceeded immediately to his revision; in a few days he was able to report,

The old term was 'Barber-Surgeon,' which seems to fit my present occupation so far as the library book is concerned. Most of the surgical work seems to have been done, and all that is left for me is the barbering. . . . I've no doubt you will hardly recognize your offspring as it leaves my chair, but I assure you that all I've done is hair cutting and shaving. . . . I fancy I had better rewrite everything, when you return it to me, chiefly for the sake of a consistent style. . . . In any case I can guess what you ought to say, whether you do or not! I'll promise not to take any undue liberties, and to return the manuscript as evidence.[30]

Meanwhile, Clements, having taken care of his political duties at the Republican Convention, made a hasty trip to New York City to meet two of the candidates for the Clements Library position. On Wednesday evening, February 28, he dined with William B. Parker, Winship's friend. Noting that Parker was 'a short stature gentleman with a pug nose, and altogether not over-prepossessing in appearance,' Clements told Burton that

I hardly know what conclusion to form. He is very modest in his talk, and if he has passed the stage of adaptability in his life I would not want him, for personally I am not interested in South America or Spanish America [Parker's field of specialization], but assuming that he has not passed this stage, he might be a very desirable man.[31]

Clements also made it a point to see the History Department's candidate, Verner W. Crane, on the same trip. As he reported to President Burton,

I paid the expenses of Parker to New York, and I thought I would do the same about Crane at Brown University, . . . and last evening I took dinner and spent the evening with Crane. Crane, as you know, is the choice of the History Department, both the European and American at Ann Arbor. He appears to be a very nice sort of a chap; very modest, and I have no doubt a good student of history. He is not a student of bibliography, whilst Parker has had considerable experience in this direction. Of course, Crane would have to materially change his line of work and thought. . . . Crane altogether is a very modest man, speaking so lowly that it is hard to follow him. . . . I am inclined to think Parker is more a man of the world and is the stronger of the two mentally.[32]

President Burton and Regent Beal had made arrangements to attend a Michigan-Harvard Alumni meeting in Cambridge on March 10. Clements urgently requested that they try to meet Parker at the same time. When Burton returned from the east, he reported, 'I like Parker very much indeed; in fact I think that he may be your man.'[33]Since Clements was in Ann Arbor on March 15 and 16, he had a chance for a conference with President Burton on the matter of the custodianship. Burton had been perfectly serious when he had put Winship forward as a possibility. The following week he wrote to Clements,

The more I think about the situation . . . the more certain I am

that you ought to see if we can induce Mr. Winship to accept the Custodianship. I believe he is the man for the place if he can be moved. I had a brief conversation over the telephone with Mr. Bishop, and I believe from what he said that I have in my mind and in conversation with you exaggerated his opposition to Mr. Winship as the appointee. In fact, I believe he has no opposition; I think he simply feels that probably there would be moments of strain and possible friction but that the advantages greatly outweight the disadvantages.[34]

It would seem however that Bishop, having been forewarned of a potentially strong candidate whom he personally did not particularly like, decided the time had come for him to make his move in regard to H. H. B. Meyer. Learning that Meyer was to be in Chicago on American Library Association business, he asked him if he could route his trip via Ann Arbor. Meyer spent the entire day of March 23 on the Michigan campus. The next day Bishop reported to Clements.

I felt that it was proper for me to tell Meyer about the situation here and ask him if he would let me present his name to the Board of Management. I took him over to your new building and went into the plans of operation. He was very much impressed with the opportunity, but naturally wanted to think about the matter before he would allow the use of his name as a candidate for the custodianship. . . . I am more than ever convinced that he is the best man we are likely to find available for the post.[35]

Harried by campus responsibilities and the approaching deadline for his manuscript, Clements called on Bishop for help in getting some of the material written. Winship had reported that the first two chapters were ready for the printer, but as Clements was only too well aware,

there still remains the Middle Colonies, which I have quite clearly outlined in my own mind – one long chapter – and another long chapter on the Revolution, but I also want to include a short chapter on the newspapers and something about the Vignaud library accession, and these two subjects I would like very much to have you write about.[36]

To Winship he said,

I have had visitors this last week and it has been mighty difficult to get anything done and there isn't much on the Middle Colonies anyway as far as I can find.[37]

But Winship did not seem discouraged with the task at hand. Noting that he had completed his revision of the chapter on the De Bry *Voyages,* he launched once more into a discussion of the custodian problem.

A long letter from J. Christian Bay tells me he wants your job. I know him only from his letters, which somehow leave me feeling rather glad each time I have missed meeting him personally. . . .
I have no personal quarrel with either Bishop or Van Tyne, but each means to control your library, and there will be trouble if either gets it away from 'tother. I gather that Bishop saw how things stand much sooner than Van Tyne, and has taken a perfectly correct attitude.[38]

Aware, no doubt, of the truth of Winship's observation regarding Bishop and Van Tyne, Clements and the regents

268

turned their thoughts in another direction. At the regents'
meeting the next week,

*On motion of Regent Leland, authority was given to Regent Cle-
ments to negotiate with a certain well-known librarian to determine whether the services of the latter could be secured as the
head of the William L. Clements Library.*[39]

The 'well-known librarian,' of course, was George Parker Winship. Immediately following the meeting, Clements left for the
East. He stopped first in New York City, where he visited
Lathrop C. Harper and told him of his plans for the custodianship. Then he went to Boston to see Winship.

But Winship could not be persuaded to come to Ann Arbor.
As Clements explained to Burton on his return to Michigan,

*I am very sorry to say that we will not be able to secure Winship.
In short, he has too many alluring connections at Harvard with
good chances for advancement with the changes in the staff of the
main library. Further, his family connections and those of his
wife, I believe, were the determining factors.*

*You must know too that Winship cannot be accused of modesty
as to his own abilities, and [he]frankly stated to me he was the
leading bibliographer in the United States, so that he could have
all the rewards going with such an enviable position as that where
he now is without entering new fields. This statement I could not
refute and the matter rested. I am indeed in a quandary as to
eligible candidates. The man in Baltimore [Lawrence C. Wroth]
has been invited to Carter Brown, I understand. There are two
men in the Huntington library whom I just know and who are
well spoken of [Clifford B. Clapp and Chester M. Cate] but they*

cannot be reached except by letter. I dislike to postpone the appointment, but if a mistake were made and an appointment made without the largest number of chances in the appointee's favor so that success were very probable, I believe it would be much better to wait until the proper man appears. The man of poor ability would be like a poor parson – difficult to get rid of.[40]

It would appear that President Burton was beginning to grow impatient with Clements' indecision on the matter of the custodianship. On receipt of Clements' letter, he sent a prompt reply stating,

I want to reiterate what I said to you in conference when you were here recently, that I believe it might be wise now to turn to a serious consideration of Verner W. Crane. My judgment has been leaning in this direction because he has had now some years of experience at the Carter Brown Library. I am conscious that with him there might be a tendency to emphasize unduly the teaching function, but I believe that we ought to be able to control that.[41]

In the midst of turmoil, a letter arrived from Harper, sounding the clear voice of calm reason. 'Don't be hurried into any decision that you may regret later,' he warned.

I think that you have in mind that it is necessary to select your librarian by the time of the Dedication in June. I don't see that this is at all imperative. Under any conditions it is going to be some time before your collection can be put to work; I don't see how it could be done by the Fall. While it would be desirable to have the Librarian selected and put in charge in June there is a world of work to be done in arranging, classifying, and locating by cards that someone in a lesser position can do.

270

If you can't locate anyone that suits I would send Miss Stewart over and put her in charge, and take my time about opening up for general use. . . .

The qualifications that you are in search of are (1) Librarian, (2) Bibliographer, (3) Historical student, (4) Personal force to put the proposition over. Now anyone combining all of these qualities can be counted on your fingers.[42]

Clements, it would seem, seized on Harper's advice as a possible way out of his dilemma. He wrote to Bishop, enclosing a copy of Harper's letter and stating his feeling about Crane.

Winship was more forthright in his judgment of President Burton's proposal of Crane. Said he to Clements,

You are letting your good nature be imposed upon by absolute selfishness, and are yielding to a definite policy of nagging. President Burton has been bullyragged into submission, till he does not dare do a thing to protect you – [he] as good as confessed as much in Boston – and they are deliberately wearing you down.

The point is just this. There has never been a single word said to suggest that Crane would make a good librarian for you. He don't [sic] want the job, as your job, and he does not want to do any single thing you want done. Miss Stewart would run the building much more to your liking. . . . He is precisely the man Van Tyne wants to have to boss, and to vote for the History Department in Faculty meetings.[43]

Well might Clements, beset on all sides by opposing factions and with his library monograph still unfinished, say,

There are times in a person's career when encouragement is needed, and at this time, with the many matters which have clogged the

accomplishment of the whole project, I am free to say I feel quite discouraged.[44]

Meanwhile, Clements had other problems at least as pressing as selection of the custodian. Because of local labor troubles, final work on his building was held up. 'I am much discouraged,' he wrote to President Burton, 'by the delays which have occurred with the sub-contractors of my building. The bronze and marble work is not forthcoming, and it now would appear that even in June the building will not be ready.' Tired and far from well, pressed with the myriad decisions attendant on his library construction, Clements said to President Burton,

I feel, possibly as a result of a disordered liver, that brick and mortar, buildings and gardens are more commended in the eyes of the public than those things which seem to me are the first essentials for the proper work of the University. Not by its buildings is the University known, but by its scholarly products. Essentials for the intensive investigation of any important subject do not seem to be so important and certainly not so spectacular as buildings.[45]

Thanks to Winship's help, the monograph dealing with his collection was making satisfactory progress. After Clements returned from Cambridge, Winship wrote,

After leaving you on Friday I went to the Harvard Press, where I found that they had become scared, with the pleasant result that three chapters of the book were actually in type. . . . The press now has all the chapters except the Spanish one ['Spanish Conquistadores and Padres']. . . . I will get it into shape today, . . . and then everything will be in hand except the Revolution.[46]

Meanwhile, Clements was hard at work on the chapters dealing

272

with the American Revolution. These he had arranged for Van Tyne to revise before sending them to Winship. By the first of May, Clements had the first chapter on the Revolution ready for the typist and was about to start the second.

Clements had asked Bishop to write the chapter on newspapers in the Clements Library. This Bishop had completed, but now Clements returned it to him, along with the catalog cards from his library dealing with further material in the Bay City collection, with the request to 'look over these cards for the newspapers and broadsides, and add, subtract, or do anything you please with the galley so as to include the whole lot, and *return* them to me at the *earliest possible time*.'[47] Whatever Bishop thought of this added intrusion on his busy life he did not say. Two days later he returned the galley proof, special delivery, with added paragraphs on broadsides and magazines. The following day, Clements sent the material on to Winship. With considerable relief, he reported the completion of the second chapter on the Revolution. 'Miss Stewart is now typing it', he told Bishop, 'and if all goes well, I will get that away not later than tomorrow evening. Then all that remains is the Foreword. I think now that inasmuch as everything is about completed we will surely get the book by the second week in June.'[48]

In September of the previous year, Clements had been asked by the Harvard College Board of Overseers to serve as one of a committee to visit the Harvard Library. The annual library inspection had been set for May 15. 'Of course,' said Clements to President Burton, 'I appreciate the honor, and I want to be present, and at that time, too, everything will be in the press to make up the completed synopsis of the library upon which I have been working for some time.'[49]

Besides attending the Harvard Library Overseers' meeting and checking with Winship on the progress of his book, Clements once again visited with Professor Crane. When he returned to Michigan, he wrote to Bishop,

I had a very interesting time in Boston, I saw Crane and I am now sure he is not the man we want. I never had much doubt.[50]

Clements was in less of a hurry to report his decision to Van Tyne; in fact he deliberately may have avoided him when he was next in Ann Arbor, on May 24. In answer to a query from Van Tyne following his visit, he wrote,

I saw Crane in Boston, in fact I invited him to attend the Club of Odd Volumes meeting by permission. To speak frankly, I cannot make up my mind that he is the man that should take the place of the Custodian. . . . No man can be educated to it; if he has not it in his soul for esthetic and sentimental appreciation of books that stand for something, then he is not the man in my opinion that is wanted. There are not many men born with such feelings I admit, and above all I do not want to make the library a mere library, which, with the spirit of many librarians, it would become if I selected one of them; neither do I want it to become a mere reservoir of historical material without an expounder of what some elements of the collection mean. A man that cannot stop and think of what a first folio or a Hariot means besides the mere sentences in the book is not the man I am after; neither do I want any man that has the spirit of our good friend [A. C.] McLaughlin, who once told me that he had no interest in an original copy if he had a good facsimile of it. Such a spirit would be fatal to the whole enterprise. To the true collector all facsimiles are counterfeits, else why should any man pay an enormous sum for an original Gutenberg or Caxton Bible? To any man with sentiment in his soul that original means the beginning of printing and the beginning of a new era in history.[51]

274

And that, at last, was that. It would seem from the fact that no more was said on behalf of Crane or Meyer, that Clements must have made it plain to those concerned that the choice of custodian was his to make, subject to the *pro forma* approval of the Committee of Management, and that he meant to wait until the right man appeared before making his move.[52]

NOTES

1   WC to Winship, December 8, 1922, Clements Papers.
2   Pound to WC, April 19, 1921, Clements Papers.
3   WC to Pound, November 22, 1921, Clements Papers.
4   WC to Pound, April 3, 1922, Clements Papers.
5   Pound to Van Tyne, April 5, 1922, Van Tyne Papers, MHC.
6   WC to Burton, November 1, 1922, Burton Papers. Burton pencilled the word 'Fine!' next to Clements' announcement that he would write his own monograph.
7   WC to Winship, December 8, 1922, Clements Papers.
8   Winship to WC, December 13, 1922, Clements Papers.
9   WC to Winship, January 6, 1923, Clements Papers.
10   Winship to WC, January 22, 1923, handwritten and partially illegible notes on Hotel Belmont, New York City, stationery, Clements Papers.
11   Burton to WC, February 5, 1923, Burton Papers.
12   Leland to Van Tyne, June 14, 1920, Van Tyne Papers MHC. Evidently Van Tyne discussed the possibility of Leland as a candidate for the position with Clements. In February, 1922, Bishop made a chart listing the qualifications of a number of potential candidates for the position. Leland was one of those listed. In October, 1922, Leland wrote to Van Tyne declining the position.
13   Bishop to WC, February 17, 1922, Bishop Papers.
14   WC to Bishop, May 12, 1922. Bishop's response to Clements' request that the History Department be brought into the decision is interesting. He said, 'It seems to me that it would be well to block out some sort of a plan on paper before the History Department is asked

to come into the discussions – this merely in the interest of definiteness and to save time. These gentlemen can talk all around the question, and generally do so' (Bishop to WC, May 13, 1922, Bishop Papers).

15   Bishop to WC, July 5, 1922, Bishop Papers.

16   WC to Bishop, July 10, 1922, Bishop Papers.

17   WC to Bishop, November 2, 1922, Bishop Papers.

18   WC to Burton, December 28, 1922, Burton Papers.

19   Lawrence C. Wroth became John Carter Brown Library Librarian in June, 1923.

20   Bishop to Burton, January 17, 1923, Bishop Papers.

21   WC to Burton, February 3, 1923, Burton Papers.

22   Bishop to WC, February 2, 1923, Bishop Papers.

23   Winship to Cross, February 3, 1923, Cross Papers.

24   Winship to WC, April 28, 1922, Clements Papers.

25   WC to Winship, February 3, 1923, Clements papers.

26   Winship to WC, February 5, 1928, Clements Papers.

27   WC to Winship, February 9, 1923, Clements Papers.

28   Winship to WC, February 12, 1923, Clements Papers.

29   WC to Winship, February 14, 1923, Clements Papers.

30   Winship to WC, February 26, 1923, Clements Papers.

31   WC to Burton, March 3, 1923, Burton Papers. William Belmont Parker (born 1871) was a Harvard graduate of 1897. When Clements met him he had been on the Harvard University English Department faculty, and had served as Assistant Editor of the *Atlantic Monthly*. Just prior to this he had been associated with Archer M. Huntington in the work of the Hispanic Society Library on a special project.

32   WC to Burton, March 3, 1923, Burton Papers.

33   Burton to WC, March 12, 1923, Burton Papers.

34   Burton to WC, March 19, 1923, Burton Papers.

35   Bishop to WC, March 24, 1923, Bishop Papers. Bishop noted in the same letter that Meyer told him that if a pending Civil Service pay raise went into effect in the near future, he might decide not to leave the Library of Congress. Perhaps this was a deciding factor in Meyer's final decision against being considered for the position (Meyer to Bishop, June 1, 1923, Bishop Papers).

36   WC to Bishop, March 19, 1923, Bishop Papers.

37   WC to Winship, March 22, 1923, Clements Papers.

38 Winship to WC, March 21, Clements Papers.

39 *Regents' Proceedings*, 1920–1923, March 29, 1923 meeting, p. 756. Of interest is President Burton's remark on the regents' meeting. 'It was a thrilling moment for me when you rather casually remarked before the Regents last evening that this Library would cost you about one-half your fortune and you wanted it to work out right. ... I suppose this letter will not reach you until you have been East. I certainly hope that your negotiations with Mr. Winship culminate successfully' (Burton to WC, March 30, 1923, Burton Papers).

40 WC to Burton, April 10, 1923.

41 Burton to WC, April 11, 1923, Burton Papers. Burton sent a short letter to the same effect to both Van Tyne and Bishop on the same date. Bishop's reaction to Burton's suggestion was negative.

42 Harper to WC, April 12, 1923, Clements Papers.

43 Winship to WC, May 5, 1923, Clements Papers.

44 WC to Burton, April 19, 1923, Burton Papers.

45 *Ibid.*

46 Winship to WC, April 10, 1923, Clements Papers.

47 WC to Bishop, May 2, 1923, Bishop Papers.

48 WC to Bishop, May 5, 1923, Bishop Papers.

49 WC to Burton, May 7, 1923, Burton Papers.

50 WC to Bishop, May 21, 1923, Bishop Papers.

51 WC to Van Tyne, May 29, 1923, Van Tyne Papers, MHC.

52 Although Verner W. Crane never became custodian of the Clements Library, he later became actively involved in its administration. Claude Van Tyne died March 21, 1930. Crane was brought from Brown University to fill his place in the History Department and on the Committee of Management.

A scholar and a leading authority on the life and times of Benjamin Franklin, Crane was selected as the Henry Russel lecturer for 1958 in recognition of his high academic achievements at The University of Michigan. He retired in 1959 and still lives in Ann Arbor.

CHAPTER XIII

THE DEDICATION OF THE CLEMENTS LIBRARY

Events moved swiftly after Clements returned from the Harvard Library meeting in mid-May, 1923. Bishop wrote to report progress on the Michigan campus during his absence.

First, as to the building: Things are certainly moving. The bronze frame for the main door is in place, and the bronze doors are promised for Monday. The marble work is practically all finished, except around the frame of the front door, and that is to go in this afternoon. The painters are nearly through the final staining of the large room, and will begin on Monday to apply the wax. The other work appears to be progressing rapidly. The sidewalk has been put in place at the rear of the building, and the building itself is receiving a certain amount of exterior cleaning. The hardware for the cases is going in rapidly, with the exception of the locks, which do not appear to have been received. The doors to the Treasure Room are here, and will be hung to-day. In fact, the only doors which are not in place are the two main front doors. I understand that the glass can go into the two large windows on either side of the front door by Monday and that it is here ready for installation. The men have been working nights.[1]

With the building nearing completion, Clements began to plan for the moving of his library from Bay City to Ann Arbor. Bishop volunteered a number of packing boxes which had been used to transport the Vignaud library from France, and these were sent on a University truck to Bay City on May 22. A load of the less rare books returned on the same truck, driven by a deputy sheriff and accompanied by a man from the University storehouse, where the books remained for the next few days. For transportation of the greater part of the library, Clements arranged for a special sealed railway car to leave Bay City Friday afternoon, June 1, arriving in Ann Arbor on Saturday. In Ann Arbor, the car was brought to the North University Avenue switch, and from there the boxes were carried, under guard, in a University truck to the Clements Library building. The most valuable books came down separately on June 4, in a University truck driven by a deputy sheriff and accompanied by Bishop and a Mr. Wilson from the University storehouse.

In the meantime, the beautifully polished parquet flooring of the main room had been covered with felt paper. The boxes were brought in through the front door of the library and set on the paper. Here the books were unpacked and distributed to cases in the main room and the rare book room. The shelving in the balcony and the second floor bibliographical room was reserved for the Americana portion of the Vignaud collection, some eighty crates of books, which were brought over from the University Library, unpacked, and made ready for display.

The date originally set for the dedication of the library was June 14, with the first formal meeting of the Committee of

Management scheduled for the day previous. However, 'a very urgent engagement in Columbus, Ohio,' on June 14 made this date an impossibility for Professor Van Tyne, 'so the whole thing was put forward one day.'[2] That this change might have been inconvenient for the two members of the Committee of Management who came from a great distance to attend the first meeting, still scheduled for June 13, does not seem to have been considered. At any rate, two thousand invitations to the dedication, with the date set for June 15, were sent out by Bishop, who had been given chief responsibility for the ceremony. Responses shortly began coming in from University representatives, book dealers, librarians, and personal friends.

Meanwhile, George Parker Winship, who had declaimed grandly that 'I have lived through two Openings, at the Carter Brown Library and the Widener, so nothing is likely to terrify me. . . . I am yours to command until the middle of June,'[3] was laboring over the last stages of getting Clements' monograph through the press, finding himself inundated with page proof. After the preface had been set in type, Clements had added a sentence regarding Bishop's contributions and one of tribute to Van Tyne. Winship reported that he had put in the sentence about Bishop without having the type reset by omitting another sentence; he was not sure if he could manage Van Tyne's.[4] With the deadline almost upon him, Winship inquired, 'How many copies must you have on the day of the Dedication? I am prepared to guarantee that you shall have one, bound, to show to your friends. More than that is in the hands of the Gods of the bindery.'[5]

Winship virtually lived at the Harvard Press during the next few days, reading proof and badgering the printers. The 29th of May saw the book in press in an edition of 2,000 copies. On June 5, with the dedication but ten days distant, Winship

280

was still pacing the floor at the Harvard Press. 'A thunder storm saved the day for us yesterday,' he wrote to Clements.

With only eight pages left to go, they had to stop the presses because it got so hot, over ninety, and the rollers showed signs of softening. Then it thundered, but in the interval I just happened to catch two misprints, so we printed cancels without any loss of time. This gives you a 'first issue, with the headline misprinted,' If I can get hold of a copy or two of the original sheet.[6]

Somehow, by the grace of the gods, thunderstorms, and hard-working pressmen, Winship managed to get the first few copies of Clements' book completed. On June 15, Clements held in his hand the result of his efforts to describe the collection he had turned over to the University that day, his book entitled *The William L. Clements Library of Americana at the University of Michigan.*

Winship always allowed Clements full credit as the author of the book, but Clements did not sign himself as author on the title page. That omission and a generous acknowledgment to Winship in Clements' preface suggests that it was a joint undertaking.[7] Winship was keenly appreciative of the solid worth of their bibliographic venture. As he wrote Clements the week following the dedication,

I have no anxieties about the book – anything that two people put as much of themselves into, as you and I did into that, has got to have some good qualities. The only question now is whether it secures recognition at once, or has to wait until some future investigator discovers it.[8]

The first formal meeting of the Clements Library Committee of Management was held June 13, in the library building. Chief action taken at this meeting was the appointment of Clements' Bay City librarian, Elsie Stewart, as Chief Assistant, temporarily in charge of the library, with a salary of $ 2,400 per year, beginning July 1, 1923. Pending the appointment of a permanent custodian, Bishop was given overall supervision.

Despite crises – such as the non-arrival of locks for the exhibit cases, a last-minute substitution of rugs, and tables delivered in such a green condition that the varnish promptly rubbed off – the library building stood ready, even to monogrammed linen towels in the rest rooms, to welcome the invited guests on Friday, June 15. At noon, regents and official representatives to the dedication from colleges and universities were invited to a luncheon held in the Michigan Union. Bishop, in charge of arrangements, asked President Burton to welcome the guests on behalf of the University. 'Mr. Clements specifically asked me to see that he was not called upon to speak at the luncheon,' noted Bishop. Instead, he suggested that President Burton might ask George Winship 'to say a word in appreciation of the occasion and of Mr. Clements' gift.'[9]

This was done. Following President Burton's short talk stressing the importance of the Clements Library 'as a place of research, as a laboratory for the intensive training of graduate students and investigators', Winship rose to respond on behalf of the invited guests. Said Winship,

The William L. Clements Library places the University of Michigan in a distinguished position for the teaching of our country's history, and for training scholars. It seems to me, and hope is parent to the thought, that this Library is likely to do something else, which I regard as not less important for an American college – to promote an appreciation of culture, of the refinements of life, among the students who are here for their college years. . . .

The building which Mr. Clements is giving to his Alma Mater . . . is, above all else, in my opinion, a centre for culture. It stands among the laboratories and class-rooms and dormitories and professors' studies and club houses as the visible illustration of the charm and the abiding value of those refinements of life which go to the making of gentlefolk.[10]

Winship's informal remarks impressed Clements to such an extent that after the dedication he asked Winship to write them up for inclusion in the dedicatory volume.

Following the luncheon, formal exercises of dedication were held in Hill Auditorium. Clements' speech of presentation opened with appropriate solemnity and embodied in carefully thought-out phrases his ideals for the library.

This day and hour mark the conclusion of a bookcollector's career. A library of American history has been created, and a disposition made of it. There has been constructed a building, that the integrity of this library may be preserved, and that there may be special facilities for historical research work. My interest in the Library is transferred, with its work and development, to its new owner – the University of Michigan. . . .

It must not be supposed that this library is for the use of the undergraduate, or for others who have not exhausted the facilities of the General Library. It is primarily a library for advanced research on the part of scholars already well equipped, rather than a library to serve as a vehicle of instruction for either the undergraduate or the ordinary graduate student. . . .

I must say a word of warning about the conservation of the treasures in this library. . . . May we use with the greatest care these materials which can never be replaced! Let those who have no valid right to examine or handle, be content with a look; and for those who would make the examination, may not facsimiles serve the purpose? Frequently, even among scholars, the aesthetic or sentimental value of a book counts for naught. . . . From him who has no sentimental or aesthetic interest, rare books should be carefully guarded.[11]

Clements spoke for the bibliographer and the book collector; the principal speaker at the dedication, J. Franklin Jameson of the Department of Historical Research, Carnegie Institution, addressed himself to the point of view of the history professor. Said Jameson,

For what is a great historical library but a means for writing history? . . . After all, these books and manuscripts are here to be used; the use of a great historical library is for the making of better and more useful histories.[12]

Jameson's words must have served as an uncomfortable reminder to Clements of the position of the members of the History Department. Even in the two principal speeches of the dedication, the battle lines about the newly formed Clements Library were drawn.

It was a day of solemn joy for Clements, and for his friends and associates who had worked with him and shared his moments of frustration and triumph in the building of his collection. The graceful white Renaissance building on the south edge of the campus which donor and guests toured after the ceremonies held a library of 20,000 rare books valued at $1,500,000. 'Tradition fades, but the written record remains

284

ever fresh,' read one inscription on the front of the building. With his gift to the University, Clements had created his living monument.

Clements had as his special guests for the dedication Henry N. Stevens, his wife, and his daughter Celia from London. He had first suggested that Stevens visit the United States in August, 1921, shortly after his return from abroad. A year later, with the walls of his library building rising and plans for the dedication set, he wrote again to Stevens, inviting him to be present in June and making a further proposition as an added inducement. He said,

I shall be glad to remunerate your services in going over carefully the De Bry which I have, so that I could retain as duplicates much of which might otherwise be sent to Ann Arbor. I believe fully fifty percent of the parts in the various lots which I have, duplicate one another.... Would it not be possible to take the twenty five parts of the Brayton-Ives De Bry which is supposed to be a set of first editions of the Grand Voyages in Latin, and use the other two lots to supplement this. The Brayton-Ives copy contains the Elenchus.[13]

Stevens was interested both in coming to the United States for the dedication and in collating Clements' De Bry collection for him. And, since Clements had brought up the subject, it just happened that Stevens had recently acquired two very rare issues of De Bry: the third edition of part three, Latin America (1630), and part four, Latin America (1644). The 1630 third edition, said Stevens, was usually found in a mixed state.

It is only the very latest copies of all ... that have every leaf of

*the distinctive third edition. The present copy has every leaf
genuine third edition, and its uniformity throughout, both as to
condition and size, shows it to have been issued in that state.
. . . I have never seen any De Bry finer.*

This issue Stevens offered for $1250 net, unbound. As for the
1644 issue of part four, Latin America, Stevens reported that
he had never before seen a copy of it; the only other known
copy was an imperfect copy in the Lenox Library. Stevens'
price for this volume was $2500 unbound.[14]

Clements was tempted, but the expenditures connected with
his library building were of such magnitude that he hesitated
to commit almost $4,000 to the purchase of only two books
– even rarities such as these. He usually consulted Harper in
affairs of this kind, but this time Winship, who had recently
offered so many helpful ideas on the revision of Clements'
gift agreement for his library, was asked to give his opinion.
He said,

*I did not approve of your going in for De Bry in the first place,
and I still think . . . Stevens over-persuaded you in this matter.
But you are in rather deep, and I do not believe you will ever be
quite happy if you try to turn back now. But this is the phase of
it that you have got to settle for yourself.*

*You can now do one of two things. You have the makings of a
perfectly good set of De Bry, probably better than any other
second rate set. You can make this up, clear out the duplicates
and minor variations, and let it go at that. Or you can go ahead
and spend a good deal more money – and have something to
brag about. This offer of Stevens makes it necessary to decide
which of the two you will do. . . . There is no use going further
unless you are going the whole way. This means everything*

286

Stevens has now offered or is holding up his sleeves; it also means the cost of printing the one and only De Bry book, to be compiled by Stevens and issued as a model of what your Library stands for in American bibliography and history. This will not interest Bishop or Van Tyne or Cross a whit, but it strikes me as a God-given chance to assume the top place, challenging Lenox and JCB and Huntington, showing each of them what they might have done.

As an answer to the often repeated statement that the De Bry *Voyages* were merely a wealthy collector's plaything, of little intrinsic importance, Winship concluded,

You question the historical importance [of De Bry].... Nobody has developed the fact that De Bry supplied the world with about all it knew of its periphery from 1590 to 1640. As so often, the contents are less significant than the bibliography.[15]

Clements discussed Stevens' offer with several other people, including President Burton, showing them Winship's letter. Then he wrote to Stevens,

I am interested in forming a working library first of all. At the same time I have played rather successfully so far in De Bry and Hulsius and the Jesuit Relations and have fairly good lots of them all.

I am not unconscious of desirable notoriety to any library, especially of the kind that I have, which has unique pieces, whether they be useful or not. I might mention many instances of this kind in American libraries. And in viewing the whole matter as a notable possession in rarity and in uniqueness, I would like to acquire the rare parts of De Bry.

But Clements was willing to take the two rare De Bry issues only as part of a larger proposition. He went on,

If I should decide to take the two parts you mention, what plan or arrangement could I make with you for you to come to the United States and spend sufficient time to go over my collection of De Bry ... and make a monograph for publication, which monograph would be published by The University of Michigan as your contribution to the literature of the bibliography of De Bry, and which would at the same time free your mind of all the stores of information which you have about De Bry, putting them in print, which would be everlastingly a memorial of your ability in that direction and secondly of the goodness of the De Bry housed in the William L. Clements Library of American History at Ann Arbor.[16]

If Clements had any thought that Henry N. Stevens was likely to agree to such an idea out of sheer altruistic desire to advance the sum of human learning, he was quickly disillusioned. Stevens' answer was equivocal. He would, of course, like to take Clements up on his proposition, but he wondered how his business would get along without the senior partner. He and his partners had talked the matter over, and had decided that the minimum value of his services would have to be set at $1,000 per month, plus travel and living expenses, for an estimated three months.

In view of Clements' other expenses at the moment, among which was his arrangement with Winship for editorial services on his library monograph, it is little wonder that Stevens' terms seemed staggering. Clements wrote to President Burton,

A letter from Henry N. Stevens of London, relative to his coming

to the United States, and writing a bibliographic [account] of De Bry in my library, has been received and is not all satisfactory. The expense will be far too great for results and I shall so advise him. I regret that he will not be with us, but I could spend what he wants to much better advantage.[17]

To Stevens, Clements sent a tactful refusal of his terms.

But Stevens, seeing that he had miscalculated Clements as a potential Maecenas, changed his tactics. He had been counting on the trip to the United States, and now that Clements seemed inclined to withdraw the offer entirely, he wrote rather humbly, proposing that he should pay Clements a visist in June, as originally suggested. He would write the greater part of the proposed De Bry bibliography in England, thus relieving Clements of this expense. For collating the Clements collection of De Bry, he suggested that Clements might want to offer him a modest honorarium, but this they could discuss when they were together.

Clements felt that this was a reasonable proposal. After a month he wrote to Stevens, renewing his invitation for the Stevens family to attend the dedication in June. As for the two De Bry variants that Stevens had offered, Clements noted that this would have to be the decision of the Committee of Management of his library, as they would control the library's funds after its dedication. He personally was prepared to offer Stevens an honorarium of $500 for his work in collating the Clements De Bry, but as for additions to the collection, 'I cannot in any way obligate the Committee of Management.'[18]

This arrangement was agreeable to Stevens, and at the end of May, Clements wrote to him,

The dedication is on the 15th of June and it will be necessary for

you to be in Ann Arbor on the following Monday, June 18, for reasons which I will explain to you.[19]

Clements did not elaborate on his 'reasons' until Stevens was in Ann Arbor. Unknown to Stevens, Clements had arranged for an honorary Master of Arts degree to be awarded him at the Commencement ceremonies on June 18. Stevens and his family arrived in Ann Arbor on June 13. They were guests at the dedication of the Clements Library, following which Professor Van Tyne gave a dinner in their honor, inviting a number of Clements' personal friends including Harper, Rosenbach, and William S. Mason.

Commencement exercises on June 18 were held for the first time at Ferry Field instead of in Hill Auditorium. Preceded by regents, faculty, and guests of honor in all the traditional splendor of academic regalia, fifteen hundred black-robed seniors filed between ranks of honor guards to the strains of 'The Victors.' The commencement address was given by Harry Emerson Fosdick, speaking on 'Private Conscience and Social Institutions.' Following this, the University conferred upon Stevens the honorary degree of M.A., with these words:

Mr. Henry N. Stevens of London, an expert and scholarly bibliographer, an authority in the maps and literature dealing with the early history of America, with high appreciation of his exacting standards and his devotion to sound learning, the University confers upon him a merited honor.[20]

Leaving Stevens in Ann Arbor to collate the De Bry collection, Clements made his way back to Bay City alone. As he said to Bishop, 'Without family or books the old home looks pretty desolate, but I am trying not to think about the matter.'[21]

290

He was back in Ann Arbor the following Monday to check on Stevens' progress. Stevens finished his work the next day, having spent six days on it. He and his family left Ann Arbor for Evanston, Illinois, on June 27, where on the following day they were taken by William Smith Mason on a bibliographical pilgrimage to the Newberry Library.

The Stevenses remained in Evanston with Mason until Monday, July 2, when they took the train for Bay City, arriving Tuesday morning at Clements' home. Here Stevens made a formal report on his examination and collation of Clements' De Bry collection.

Taking the Stevens set of 100 [i.e. 104] volumes as the ground work for the main collection, I am now able to report that the eighty Huntington duplicates have furnished you with twenty-five accessions, whilst the remaining fifty-five volumes are duplicates. Amongst these fifty-five duplicates there are of course many which will supersede or improve the Stevens copies. . . . In a separate letter I will send you shortly a list of very rare parts which I can now offer you from stock. These would add greatly to the interest and importance of your set of De Bry and probably establish its pre-eminence over all other collections.

Two days later Stevens offered from his stock twenty of 'the very rarest parts and variations in the whole series of De Bry and the majority of them are the only copies I have ever possessed or even seen.'[22] For these rare variations, the so-called 'Stevens Addenda,' Stevens asked $10,000. The Clements Library Committee of Management purchased the Stevens Addenda, but the matter of the publication of Stevens' De Bry bibliography hung fire for many years and was never carried through, although the Committee discussed the matter on several occasions.

NOTES

1   Bishop to WC, May 19, 1923, Bishop Papers.

2   WC to W. S. Mason, May 23, 1923, Clements Papers. The nature of Van Tyne's 'engagement' is not known.

3   Winship to WC, May 12, 1923, Clements Papers.

4   Winship to WC, May 28, 1923, Clements Papers. Although Winship may have been reluctant to take any extra trouble to insert a tribute to Professor Van Tyne, he did manage to find room for it, a single sentence at the bottom of p. xi.

5   Winship to WC, May 23, 1923, Clements Papers.

6   Winship to WC, June 5, 1923, Clements Papers. Winship's allusion was of course to the collector's pursuit of variant issues of rare books – which often came about in just such a fashion in the early days of printing.

7   Clements paid Winship $1500 for his editorial services (WC to Winship, June 22, 1923, Clements Papers). That Clements was taken aback when he received Winship's bill for services is evident from his letter to President Burton of July 20, 1923: 'I paid Winship myself for his time in seeing to the Press work, and for the time he spent in checking the facts of history. He made no radical changes in my manuscript [!] and I do not believe there are many errors in the facts. As stated, his bill was of such an amount that I shall respect in the future the services of any literary man.' (Burton Papers)

The University of Michigan budgeted $1800 to pay for the press work (WC to Bishop, July 20, 1923, Bishop Papers) but the bill from the Harvard Press was almost double this amount, possibly because Clements had requested, and received, the services of Bruce Rogers (Winship to RGA, March 14, 1947: Bruce Rogers designed the title page and also drew the vignette of the library on the title page). In September, 1928, $1,775 was added to the original appropriation. Cf. *Regents' Proceedings*, 1923–1926, September 27, 1923, meeting, p. 29.

8   Winship to WC, June 27, 1923, Clements Papers.

9   Bishop to Burton, June 14, 1923, Bishop Papers.

10   George Parker Winship, 'Remarks,' in Michigan. University. William L. Clements Library, *Dedication* (Ann Arbor: University of Michigan, 1923), pp. 21–22.

11   Clements, 'The Presentation,' in Michigan. University. William
L. Clements Library, *Dedication*, pp. 11–15.

12   Jameson, 'The American Historian's Raw Materials,' *Ibid.*, p. 38.

13   WC to Stevens, October 4, 1922. Clements got the Brayton-Ives
De Bry from George D. Smith in 1918.

14   Stevens to WC, November 10, 1922, Clements Papers.

15   Winship to WC, December 11, 1922, Clements Papers.

16   WC to Stevens, December 28, 1922, Clements Papers.

17   WC to Burton, February 3, 1923, Burton Papers.

18   WC to Stevens, March 22, 1923, Clements Papers.

19   WC to Stevens, May 31, 1923, Clements Papers.

20   'The Seventy-ninth Commencement,' *Michigan Alumnus*, XXIX
(June 28, 1923), 1049–54. It is interesting to note how many of
Clements' bibliographical friendships resulted in honorary degrees.
Winship was awarded the Litt. D. in 1917; Worthington Ford re-
ceived the L.L.D. in 1920; Harper was given an honorary M.A. in
1928.

21   WC to Bishop, June 22, 1923, Bishop Papers.

22   Stevens to WC, July 5 and 7, 1923, Clements Papers.

CHAPTER XIV

THE CUSTODIAN AT LAST

The weeks following the dedication of the library were lonely ones for Clements. As he told Worthington C. Ford,

The dedication of the new library building at Ann Arbor has taken place and I have returned home to a house empty of nearly all books, so that it is needless to tell you how totally lost I am. . . . I am still looking for a custodian, and of the four kinds of ability necessary for the perfect one, I am fearful I will have to wait quite a time to find them. But I am going to be patient and try and get the spirit of the book collector interwoven with a good bibliographer and historian. . . . Even these three qualities in one man I have not yet found.[1]

Ford, having lived through the John Carter Brown Library's long search for a custodian, was philosophical. He answered,

I do not think you need actually worry over a custodian or about getting immediate results. It took years for the JCB to receive

294

even moderate recognition and yet it was a fairly well advertised library when in the possession of Mr. Brown. . . . Yours has not been so well advertised in the past and it is placed in a position where after all it must create a following, not find one already made. It is its capacity for creating a school that appeals to me most strongly, for that is the thing that is much needed and is not yet supplied from any other source. The New York Public Library has no university connection; the JCB is in a university where little attention can be paid to graduate or higher studies; . . . and the Huntington Library might be at the bottom of Mount Etna. Yours alone has an immediate university connection with an active teaching element, which makes it an essential part of the historical department, and I think that it will be in rather exaggerating a historical part as against mere library management that you will win your best returns.[2]

But Clements *was* worried – both over the problem of the custodian and the problem of what to do about his library for the rest of the summer. The new building was to be kept open through Commencement day, and then closed indefinitely pending completion of carpenter work and the arrival of more furniture and the rugs. Elsie Stewart assumed charge on July 5 and began checking the collection against the card catalog to make sure that all the books sent down from Bay City were accounted for. Almost immediately, people began coming to the campus with the expectation of using the facilities of the new library. But Clements was not anxious to set a date for the opening of the library to the public. As he confided to Winship,

That we are not running the ordinary type of library with open shelves and free access to every book and document in it is hard for many people to understand, particularly the teacher. There

has been an insistent demand that the library be open this summer for work, and I have asked the question, 'What is that work?' The work generally seems to be that of men who are here for the summer, far from the advanced student status and not in any way qualified, even if the library were in order, to be granted facilities, and I shall certainly be insistent upon the library having first of all the proper staff, and then after that the proper arrangement made for the care of the books, before it shall be used. I shall have a good deal of difficulty in maintaining this position.[3]

In the last weeks before the dedication of the library, Clements had thrust the problem of the custodianship from his mind, but now the selection of the right man became of paramount importance. He wrote for advice to Victor H. Paltsits of the New York Public Library, saying, 'I am still looking for a custodian, and wish someone would guide me to an ideal man for this very important post.'[4] Paltsits suggested Dr. Edward Luther Stevenson of the Hispanic Society of America in New York City, a man who, according to Paltsits, could 'administer your library, edit exquisitely texts, write good papers, and lecture or teach.'[5] Clements knew Stevenson through his contacts with the Hispanic Society and was not overly impressed with Paltsits' recommendation.

About the same time, Henry R. Wagner, author of the bibliography entitled *The Plains and the Rockies* and collector of western Americana, wrote strongly urging the candidacy of David Bjork, a young man holding a Ph.D. in history from the University of California with a specialty in Americana. Clements considered Wagner's proposal for several weeks without reaching a decision. He finally wrote Winship, enclosing Wagner's letter. 'The points in Bjork's favor,' averred Clements,

296

are that he seems to be well prepared historically. He is a young man, healthy and full of energy; further than that I know not, or whether he is a book lover and has that spirit so necessary for success.

. . . On the other hand, generally speaking, I am not convinced of the fact that such a foreigner could be intensely interested in American history.

Having virtually disposed of the hapless David Bjork, Clements turned his attention next to Lawrence J. Burpee, Canadian secretary of the International Joint Commission, who, with the elimination of H. H. B. Meyer, remained Bishop's preference. Regarding Mr. Burpee, Clements said,

My impression of him was that he was not neat in his person. He is rather fat and like many fat people his collar was wilted and did not look to me absolutely clean. To me that would be a terrible objection, for an untidy person with himself and about the building personally I could not tolerate. If he did not insist upon neatness throughout the building he could not be tolerated.[6]

At this late date, Clements began to regret that he had not pursued Lawrence C. Wroth, now librarian of the John Carter Brown Library, with more vigor while he was still available. Wroth's review of Clements' monograph on his library, a detailed, thoughtful, and favorable analysis of the book and of the collection, had just appeared; Clements suddenly joined Winship in his long-held opinion that Wroth was 'in a class by himself, with nobody anywhere near him.'[7]

Winship's sage analysis of the situation was helpful. 'Of the men you are considering,' he wrote,

Burpee I know absolutely nothing about, but supposed he had been eliminated . . .. I would accept Wagner's opinion [of Bjork] at face value, but all the same I do not like Swedes. . . .

There is this about Miss Stewart as 'acting' custodian; she would not have to settle any matters of permanent policy, and could always fall back on the fact of her ad-interim status as an excuse for not doing the things you do not quite like to forbid, but which you do not want done. Also she would not be over-awed by any of us Committee-men who might claim ex-officio rights, but she would always look to you as the only person she recognized as giving instructions. There is a great deal to be said for leaving things as they now are until after next year's graduate students are well settled for their year's work. If I were you, I would stop trying to hurry up the contractors, and have things 'not yet ready' on October 1. I do not believe in dodging trouble, when it is sure to come, but there is no use in interfering with the mills of the Gods. And I suspect Miss Stewart has the makings of a very good miller.[8]

Clements was in Ann Arbor during the last week of July, and he found both progress and friction. Except for the arrival of one last rug, the building was ready for opening. Miss Stewart was working steadily, checking the collection against the card catalog. But Miss Stewart, who it would seem was not entirely easy to get along with, was having trouble with the janitors. 'My mission to Ann Arbor,' wrote Clements to Winship,

was to pour oil upon the troubled waters. The head janitor and the acting custodian were at odds, but the acting custodian, Miss Stewart, was certainly in the right. She insisted upon proper care of the building and furnishings. However, all these matters are now straightened out.[9]

298

By the end of the week, the last rug had arrived, and Clements decided to open the building to visitors, with the caution that ropes be placed 'so that when the room is opened the public cannot roam about the entire room.'[10] Clements, in Grand Rapids for a few days' rest, seemed to have resigned himself to the fact that not only was his library to be opened, but that the fall semester at the University was likely to begin without a permanent custodian for the library.

'There is no use in interfering with the mills of the Gods,' had said Winship. But the gods, although their summer's activities had not yet produced any visible results, were about ready to take a hand in Clements' affairs, again through the agency of the same 'somewhat puckish individual'[11] who had already had such a large share in the shaping of the Clements Library.

The ninth of August, 1923, had dawned unusually cold in Cambridge. George Parker Winship sat before his typewriter at his cluttered desk in the Widener Library. He was answering the latest letter from Clements. Another prospective custodian that Clements was considering, and what did Winship think of him? Winship became aware that someone had entered the room. He looked up, to see a pleasant-faced young man and an attractive girl, with one of Winship's casual acquaintances, standing before his desk.

Twenty-three years later, the same young man' now somewhat older' set down his recollections of that momentous meeting.

Late in August, a young assistant professor of American history from a small southern college was catapulted into the Widener Room at Harvard by an imperious dowager-cousin whose addresses were Beacon Street, Boston, and Hingham, Mass. – names which, apparently, mean something in the Boston area. GPW had neither met nor even heard of the young assistant professor – nor had the latter ever heard of GPW. To add confusion, but no gaiety, the aforementioned Beacon Street matron could not remember GPW's name, although she had met him at tea the previous winter. Nothing daunted, she barged into the Widener Room à la a Helen Hokinson drawing, introduced the young assistant professor and his wife, and promptly rushed away to shop at Jordan Marsh's. GPW was stuck with the young couple. He had every reason to be annoyed. He had been interrupted in the writing of an important letter. It was addressed to his friend William L. Clements, and it was a last attempt to get Mr. Clements to make up his mind about the vacant librarian's chair at the Clements Library.

The young man . . . has never been quite certain what happened next. The half-finished letter on GPW's desk was forgotten. The Winship charm was turned on. He enquired whether there was any particular book the visitors would like to see. The young assistant professor was groping frantically for some title to suggest when his eyes spotted the bright morocco backs of a row of solander cases which obviously (they were labeled) contained a set of Purchas' Pilgrimes (London, 1624–25). He asked to see the first volume. This was a lucky break, for Harry E. Widener's set of Purchas is noteworthy as the only known presentation set from the compiler.[12]

Winship never finished his assessment of R. W. G. Vail, Clements' new prospect for custodian. His letter closed, much later, with a hasty scrawl.

At this point a friend introduced me to Randolph Adams and wife . . . .I have known him four hours. One hour talk about books,

300

*an hour going over the library building, two hours at luncheon.
On this, I am prepared to guarantee him.*[13]

The next day, Winship wrote, still in a state of excitement,

*As to the Adams man, it is a straight case of love at first sight. . . .
The ice was broken by a presentation Purchas, which led him to
tell me of his efforts to get a copy for his college library, and
that to talk of bookbuying and librarians. In half an hour I had
decided that his ideas fitted our ideal very closely, that he was
personally likeable, and in general was more like Wroth than
anyone you have considered. So I gave him a copy of The Book, as
a souvenir, and as bait to my line. He played up at once; knew
a little about your library, opened to the Revolution chapter, and
remarked that that was the subject of his book, which Van Tyne
had reviewed favorably. . . .*

*In an hour, I had decided that he would do; for another three
hours I grilled him all I could over the luncheon table, without
discovering what his fault is. Of course he has faults – being taught
to like books by [A. E.] Newton is something of a handicap, but
I guess I can provide antidotes for that, in time. But this means
that your books will be safe in his hands. . . .*

*I suggested that you make up your mind now rather than later,
because, although I detected nothing in the way of idealistic
sentimentalism about such things, I did once or twice think that
I detected signs of rigidity in matters of principle – most unusual
in a Philadelphian. It would not surprise me if he declined to break
an agreement to teach this next year, if he should decide that you
had kept him waiting until it was too late to secure someone to
supply his place.*[14]

Meanwhile, completely unaware of all the excitement, Clements had spent the week in Grand Rapids. He did not reach Bay City until August 16. As soon as he read Winship's letters concerning Adams, he telegraphed, suggesting that they arrange a meeting with Adams. He then called Bishop in Ann Arbor, and asked him to send him a copy of Adams' book, *Political Ideas of the American Revolution*, which had just been published. Bishop sent the book the same day by special delivery commenting that

It looks interesting, and certainly shows, from a hasty glance, a very wide acquaintance with the sources. . . . I plan now to leave here tomorrow . . . [He was spending most of his vacation at Camp Davis]. It is perfectly simple to reach Ann Arbor from Camp Davis by rail, and I should be very glad to come down to see Mr. Adams if you think it wise to bring him out here.[15]

Having read Adams' book, Clements wrote to Adams himself,

I have been very much interested in the reports which Mr. George Parker Winship . . . . has sent me, all relating to your intense interest in historical subjects and in libraries of American history. The collector's standpoint of rare Americana from all I have learned – seems to be reflected in you although [you are] not a collector yourself . . . .

Mr. Winship and myself have been casting about for a custodian . . . . I write you this letter with a view of having a conference whereat all questions might be discussed pertaining to the management and future of the library, and all with a view of coming to some conclusion relative to the office of custodian. I have been wondering therefore whether it would be possible for me to meet you in New York for a conference of possibly two or three days.[16]

Clements spent the following weekend in Ann Arbor. While there, he talked to Van Tyne about his plans and also saw Regent Beal. Then he left for New York and his meeting with Adams and Winship.

Just what Clements and Winship and Adams talked about during their long interview none of them ever said. Adams set down one incident some twenty years later, perhaps remembered over the years because it was hardly what he had been led to expect of Clements. Adams said, 'When I met [Clements] for the first time, in 1923, he told me that he wanted to acquire a good Abraham Lincoln collection.'[17] But more than a good Lincoln collection, Clements wanted to acquire a good custodian for his library. By the end of their interview he had been completely won over by this young man of thirty, a sparkling conversationalist, witty, charming, yet obviously scholarly. His studies, first in law – which he hated – and then in history, at the University of Pennsylvania had been interrupted by military service during the first World War. He had returned to the University of Pennsylvania following his discharge in 1919, to obtain his Ph.D. in 1920. His dissertation, *Political Ideas of the American Revolution*, was of such high quality that it was published in 1922, and he was appointed assistant professor of history at Trinity College (now Duke University) in Durham, North Carolina, the position he held when Clements met him. He was well along with research and writing on a second book, *A History of American Foreign Policy*, and this appeared in 1924. As for Adams' love of rare books, A. Edward Newton, Philadelphia book collector and author of *This Book Collecting Game*, took credit for the early direction of Adams' library experience. Newton wrote to Winship after Adams' appointment to the Clements Library post, 'I have known Randolph Adams always. He has practically grown up in my library and amid bookish influences.'[18] Clements summed up his feelings about Adams in a letter to President Burton shortly after Adams came to Ann Arbor: 'I thoroughly believe he and Wroth of JCB will be the forthcoming bibliographical authorities in this country, and their work will redound to the credit of Michigan.'[19]

On August 28, Clements sent a brief but triumphant telegram to Elsie Stewart: 'Arrangements made with Adams.' The decision was made; the quest was at an end. Clements had found a custodian. As Winship put it, in an undated note which he slipped onto Clements' nightstand in his New York hotel room, 'Good bye . . . I go back – feeling that this is the best time – taking everything into account – I ever had in New York. GPW.'[20] And Clements echoed his feeling when he returned to Bay City. 'We did a mighty good piece of work this week, and I think the selection made is a wise one.'[21]

Randoph G. Adams was officially appointed to the custodianship of the Clements Library by the regents at their meeting on September 27, 1923. He entered with the rank of full professor, at a salary of $ 5,000 per year, dating from September 1, 1923. The selection had indeed been a wise one. Adams came to Ann Arbor in October, 1923, and remained nearly thirty years, until his untimely death early in 1951, as the first director of the William L. Clements Library.

NOTES

1   WC to Ford, June 27, 1923, Clements Papers.
2   Ford to WC, July 2, 1923, Clements Papers.
3   WC to Winship, July 10, 1923, Clements Papers.
4   WC to Paltsits, June 27, 1923, Clements Papers.
5   Paltsits to WC, June 30, 1923, Clements Papers.

6   WC to Winship, July 16, 1923, Clements Papers.

7   Winship to WC, July 24, 1923, Clements Papers. Wroth's review, titled 'Americana for Americans; Collector's Story of the Clements Library,' appeared in the *New York Times Book Review and Magazine*, July 22, 1923, p. 3, 25. In a nicely phrased tribute to Clements, Wroth said, 'Books have been to this collector as documents in the history of the human race. He has not confused them with snuff boxes, old pipes, or little china dogs.'

8   Winship to WC, July 24, 1923, Clements Papers.

9   WC to Winship, July 31, 1923, Clements Papers.

10   WC to Bishop, August 3, 1923, Bishop Papers.

11   Adams to Regent J. O. Murfin, December 15, 1935, Adams Papers.

12   Randolph G. Adams, 'GPW & WLC,' *The [Clements Library] Quarto* (April, 1946), [1–2].

13   Winship to WC, August 9, 1923, Clements Papers.

14   Winship to WC, August 10, 1923, Clements Papers.

15   Bishop to WC, August 16, 1923, Bishop Papers. Neither Bishop, Van Tyne, nor Burton met Adams before he had been hired for the position.

16   WC to Adams, August 21, 1923, Adams Papers.

17   Randolph Adams, fall 1943, untitled paper, in Librarians' Advisory Committee Folder, MHC #17.

18   Newton to Winship, October 6, 1923, Clements Papers.

19   WC to Burton, October 10, 1923, Burton Papers.

20   Winship to WC, undated message on Hotel Belmont, New York City, stationery, Clements Papers.

21   WC to Winship, September 1, 1923, Clements Papers.

CHAPTER XV

THE GREAT MANUSCRIPT COLLECTIONS

'This day and hour mark the conclusion of a book-collector's career.' With these words, William L. Clements transferred his library to its new owner, The University of Michigan, at the dedication of the library on June 15, 1923. And when Clements returned sorrowfully to his home, now empty of family and empty of books, he did not think at that moment that he would begin anew to fill the shelves of his library.

But bibliomania is an incurable disease, and, like many another collector who disposed of a first library only to begin a second, Clements had simply completed the first period of his development as a collector. He had been twenty years in building the collection that formed the original gift to The University of Michigan. He was to spend the next decade, the final years of his life, in further collection building, but in a different area.

In April, 1924, Clements, thinking perhaps of Henry E. Huntington's method, wrote to Stevens,

I have had it upon my mind to write you relative to any English

libraries which might be offered and for sale as a whole, pertaining to American history. It would seem, however, that such libraries in England would be few. I would be interested in acquiring such libraries with a view of adding possibly parts of them to the library at Ann Arbor and using the balance for my own amusement. Should you have anything really worth while, either in manuscripts or in books, I might make a visit to England.[1]

Stevens was not long in responding. In October, he sent Clements a clipping from the *London Times*, protesting the number of significant collections of English manuscripts which had left the country through sale to purchasers abroad in recent years. The Shelburne manuscripts, which Clements had purchased in 1921, were singled out as a notable example. Said Stevens,

Some time ago you wrote to me to be sure and let you know if any similar collections came into the market, or could be bought privately. I heard some time ago that the Papers belonging to the Clinton family, namely those of George Clinton, Governor of New York, and Sir Henry Clinton, Commander in Chief of the English Forces during the War, were coming on sale at Hodgsons. I have tried to negotiate with respect to these, but so far without much prospect of success. But owing to this correspondence in the Times I learn from my friend Mr. Hodgson ... that possibly something might be done in the way of buying the collection en bloc, provided you would undertake to keep it intact.[2]

Clements' cabled answer expressing interest in the proposition was the start of more than a year's negotiations that turned out to be a drama involving cloak and dagger intrigue, complete with a cast of characters starring William L. Clements and an aristocratic old lady who, as Stevens put it, 'appears to have a wobbling mind,' plus a supporting cast of self-interested and sometimes double-dealing agents, and even a couple of genuine villains worthy of a Victorian melodrama.

It was February, 1925, before J. E. Hodgson, agent for Miss Frances Clinton, owner of the papers, managed to talk her into considering dealing with Stevens as agent for Clements. As Stevens was to explain more than once in the next year, 'the negotiation has been a long, difficult and delicate one, as often happens when one has to deal with a lady who is of a wavering mind, with no experience of business methods, and who is continually being influenced by the advice of friends.' But now Hodgson had the papers at his London store, and he and Stevens were making a detailed evaluation of them, so that they could arrive at a fair price for the collection. Said Stevens,

I am absolutely overwhelmed with the historical importance and interest of the marvellous collection, which surpasses anything I have ever seen or imagined. Whatever the valuation agreed to, I tell you most emphatically that you must *rise to it, because the Collection would be the very essence or corner stone of your Revolution Collection, already the best in existence.*[3]

He grew more excited as his examination continued. A week later he wrote,

The more I see of the Collection the more I am impressed with it. . . . You simply cannot afford to let this Collection pass into other hands, if it is in any way possible to secure it. It would be the glory of the Clements Library for all time. Whilst the Lansdowne Papers [Shelburne Papers] cover the political side of the Revolution and events leading up thereto in England, these Clinton Papers fill the gap which has always been a weak point in American

308

*history, viz. the true details of the military operations in the con-
duct of the war on the spot.*[4]

Stevens' tantalizing descriptions served to whet Clements' enthusiasm. In March, Stevens reported on some of the papers of
Major John André, aide to General Clinton, which he had discovered. These included secret information on spies and deserters,
drafts of letters in André's own hand, a large quantity of material
pertaining to the negotiations between André and Benedict
Arnold, including correspondence dealing with André's capture,
his farewell letter to Clinton, and his execution by American
forces. By this time, Stevens was ready to give Clements
a tentative idea of the valuation of the papers, which he thought
would run to more than £15,000, or about $75,000.

But complications, in the shape of the ubiquitous Dr. Rosenbach, suddenly made themselves manifest. A hasty cable from
Stevens followed his letter.

*Although valuation incomplete strongly advise opening negotia-
tions immediatedly with preliminary firm offer £15,000. Other
enquiries dangerous quarters just intervened.*[5]

Dr. Rosenbach had not been the only one making inquiries.
Leon Kashnor of the Museum Bookstore and Ernest Maggs of
Maggs Brothers had been around to call on Hodgson. To forestall these potential rivals, 'we thought it very desirable that
negotiations should be opened at once, before anyone else approached her [Miss Clinton] direct,'[6] said Stevens.

Meanwhile, Clements had consulted Van Tyne as to his opinion of the advisability of the purchase. On the basis of information received thus far from Stevens, Van Tyne reported that
'Altogether there are quantities of Sir Henry Clinton's letters in

print and it is probably fair to ask the question as to whether the cream has not been already skimmed from the collection Stevens has for sale?'[7] After reading Van Tyne's report, Clements seemed to lose interest in the papers. He enclosed the report in a letter to Stevens, saying,

That I value your judgment in appraising such materials goes without saying. But from my own and my Library's standpoint much depends upon whether the material is published or unpublished. Of course, much of the Clinton, Andrè and Arnold correspondence has been published and the story has been long written.[8]

Meanwhile, Stevens, in panic lest the bird slip from his grasp, took it upon himself to make Hodgson a firm verbal offer of £15,000 on Clements' behalf. Hodgson, however, was having his own troubles. Miss Clinton was spending the winter in southern France. Although Hodgson wrote to her immediately about the offer, she did not reply. 'In the meantime,' said Stevens,

one of the dangers I anticipated has materialized. Dr. Rosenbach from Philadelphia has seen Hodgson and asked for information, but so far has not asked to see the Collection. Dr. R. is such a bluffer that the danger is that if he should approach Miss Clinton direct and learn that an offer of fifteen has been made, he would be likely to make a bluff offer of twenty without having even seen a single paper, but acting merely on my judgement in offering fifteen.

I have spent the best part of my time for six weeks or more looking through these papers leaf by leaf, and the more I see the more I am convinced that you must not let them pass even at £20,000.[9]

310

By May, Miss Clinton had returned to England, but after all Stevens' and Hodgson's work, the lady could not her make up mind what to do. The only thing she was sure of was that she would not accept £15,000 for the papers. But Miss Clinton's 'wobbling mind' was only the least of the difficulties. Stevens continued, 'Then again Rosenbach has been nibbling strongly but had to sail for home this week without seeing the collection, but he has asked to have a report sent on to him.' If this were not enough, Ernest Maggs of Maggs Brothers had also applied on behalf of a mysterious American client to see the papers. 'The only thing to do,' concluded Stevens, 'is for you to come at once and judge for yourself.' Although Clements' offer of £15,000 had been rejected, Stevens felt that a firm offer of £17,500 might succeed.[10]

The cable Stevens sent the same day that he mailed his long letter reached Clements in New York City. Up to this point he had kept his negotiations for the Clinton papers confidential, except for a request for information and evaluation from Adams and Van Tyne. He had not even confided the proposition to Winship. But when Stevens' cablegram reached him, he decided to take Lathrop C. Harper into his confidence. He told Randolph Adams about their conversation after he returned to Michigan.

I related the story of the whole negotiation.... When I had finished he said he knew all about the matter and that Hodgson had made a public statement, offering them for sale when he should not have done so, for he had no authority from Miss Clinton. That was some months ago and probably six or eight weeks before I had my first letter from Stevens. It was then thought that the Papers would be offered piece-meal at auction, but Miss Clinton objected to this procedure as she wanted them held intact. At any rate, complete changes of plans were made. At Hodgson's invitation, Harper personally inspected the papers. He told me that the job was such an extensive one that he could only go over them in a casual way, but that he was greatly impressed with the extent of the collection. . . . I think we can accept what Mr. Stevens has told us about the Papers as correct. . . .

Mr. Harper said that he saw enough of the Papers to convince him that he would make an offer forthwith, without further examination, of £5,000, and he said he came away with the feeling that he would give possibly £8,000 or £10,000; beyond that nothing more. He thought that the price of £15,000 without Stevens' commission had been worked up through Hodgson and Miss Clinton, and he did not know now whether they could be purchased, with Miss Clinton's attitude, even at that price, but he said he would not personally pay over $50,000.

But now the important phase of the matter was told to me – namely that with the friendship that exists between Rosenbach and Harper, the latter asked Rosenbach and Rosenbach agreed to keep off the premises so that the Doctor will not make a bid while Harper is in the field. If I had not seen Mr. Harper in New York and talked this over with him as I did, I have grave doubts whether, if Harper had secured the Papers, I would ever have heard of them. I do not know where they would have gone. . . . We talked it over very carefully and I came home with the feeling that under the circumstances, with the promise on Harper's part that if he could purchase them he would turn them over to me with a reasonable commission added to the best price for which he could get them, I had better withdraw for Harper did not think that there would be any other bidders, with Rosenbach out of the way, unless it would be the Museum Bookshop.[11]

Armed with this information, Clements said to Harper, 'I very much desire this material and I believe you are in a position to save me many thousand dollars. If Rosenbach will keep off as you report and the Museum people will do the same, I think they will come off their high horse.'[12] Then he sent a cablegram to Stevens, 'Much disappointed: cannot consider such an extensive purchase.'[13]

In the meantime, Rosenbach, now back from his trip to England, had had a visit with Harper. Harper wrote to tell Clements what he had learned.

Dr. Rosenbach saw Hodgson and had some talk about the Clinton papers. He would say nothing definite as to a price. He said that a London dealer [Stevens?] had a 'rich American' who was very anxious to get the lot, and he could not say how much they could get for them. Wanted Doctor to take the matter up. But Doctor told him he would do nothing except in connection with me. Of course they wanted Doctor to make an offer which would help boost the price. Doctor tells me that even if he had not wanted to keep off on my account, he would have had nothing to do with the lot. He did not like the way it was being handled. Miss Lone [Harper's assistant, E. Miriam Lone] sails 30th and will see what she can find out. Your cable ought to help.[14]

Clements, who doubtless did not take kindly to being characterized by his London friends as a 'rich American,' was evidently little impressed by Stevens' long and rather frantic letter sent on receipt of Clements' telegram terminating negotiations. He returned a cool reply to Stevens, reiterating his decision not to renew his offer of £15,000 for the papers. Said he,

The negotiations have taken so many turns and the lady who has the Papers for sale is so erratic . . . that I feel that as much as I

desire to secure them, I am not going to commit myself again to any offer without first knowing that it will be accepted, secondly without a personal examination of the Papers.[15]

Meanwhile, Harper had heard from Miss Lone in London. He reported her findings on the Clinton papers:

The matter is still in shape where they will not say anything defi-nite. They are talking big and increasing their ideas daily. Under these circumstances it would be folly for me to make any offer. I shall be in London in September and by that time they may have cooled off somewhat. I shall try and see Miss Clinton. I feel that I ought to deal with her direct.

I told Miss Lone to talk it over with [Leon] Kashnor [of the Museum Bookstore], and from him she got some interesting infor-mation. The lot has been offered to him, and they have tried very hard to get him to make an offer. As he looks at the matter the same as I do, he has refused. He offered the lot to Harmsworth, and Sir Leicester made an offer of £400 for the early (Governor Clinton) portion. This was of course absurd, and I expect that Kashnor had something to do with such a low offer, wishing to discourage them. As it now stands they have promised Kashnor not to sell without giving him the last chance.

Kashnor says that he hears the lot has been offered to Mr. Mason, Mr. Huntington, and yourself, but that you are regarded as the best prospect. Dr. Rosenbach has just returned from California. He did not hear any talk of the Clinton matter there. Mr. Hun-tington is not buying at present as he has made some very heavy art purchases.[16]

In London, Hodgson and Stevens had been busy. 'Mr. Hodgson,' wrote Stevens,

314

is absolutely in despair at not being able to get any definite instructions from Miss Clinton. He had an interview with her the first week in July. . . . He told her that the time had come when she must decide on a definite price she would be willing to accept for the Collection. . . . Hodgson advised her that as she would not accept £15,000 she should give you a definite two months option at a price not exceeding £17,500, thus allowing you time to come over and inspect, if you desired to do so . . . .

Miss Clinton appeared favorable to this course of action and left with the understanding that she would consult her friends and write Mr. Hodgson.[17]

But alas, whenever Miss Clinton consulted her friends the result was never a firm decision. After some considerable delay, Hodgson received a rambling letter from the lady stating that if Mr. Clements cared to make an offer of £20,000 for the papers, she might be willing to consider it. On Hodgson's reply that this would not be satisfactory, she set up a further appointment 'to meet Hodgson again with a friend who would advise her what to do after hearing Hodgson's advice.' And that is where the matter stood[18]. Finally, Stevens hastened to give his version of Hodgson's tentative offers to 'two parties on this side of the Atlantic.' He said,

Firstly I may tell you emphatically that you are the only person who has seriously negotiated for the Collection. I am the only person who has been allowed to view the papers in detail, and who has gone through them and made an independent valuation. I spent many weeks on this job as you can imagine from my reports. . . . Hodgson tells me definitely that the papers have not been offered to two parties on your side as you say you have been privately informed. . . . When Harper was over here last year he saw a few of the pieces and spent merely an hour or two on two days looking at a few pieces. The bulk of the Collection had not then been even unpacked and examined by Hodgson himself. He thinks Harper did make a sporting offer of £4,000 or £5,000, which Hodgson says he did not take seriously. As to who the second party can be to whom you refer, he cannot imagine. . . . I may tell you also that Doctor Rosenbach when here this year made some enquiries, but no price was named.[19]

Clements, busy the next few weeks with important University business, did not reply until September. Once again he indicated his interest in acquiring the collection. But he pointed out that, even if his original bid of £15,000 were to be accepted, 'the difference in exchange alone is an item of some 10 %, for sterling is about par at this time.' Therefore, he was willing to reopen negotiations, but on a dollar basis.

I will make you a proposition in dollars which shall include all commission, of whatever nature, either to yourself or to Mr. Hodgson, of $88,500.00, subject as was my first proposition to an examination, and with the further condition that I should be allowed ample time to prepare for my trip for such inspection, should the proposition be acceptable, such time not to exceed four months.[20]

Still difficulties with the fractious Miss Clinton were not at an end. As Stevens said, when he turned Clements' offer over to Mr. Hodgson, 'she is such a difficult lady to deal with that although [Hodgson] will advise her to accept the offer, he is by no means certain that out of pure contrariness she may not turn it down.'[21] And sure enough, 'after wasting three more weeks,' Miss Clinton declined it absolutely. She had decided that the price of the papers must be £17,500 net to her. 'That is to say, Hodgson must charge his commission to the purchaser on that amount.' The two agents agreed to reduce their commissions to meet Miss Clinton's figure and yet stay within Clements' limit; Hodgson was willing to take 10 percent instead of 12 1/2 percent, and Stevens would reduce his 10 percent to 7 1/2 percent, if Miss Clinton would meet them at £15,250 net. But Stevens expressed some private doubts as to Miss Clinton's willingness to come down. Would Clements by any chance be willing to raise his offer to $100,000? 'I will tell you in strictest confidence,' concluded Stevens, 'that Hodgson is instructed (if you do not accept her counter offer within fourteen days) to offer the Collection to the Library of Congress.'[22] Clements, however, wise by now to the ways of Miss Clinton, quickly ascertained that the Library of Congress was in no financial position to pay for the papers and cabled Stevens that he declined to raise his offer.

Thereupon Miss Clinton had a sudden change of heart. Clements' cablegram was answered by one from Stevens. 'Clinton suddenly reopened negotiations ... accepting your offer, subject 5 % forfeitable deposit which we rejected absolutely. Think probable unconditional settlement will result.'[23] But Clements stood his ground. 'No forfeiture,' read his cabled reply to Stevens. A second, longer cablegram followed in two days, in which Clements told Stevens,

My confidence your report induced me make the last proposition. You should have confidence in my sincerity. Expense trip London considerable. Will not agree penalty. With winter at hand very inconvenient if not impossible make examination before April next possibly sooner. Terms payment one third cash acceptance, one third three months, one third six months thereafter without interest.[24]

Stevens immediately communicated Clements' message to Hodgson, 'who in turn informed Miss Clinton's representative. They are now chewing it over and Hodgson has told them pretty straight that if they don't make haste to get down to business on proper lines, they are likely to lose the sale altogether.'[25] Miss Clinton and her friends 'chewed' until the end of November and at length proposed a compromise. Stevens at once cabled Clements,

Clinton will not wait till April but will waive deposit if you will come inspect at once, or preferably close without inspection on my recommendation, Hodgsons as experienced valuers giving certificate of value. Strongly advise this course.[26]

On December 3, 1925, Clements cabled authorization to Stevens to purchase the Clinton papers for the stipulated $88,500, without his examination. The long negotiation was at an end. But only by a hair's breadth did Clements get the Clinton papers. A few days later Stevens sent him a letter marked 'Private and confidential.' Stevens said,

You may like to know how nearly we lost the Clinton collection. On the morning of Friday, December 4th, the very day I received your cable authorizing me to conclude the purchase, Maggs rung up Hodgson on the 'phone to say he had just received a cable from Mr. Huntington authorizing him to treat for the Collection, and asking for particulars. Hodgson replied that acting on Miss Clinton's instructions he was already in negotiation with a party, and by the same instructions he was not permitted to give particulars to anyone else or allow anyone to see the papers whilst that negotiation was still in progress.

318

On the same day, Stevens notified Hodgson of Clements' cablegram; the following day, Miss Clinton's representative wrote Hodgson to accept the proposition. 'By the same post,' continued Stevens,

he received a very insolent letter from Maggs . . . telling him that it was clear he was not acting in the best interests of his client by negotiating with one party without allowing anyone else to make a better offer.

Hodgson 'phoned me up to say that he was authorized to complete [the transaction], so I went down at once to his office. In the meantime Maggs had gone to Hodgson's to look at some lots that were on view for this week's sale. Hodgson seeing him in the Sale Room asked him to step into the office. I arrived whilst he was there and waited in a private room till Maggs had gone. When I saw Hodgson he was evidently very angry and annoyed and he told me he had given Master Maggs a good dressing down for daring to insinuate that he had not acted for the best interests of his client. He told Maggs definitely that the papers were sold and Maggs said, 'I suppose Mr. Clements has got them for Mr. Huntington says he knew he was after them.' He then made some disparaging remarks about you which Hodgson resented. . . . Finally Maggs told Hodgson that the owner ought to be informed that his client would have been prepared to give several thousands of pounds more, and expressed surprise that you could afford to buy them at all.[27]

But this was not the last Hodgson was to see of Ernest Maggs. Two weeks later, after several routine cables and letters regarding final arrangements, Stevens wrote again.
You will hardly believe it that Maggs went behind Hodgson's back and wrote to Miss Clinton direct, and told her that his client

would have given more if he had had the chance, and if Hodgson had negotiated on a proper basis. Result is Miss Clinton's representative wrote to Hodgson to enquire whether he was quite sure the best price had been obtained after all. . . . This is of course very unfortunate and annoying and owing to the unbusinesslike nature of the lady she will no doubt for evermore think she might have got a bit more.[28]

Stevens had the last of the Clinton papers in the mail by February 5, 1926, and they were received in Bay City by the end of the month. Consisting of more than 16,500 separate documents and 360 manuscript maps, the collection included 'not only the letters received by the British Commander in Chief and his subordinates, but also [3,500] retained copies of the letters [in 50 letterbooks] sent out from his office.' At the time of purchase, most of the letters, having been in the possession of the Clinton family since Sir Henry's death in 1795, were unknown to historians. Van Tyne was wrong in believing that many of them had been published or existed in other copies in other depositories.

Inasmuch as Clinton arrived in Boston before the Battle of Bunker Hill and remained until May, 1782, the documents illustrate some of the most dramatic episodes in the Revolutionary War. They begin with an unpublished manuscript account of the battles of Lexington and Concord written by Lieutenant William Sutherland and end with Cornwallis' letter announcing his surrender at Yorktown on October 19, 1781. Included are cipher letters and masked letters, complete with the mask that served as a key, between General Burgoyne and Sir Henry Clinton. The full correspondence between Major John André, Sir Henry Clinton, and Benedict Arnold tells a shabby story of intrigue and betrayal, ending with André's pathetic farewell letter to his well-loved superior, Sir Henry Clinton. As Randolph Adams observed,

320

This great collection of manuscripts seems to have been held together by Sir Henry Clinton in order that he might write his account of the War of American Independence. That book was written . . . in full, annotated by scholarly footnotes and citations to the documents in the collection – material for two stout volumes. That it was never published is probably due to the fact that by 1795 London publishers had a great many other things on their minds besides the details of how England lost the United States of America. Yet today it is a fascinating story . . . the story of the American Revolution by the British Commander in Chief.[29]

Sir Henry Clinton's manuscript, also included with the papers, was edited by Professor William B. Willcox and published by Yale University Press in 1954 under the title, *Sir Henry Clinton, The American Rebellion*. Similarly, the whole story of Arnold's treason and his wife's involvement was related correctly for the first time in *Secret History of the American Revolution* (1941) by Carl Van Doren, after his exhaustive study at the library.

During the same year of 1925, Clements acquired for $30,000 the papers of General Nathanael Greene, Washington's ablest general during the Revolution. This collection, consisting of approximately 5,000 items, deals chiefly with Greene's conduct of the Southern campaign during the Revolution, 1780-1783. Joseph Sabin had acquired them from a New York banker, James A. Garland, in 1905. He tried for several years to sell them *en bloc*, and failing this, began to sell them piecemeal. About 400 letters from the original collection had been sold when Clements first learned of the letters in 1924; some of these he either bought back in separate transactions or they were purchased later by the library. Greene's letters are detailed and well written. At the time that Clements acquired them, few of the papers were known to historians. As Randolph Adams put it, 'The acquisition of these papers by Michigan will make the rewriting of the life of Greene necessary.'[30]

The fourth great manuscript collection, the papers of Lord George Germain, Secretary of State for the American Colonies 1775-1782, was added to Clements' personal library after a series of contretemps in September, 1927. Henry Stevens discovered the existence of the Germain papers through some bibliographic work he was doing with the *Atlantic Neptune*, one of his perennial projects. As an expert, he was asked to go to Drayton House, the ancestral home of the Sackville family, about seventy-five miles from London, to appraise a copy of the *Neptune* for probate. In talking to Mrs. Stopford Sackville, and her son, Sir Nigel Stopford Sackville, he learned that they had just inherited through the death of an uncle the papers of Lord George Sackville, otherwise known as Lord George Germain. To pay heavy death duties, they would be interested in selling the collection. At Stevens' urging, Clements made a trip to England in September, 1927, chiefly to inspect the papers. After he returned in October, he told Winship of his troubles in negotiating with the family:

I supposed all of the plans had been perfected before I left home, but when I arrived in London, I was met by Mr. Stevens, who told me the lady had changed her mind. I was indignant, and even the serene Henry was angry. The next day he wrote a letter to the lady in which he stated that international relations might be disturbed if she did not keep her promises. He also wrote to the lady's son, and he was the person who worked out salvation.

All this would appear plausible on the surface, but Henry's ambition to purchase [the Sackville] set of the Atlantic Neptune at a price of £300 . . . was the cause of all the trouble. Henry as a purchaser is a different man from Henry as a seller. Because of

322

some good advice the lady received, she did not sell her Neptune for £300. All the confidence she had in Henry's advice as to prices, valuations, etc., was destroyed. The materials were taken from him and given to Sotheby's. Henceforth my dealings were with them. To make a long story short, I purchased the manuscripts, after much delay, at Sotheby's valuation. I might add that Henry wanted the Neptune so badly, he paid twice his offer, and I paid nearly twice his valuation [which had been just under £2,000, cf. Stevens to WC, August 12, 1927] for the manuscripts. Nevertheless I am very fond of Henry for I believe him honest.

We will add to the Library the Lord George Germain manuscripts, which are not very voluminous but are full of meat. There are thirteen folio volumes, poorly bound but mounted in a way ready for recording. They are a wonderful accession to the Library. They dovetail with what we have and nowhere in the United States is there such a lot of source material as we now have.[31]

Unfortunately, this was not the end of the transaction. Shortly after Clements wrote his letter to Winship, he and Randolph Adams made a careful check of the Germain volumes, just received in Bay City, and discovered that one of the volumes described in the Historical Manuscript Commission's report on the collection, labeled America 1778, was missing. Clements cabled forthwith to Stevens asking him to check into it. Stevens called Nigel Stopford Sackville; Drayton House was searched, but the missing volume did not appear. Stopford Sackville, reported Stevens, greatly regretted this, but he pointed out that the lot had been evaluated on just what Stevens had seen, not including the missing volume, so Clements had not been cheated. He also promised, if the 1778 volume ever turned up, to give it free of charge to Clements.

It was three years before Clements was to see the missing

volume. Randolph Adams was in London in March, 1930, doing some work at the Public Record Office. While there he made a startling discovery, which he shared with his wife in a letter.

While I was talking with Stamp and Ratcliffe the subject of the Stopford Sackville papers came up. You remember that when WLC brought them back from England the 1778 volume was missing? And that we were never able to find it? Well, Stamp said he thought he remembered something about it – that it had been sent to the Public Record Office as a loan many years ago and never returned to Drayton House. He promised to look it up. I had hardly gotten back to the hotel before Stamp called me up and said to come back. I hurried back to the Public Record Office. Stamp was standing in the middle of his huge office – walls lined with folio volumes – thousands of them. He was grinning hard.

'Well, Mr. Adams,' he said, 'do you think you could recognize the missing volume?'

I said I knew I could.

'All right,' he said, 'find it !'

It took me just twenty seconds by his watch to find it where he had just placed it on a shelf!

Sure enough, that's the volume, 1778, the one we have been looking for all these years. . . . It is a ten-strike and will please the old man greatly.[32]

Nigel Stopford Sackville kept his word, and turned the missing volume over to Clements without charge. But in his search for the 1778 volume, Stopford Sackville unearthed an old family chest containing further Germain letters. These he sold to Clements through Stevens, who called them 'quite a number of important and interesting pieces relating to the Revolution,' for a total of £607/5/7. [33] Clements, however, was disappointed in

324

the lot, stating that 'with the exception of a few letters, they add little to the main body of the Germain papeis.'[34]

When Clements made his initial purchase of the Germain papers in 1927, he found upon inspection that not only was the 1778 volume missing, but also that the collection lacked manuscript maps, 'which struck him as odd, as the Clinton Collection had been accompanied by such maps.'[35] In 1931, the year following Henry N. Stevens' death, a Stevens sales catalog appeared offering 'The manuscript maps of Lord George Germain,' for £950. Randolph Adams, in a letter written after Clements' death, told what happened next.

Mr. Clements said he was going to have those maps and directed me to get my hands on them. Naturally, I did, and had them sent to me at Ann Arbor, without discussing the price or who was to pay for them. . . .

When the maps came here, Mr. Clements came down and inspected them, and saw at once they were exactly what they purported to be – the maps which should have been with the collection he bought in 1927. This did not improve his temper.

In the summer of 1931, Mr. Clements went to England and saw [Henry] Stevens [Jr.] personally. He ascertained that what had actually happened was this: After I had located the 1778 volume, Sackville decided to look again through his own library, and there he found these maps. He should have offered them to Mr. Clements. They were not part of the original deal. With characteristic British nonchalance, Sackville decided America was rather unimportant anyway, and instead of notifying Mr. Clements, he sold the whole lot to Stevens for about £500. Stevens' mistake was his failure to notify Mr. Clements and to pass the material along at cost plus the customary ten percent. Instead of that, Stevens catalogued the maps, and put them on the market at cost *plus nearly one hundred percent profit. Naturally this enraged Mr. Clements still further, because he thought that was a pretty shabby trick played on him by a man who had been his agent for thirty years. After a good deal of discussion in London in 1931, Mr. Clements finally agreed to have the Library pay Stevens £700, which at the then rate of exchange was about $3400, and it seemed as though peace had been restored.*[36]

The Clements Library did pay for them, although the transaction was not completed until after Clements' death in 1934.

The fifth and last great manuscript collection, the papers of General Thomas Gage, was added to Clements' Bay City library in 1930. Gage was commander-in-chief of the British forces in America for the twelve years preceding the American Revolution and during the first months of the war. His papers, approximately 21,000 letters and documents, span the years between 1763 and 1775. They include a number of extremely important letters bearing on the battles of Lexington, Concord, and Bunker Hill. Of particular interest is Gage's letter to Lieutenant Colonel Smith ordering him to seize illegal ammunition and supplies hidden by the American rebels at Concord; this order precipitated the Revolutionary War.

The Gage papers had been known to historians since Henry Belcher used them at Firle House, ancestral home of the Gage family, in writing his *The First American Civil War* (1911). Sometime between 1911 and 1926, the sixth Viscount Gage transferred most of the family papers to the Public Record Office in London for safekeeping and also so that they could be recorded. A number of historians wanted access to them; about 1926, Clarence E. Carter, Professor of History at Miami University, Oxford, Ohio, obtained Gage's permission to use the papers. He had not, however, begun his study when Allen

326

French, also a historian, happened into the Record Office in 1926 on a similar quest. Some years afterward, French wrote to Adams,

Unaware of [Gage's permission to Carter to use the papers], . . . I was at the Public Record Office and asked the director, Mr. Stamp, where the Gage Papers were. He said, 'They are underneath my feet.' Because of the permission given Carter by Lord Gage . . . I was denied permission to work in the papers.

In 1927 . . . when I was again in England, I got permission to work in the papers. For two months my wife and I worked daily in the documents of 1774-5. On returning, I wrote Mr. Clements concerning the papers, telling him that in my opinion he ought to buy them.[37]

By somewhat of a coincidence, when French returned from England late in August, 1927, Clements was just on his way to London. Stopping in Ann Arbor on his way to Bay City, where he hoped to have permission to use the Clinton Papers, French left a short description of the Gage Papers with Randolph Adams, including the statement that Lord Gage might consider selling them. Adams cabled this information to Clements, who was at that moment having a discouraging time with his negotiations over the Germain Papers. But when Clements checked with the Public Record Office, he received no encouragement. He returned from his summer in England with the Germain negotiation successfully completed; he did nothing further about the Gage papers until the next year. Professor Carter had spent the summer of 1928 in London preparing an edition of some of the correspondence of General Thomas Gage. Again he heard the rumor that Lord Gage might be thinking of disposing of the manuscripts. Carter, hearing that Clements 'had shown some inclination toward attempting negotiation for them,' wrote to him, offering to come to Ann Arbor to show Clements his notes on the Gage Papers.[38]

Carter was in Ann Arbor on December 7 and 8, 1928, and in Adams' absence, talked to Professor Van Tyne. He gave Van Tyne a fairly long report on the papers, his findings from his summer's work.

The papers are contained in twelve large chests, each with two tills, with one exception, and they number approximately 20,000 items. The correspondence and other papers in the collection consist of office copies of letters from General Gage, original letters to him, letters from various persons to people other than General Gage, and miscellaneous documents. Some 600 persons are represented in the correspondence. . . . The papers are not arranged in the chests, however, according to the above classes. They appear in neatly tied bundles, resting in small compartments, and are arranged according to geographical and chronological sequence.[39]

Van Tyne passed Carter's report on to Clements. After reading it, Clements wrote directly to Lord Gage, introducing himself as 'the donor of a Library of the University of Michigan,' and describing his library and the building. Explaining that he had already secured the papers of Lord Shelburne, Sir Henry Clinton, and Lord George Germain, he said,

The papers of both Lord George Germain and Sir Henry Clinton are of course associated intimately with the papers of General Gage, your illustrious ancestor . . . . These papers are so intimately connected with American Colonial History and the early American Revolutionary period, supplementing in such a marked degree those papers in the Library that I am emboldened to ask

*whether some arrangement cannot be made for the purchase of
these papers so that they may be forever stored in the vaults of
the Library.*[40]

To this letter, Lord Gage made no reply; this might have
been the end of the matter except for an unexpected quirk of
fate. V. C. Clinton-Baddeley, the great-great-great grandson of
Sir Henry Clinton, was in the United States on business connected with the new edition of the *Encyclopaedia Britannica*, of
which he was one of the editors. As he told the story,

*I was in America in 1929 and an old friend of mine (Tom Harris)
was a chaplain at Ann Arbor. Before going home I did a whizz
round the States and Ann Arbor was one of the places I went to.
He told me that Clements had purchased the Clinton papers. I didn't
even know – for though I knew of Miss Clinton I didn't know her –
she was about a 4th half cousin. I was nobly received by the Clements Library and invited (with Tom Harris) to stay a night with
Mr. Clements at Bay City. I remember him showing me a mask –
a paper shape to put over a letter – the part that showed being
the real message. As he was handling the mask his finger shook
and he tore the paper slightly with his nail. 'If anyone else had
done that I would have been very angry,' he said. . . . While I was
with Clements he remarked that he had several times tried to get
hold of Lord Gage but could never get an answer. I told him that
I knew Lord Gage and could easily speak to him.*[41]

Clinton-Baddeley was as good as his word; he visited Lord Gage
on his return to England and told him about Clements' proposition and his library. Lord Gage wrote to Clements. 'I had a
visit the other day from Mr. Clinton-Baddeley,' said he,

who tells me that he visited you while in America and that you mentioned, during the conversation, that you had written to me about the Gage papers.

I fully understand and appreciate your desire to have accurate records of what are, after all, documents highly important to American historians, and although I cannot, I am afraid, be definite on this point, I feel inclined to think the best course would be for you to arrange that Photostat copies should be made of such documents as your representative considers desirable.

. . . I must say at once I should think it very improbable whatever my own feelings might be, that my trustees would give permission for family papers of this description to leave the country.[42]

In May, Clinton-Baddeley wrote again to Clements, telling him that he had been to the Public Record Office to see the papers stored there. 'Also,' he continued,

I have been to Firle to see the other papers – papers which Mr. Carter never saw. There are a very large quantity – excellently preserved – but much out of order. These the Record Office are going to sort out. They have not the same interest as the Clinton papers, as they refer mostly to before the war, but many are most interesting and some amusing. . . .

Lord Gage is less than ever inclined to part with them, and I don't think he will. He would be, however, perfectly friendly to anyone wishing to study and make copies of them.[43]

In the meantime, Randolph Adams, who had been in Great Britain since the first part of the year investigating the Anglo-American peace negotiations of 1782-83 and who therefore had not met Clinton-Baddeley in Ann Arbor, wrote to him about

330

the Gage papers. The obliging Mr. Clinton-Baddeley returned a friendly reply, stating that 'Lord Gage expresses amiability and would like to meet you some time. He is sending his stuff up to the Record Office early next week, and therefore he suggests that he meet you *there* some day.'[44]

The proposed meeting between Adams and Lord Gage finally took place over a luncheon table on July 16. Clinton-Baddeley wrote to Clements afterward,

It is clear that Lord Gage has no objection to your photostating the whole collection. The question of purchase was touched on. It seemed that he would conceivably *sell. But it would depend upon (1) it being a tempting figure because he doesn't really* want *to sell; and (2) upon his trustees agreeing to sell. So it's not highly likely.*[45]

No further developments took place until Adams returned to Michigan in September, 1929. At this time, Clements asked Adams to write to Gage, offering £12,000 for the collection. He replied from India, stating that he considered Clements' offer too low, but that he would agree to sell the collection for £20,000. Clements did not hesitate; on December 6, 1929, he wrote Gage, agreeing to his terms. Since Gage was in India, the papers were not to be delivered until his return to England in March, at which time Clements proposed that he and Mr. Adams should go to England 'for the consummation of this agreement.'[46]

Clements wrote to Van Tyne, to tell him of his letter to Gage, but warned him to secrecy. Adams, however, could not resist hinting at the great acquisition. He wrote to Samuel Eliot Morison,

We have just purchased a manuscript collection which, among

other trifles, contains a sheaf of letters written by Joseph Warren in May of 1775 – and reams of similar items. How about four unpublished letters of John Hancock? How about seventeen letters from Francis Bernard and sixty letters from Thomas Hutchinson, 1763-1774? How about hundreds upon hundreds of letters to and from Boston merchants before the Revolution – letters which Schlesinger never saw? . . .

No, it is not the Clinton or Germain Collections – it is something bigger than both of them put together that we have hooked this time.[47]

News of such importance could not be kept secret too long, however, and on January 1, 1930, the *Detroit News* ran an article on the acquisition, complete with a picture of William L. Clements. It is probable that this publicity, together with a news item on Clements' purchase in the *New York Times*, January 2, 1930, alerted not only historians and fellow book collectors to the transaction, but also a dangerous competitor, Dr. A. S. W. Rosenbach.

Although Clements had received an informal letter from Lord Gage agreeing to the sale of the papers, final arrangements were not to be taken care of until Lord Gage's return from India on March 25. Clements, who planned to take care of the official consummation of the sale himself, had decided not to meet Lord Gage when he arrived, but to wait until later in the spring. But these plans did not work out. On March 22, he wrote to his daughter Betty from New York,

I have had a hectic two weeks. I am here in a hurry after a tip from Mr. Harper that all was not well for securing for the Library the Gage Papers. So I came here, found the situation was serious, and decided I must send Mr. Adams at once to England or go

myself. Mr. Adams has gone – left on the Bremen four days after my coming [he sailed March 15], and that together with arranging the financial part has about put me in nervous collapse. . . . A certain book dealer here [Rosenbach] was about to offer $50,000 to break the deal and went over, just one day after Mr. Adams sailed. I hope good news from Adams will be forthcoming.[48]

On March 29, Clements had a cable from Adams stating that Lord Gage had accepted the first payment of £10,000 as a binder on the sale of the papers. The prize was safe. But Adams did not leave England until the papers were ready for shipment; when he returned to America on April 24, the papers, packed in four large trunks, were brought with him as his personal baggage. Through the good offices of Clements' friend, Senator Arthur H. Vandenberg, the papers were cleared through customs without inspection. Clements did not rest easy until Adams and the papers had reached Bay City. As he wrote to Harper,

You cannot imagine the feelings that occur to me when it becomes evident that the Doctor must have written or approached Lord Gage as a third party interfering in a contract! I can hardly believe it of any fairminded or generous man, especially when he knew that the coveted property was to be used in a worthy and impersonal way for research in history. I think the whole episode is contemptible on his part. . . . I am exceedingly glad that I took the course I did in sending Mr. Adams to England, although I have always thought that Lord Gage would stick by his word.[49]

NOTES

1   WC to Stevens, April 10, 1924, Clements Papers.
2   Stevens to WC, October 7, 1924, Clements Papers.

3   Stevens to WC, February 20, 1925, Clements Papers.
4   Stevens to WC, February 27, 1925, Clements Papers.
5   Stevens to WC, March 23, 1925, Clements Papers.
6   Stevens to WC, March 31, 1925, Clements Papers.
7   Van Tyne, 'Report on Clinton Papers Already in Print or Known to Exist in Manuscript Copies in Public Repositories,' [1925], WLCL.
8   WC to Stevens, March 31, 1925, Clements Papers.
9   Stevens to WC, April 9, 1925, Clements Papers.
10   Stevens to WC, May 15, 1925; also cable, Stevens to WC, May 15, 1925, Clements Papers.
11   WC to Adams, May 19, 1925, Adams Papers.
12   WC to Harper, May 16, 1925, Clements Papers.
13   WC to Stevens, May 18, 1925, Clements Papers.
14   Harper to WC, May 25, 1925, Clements Papers.
15   WC to Stevens, June 19, 1925, Clements Papers.
16   Harper to WC, July 11, 1925, Clements Papers.
17   Stevens to WC, July 20, 1925, Clements Papers.
18   *Ibid.*
19   *Ibid.*
20   WC to Stevens, September 3, 1925, Clements Papers. Clements' action in reopening negotiations with Stevens evidently ended Harper's interest in the papers. He took no further action on them.
21   Stevens to WC, September 18, 1925, Clements Papers.
22   Stevens to WC, October 16, 1925, Clements Papers.
23   Stevens to WC, November 6, 1925, Clements Papers.
24   WC to Stevens, November 15, 1925, Clements Papers.
25   Stevens to WC, November 17, 1925, Clements Papers.
26   Stevens to WC, November 29, 1925, Clements Papers.
27   Stevens to WC, December 8, 1925, Clements Papers.
28   Stevens to WC, December 24, 1925.
29   Randolph G. Adams, *The Headquarters Papers of the British Army in North America during the War of the American Revolution*, Clements Library Bulletin, XIV (Ann Arbor: Clements Library, 1926) p. 9.
30   Adams, 'Papers of Greene at Michigan' [1926?] (Typescript), MHC #13.
31   WC to Winship, October 14, 1927, Clements Papers. Date of sale was September 23, 1927. Price, with Stevens' commission, was £4, 410/3/2. Stevens invoice, September 30, 1927, Clements Papers.

32   Adams to Mrs. Helen Adams, March 26, 1930, Adams Papers.

33   Stevens to WC, February 3, 1928; WC to Stevens, February 19, 1928, Clements Papers.

34   WC to Stevens, April 12, 1928, Clements Papers.

35   Adams to Harry Finkenstaedt, December 15, 1934, Adams Papers.

36   *Ibid.*

37   French to Adams, October 22, 1938, MHC #12.

38   Carter to WC, October 8, 1928, MHC #9.

39   Carter, 'Notes on the Lord Gage Collection,' undated, WLCL.

40   WC to Gage, January 10, 1929, MHC #1.

41   Clinton-Baddeley to M. Maxwell, June 22, 1970.

42   Gage to WC, April 30, 1929, MHC #1.

43   Clinton-Baddeley to WC, May 18, 1929, MHC #1.

44   Clinton-Baddeley to Adams, May 30, 1929, MHC #1.

45   Clinton-Baddeley to WC, July 16, 1929, MHC #1.

46   WC to Gage, December 6, 1929, MHC #1.

47   Adams to Morison, December 12, 1929, MHC #19.

48   WC to Betty Clements Finkenstaedt, March 22, 1930 (Mrs. Finkenstaedt's personal files).

49   WC to Harper, April 10, 1930, Clements Papers.

CHAPTER XVI

AN APPRAISAL

The Gage papers were Clements' last major addition to his library. Their acquisition may have been the only happy event of 1930. The stock market crash of the past autumn was turning into a widespread economic depression. Mrs. Clements, who had been separated from her husband, obtained a divorce. Professor Van Tyne, deeply respected as an American historian by Clements, died. The only satisfaction rising from the loss was the subsequent award of the Pulitzer Prize in history to Van Tyne's book, *The War of Independence*, dedicated to Clements and written largely out of his manuscripts and his library. Then Henry N. Stevens died in London. He was more than an agent; he was a bibliographer Clements admired and a friend he enjoyed.

The clouds lifted for a short time in 1931. On April 22, Clements was married to Miss Florence Kathryn Fisher, an old friend in Bay City. They set off on an extended trip to Europe, but the tour was interrupted by a cablegram which Clements received in England. It told of financial difficulties involving the Bay City bank of which he was president. Mr. and Mrs. Clements returned home as quickly as possible, arriving about the end of August. Almost immediately thereafter the bank closed. Clements summarized the events of the next few months as follows:

Banking conditions in Bay City have been terrible since the failure of the Bay City Bank in September. Withdrawals amounting to 40 % of the total deposits have taken place, and liquidation of securities simultaneously followed. This was without loss, but rather than continue with a loss, the closing was decided upon by the Board of Directors. It was not forced. We made the best fight possible, and the burden fell principally upon me. I shall be a terrible sufferer financially, but I have a few shillings left and I hope to be able to function for my allotted time.

. . . I am determined that the humiliation of being connected with anything defunct – something I never before experienced – will not get me. Many others are in the same predicament, and I do not think we have yet reached the end.[1]

The bank was reopened during the summer of 1932, but Clements' assessments on his stock, together with other stock losses,[2] were of disturbing magnitude.

Clements was renominated by the Republican party for the Board of Regents, but the spring election of 1933 was a replay of the Democratic sweep nationally in the previous fall. After three terms totalling twenty-four years, Clements was defeated along with other Republican candidates. He had long served as chairman of the regents' committee on buildings and grounds, and during the last dozen years of his tenure the University had erected more buildings than ever before in its history.

By 1934 Clements' health was giving him concern. He had

suffered a heart attack that winter while vacationing in Florida. He also realized that he was unable financially to give to the Clements Library, as he had planned, the several manuscript collections he had gathered during the preceding decade. Accordingly he opened negotiations with the University for their sale to the library.[3] In September the University bought one collection for $15,000. It was the extensive papers of John Wilson Croker, secretary of the British Admiralty, 1809–1830, and a literary critic. The collection was virtually Clements' first purchase in the field of manuscripts, having been obtained in England in 1924. Nothing further had been settled before Clements died on November 6, 1934, in Bay City. He was buried in Ann Arbor.

'In character,' wrote Randolph G. Adams, 'Clements was a born connoisseur, whose good taste was apparent in whatever he touched. The extent of his charity and kindness to others can never be known, but it was marked and considerable. Like other successful American business men of his period, he was essentially a builder, with somewhat of the soul of an artist. Like so many Americans of his generation, book-collecting was no fun to him unless he was able to share his pleasures with others, and the gift of his collection to the principal educational institution of his state is the supreme evidence of this.'[4]

In his will he expressed regret that financial consideration for his family prevented him from turning over the manuscript collections in his house as gifts to the Clements Library. Instead he must ask the University to buy them; in the event of refusal they would have to be put up for sale. The difficulty was that the University was also caught in the depression with a reduced appropriation from the state and falling enrollment. After several discussions between the executors of the estate and University officers, the former invited Charles Goodspeed, well known antiquarian book dealer of Boston, to appraise the collections. After he submitted his figures, the executors set a price of $300,000 on them.

The sum was out of the University's reach. But Tracy W. McGregor, book collector and philanthropist of Detroit and Washington, had come on to the Committee of Management in 1933, after George Parker Winship resigned. He comprehended the stalemate and felt strongly that the collections must be added to the Clements Library, as everyone wanted. Generously he offered $100,000 toward the settlement, and the estate agreed to accept the balance in annual installments of $15,000, the amount of the yearly appropriation to the library for acquisitions. Agreement on these terms was concluded in 1937, and the manuscripts were transferred to the library at last.

It is clear now that William L. Clements was the last of the great 'classic' collectors of Americana. No one, starting after he did, could put together a duplicate or even a similar collection of source books of the same magnitude, simply because many of them would not come on the market again. Clements missed some titles because he was almost too late in the field himself. John Carter Brown and James Lenox collected more books and had an easier time of it just because they started earlier. Henry E. Huntington was financially able to buy the collections of others and amalgamate them. The luck of later collectors reveals the changed conditions. Thomas W. Streeter of Morristown, New Jersey, began collecting right after World War I and continued until his death in 1965. He managed to assemble a library of rare Americana amounting to approximately 6100 titles, but to accomplish even this much he extended his coverage down to 1900 and emphasized the history of Texas. His unequalled Texas collection of nearly 1700 rarities was bought by Yale University, leaving his general Americana of about 4400 titles to be sold at auction. To be sure, he had some books that Clements was not able to find (and the Clements Library bought some at auction), but the difference in size and concentration between the libraries of the two men is striking.

Similarly, Tracy W. McGregor, mentioned above, started collecting in the 1920's and died in 1936. Much richer than Clements, he created a collection of about 8500 volumes, but 1,000 of them were English literature. The remainder was early Americana. He did well in a short time, but his opportunities in historical sources were diminishing rather than increasing. McGregor was influenced by Clements' example, and in accordance with his known desires and his will, his executors gave his collection to the University of Virginia in 1938, where it has continued to grow and attract other gifts.

J. K. Lilly, Jr., of Indianapolis also started collecting in the 1920's, but began with American and English literature, an ample field. Later he picked up some choice Americana, but never emphasized it because of its growing scarcity. Like Clements and McGregor, he too became a library founder at Indiana University in 1960. The Lilly Library houses his own collections and several special collections owned by the University.

Other collectors of Americana learned to specialize in particular periods, persons, or places.

Considering that Clements, although well-to-do, was never rich in the way that Henry E. Huntington or J. P. Morgan was, he did astonishingly well in forming a library. Lathrop C. Harper, who knew Clements and his collecting activity as well as anyone did, said of him while he was still living:

When it comes to the question of buying, Mr. Clements is very

340

clever. He has in most cases got the right stuff and splendid value.... In fact, the gathering of the Clements Library was a remarkable achievement, and there is very little in it that today [1924] is not worth 50 % to double what Mr. Clements paid.... Forming such a collection as Mr. Clements has is not an easy matter. There is a good deal more to it than footing the bills – but he has always been 'in right.'[5]

If the increase in value was so high in 1924, it staggers the imagination to try to figure the monetary worth of the library's contents today. Market value, however, is but one measurement of the library's worth, and not the most important.

The satisfaction that Clements derived from acquisition was multiplied by his intention to have those acquisitions used by those scholars who could appreciate them. At what better location than a university? He had in mind a dual purpose for this library: bibliographical and historical. The primary objective, he said, was

to create a love for books, and in particular for those books which stand for something in American history; to create a bibliographical love for books and a sentimental appreciation of the important and beautiful.[6]

Small wonder that he insisted on a magnificent building to house his collection. As a concomitant to his primary end, Clements went on to enlarge his library with more materials,

additions costing many thousands of dollars, so that the scholar might find material there for an exhaustive if not complete survey of American history in the Discovery, Colonial, and Revolutionary period ....

The wonderful source books of the Discovery period – not to be purchased at any price today for none seem to be available – and those of the Colonial period, almost equally scarce – who can view them without exhilaration? And in the Revolutionary period the Library has a collection unapproached in completeness by any one library anywhere in the United States.[7]

The word 'exhilaration' may be the key to his motivation. It was an emotional as well as intellectual accompaniment of his collecting activity. It kept him going. It was what he hoped to communicate to the University faculty and graduate students. If he inevitably built a monument to himself, that was incidental; his purpose was much broader, his impact much deeper, his vision much more acute. Keenly aware of the educational value of his collection, he wanted it as well to inspire the research worker whom he welcomed.

The University of Michigan was doubly fortunate to have Clements as both regent and benefactor. Even the administrative organization of the library, with its own budget and director under the control of a Committee of Management, which in turn is responsible to the Board of Regents, has functioned smoothly for fifty years and without any changes in the original provisions of the gift agreement. On his part, Clements was fortunate to see the beginnings of that stream of contributions by historians, biographers, editors, and bibliographers who have used the resources of his library. They demonstrate the sagacity of his decisions regarding the development and disposition of his collection. Not all men of good intentions find such vindication.

Clements would applaud the University's fidelity to its contract. It is quite aware of the prestige that the library contributes to the University's reputation for excellence. It

342

has maintained the building in good repair, improved its lighting, and added more shelving, air-conditioning, and an automatic alarm system. It has provided for a growing staff. It has gradually increased its allocation for acquisitions. It has also utilized the building on occasion as a proper place in which to welcome heads of foreign states and other distinguished visitors. Bequests have enriched the holdings of the library and created modest endowment funds for the benefit of the institution. Clements' vision inspired friends of the library who never knew him to form in 1947 the Clements Library Associates, whose annual contributions are likewise used for acquisitions. Thus the library has grown steadily and impressively on the solid foundation William L. Clements provided through books, building, and university ownership.

NOTES

1   W. C. to Albert Kahn, Dec. 9, 1931, MHC #1.

2   Adams to Winship, June 6, 1932. MHC #3. Adams told one anecdote which illustrates Clements' determined optimism in this regard. Clements suffered considerably from arthritis during the spring of 1932. He was admitted to the hospital in Ann Arbor for a series of shots. Adams, going to visit him, told what happened. 'He was sitting in his dressing gown reading the Commercial and Financial Chronicle. He was laughing uproariously when I arrived. I enquired the reason. He replied 'I bought my Packard stock at 80 and here it is down to 2!'

3   Adams to Bishop, Sept. 5, 1934, MHC #8. 'In my talks with Mr. Clements in the spring and summer, he repeated again and again that the manuscripts and other collections were much on his mind, that it was now apparent he could never *give* them to the University, that some other plan must be devised, that he would reduce the price by at least 50 % of what he paid, etc., etc. . . . .'

4   From sketch of WLC in *Dictionary of American Biography*, Supplement vol. XXI, 181.

5   Harper to Adams, May 23, 1934, MHC #14.

6   W. C. to Adams, Nov. 10, 1925, Adams Papers.

7   W. C. to Adams, May 13, 1927, Adams Papers.

I have supplemented the material contained in the Clements Papers with additional correspondence and information concerning Clements and his collection, chiefly from the papers of University of Michigan presidents, regents, faculty, and staff, housed for the most part in the Michigan Historical Collections at the University. Also of great value were the papers of William Warner Bishop, University Librarian during most of the period of Clements' collection building. These are to be found in the General Library of the University. Much helpful information, particularly pertaining to the last decade of Clements' life, is contained in the correspondence and records of Randolph G. Adams, first director of the Clements Library (1923–1951), located in the Clements Library and in the Michigan Historical Collections.

I am indebted to many people for advice, information, and helpful suggestions given during the two years in which I have been studying Clements and his world. Betty Clements (Mrs. Harry S.) Finkenstaedt, William L. Clements' daughter, of Hyannisport, Massachusetts, has shared family pictures, memorabilia, and information which could have been obtained in no other way. James Shearer II, Chicago, an associate of Clements in the Industrial Works during his younger days, author of several interesting articles about Bay City and about Clements, and longtime friend of the Clements Library, has given me much invaluable information, often the results of his own research. Douglas G. Parsonage, surviving member of the original firm of Lathrop C. Harper, Inc., in New York City has given freely of his knowledge of Mr. Harper and of other members of the book trade, both by correspondence and by personal interview.

For helpful assistance and for a careful reading of my entire manuscript I am indebted to Wallace J. Bonk and Edmon Low, both members of my doctoral committee. I am grateful to the chairman of my committee, Russel E. Bidlack, Dean of the School of Library Science at The University of Michigan, for his overall direction of the study and for his generosity in sharing his knowledge and in helping me to get necessary information for the section dealing with early Ann Arbor history and the Clements family genealogy.

The Clements story could never have been written without the full cooperation of the Clements Library staff. Howard H. Peckham, Director of the Clements Library, and also a member of my committee, provided the initial inspiration for this study with his suggestion that an investigation of the Clements Papers might prove valuable to one interested as I am in library history and in rare books. Mr. Peckham has sustained me through the entire study by his continued interest in my findings, and by sharing with me his knowledge of Americana and of the Clements Library collection. To others on the staff, particularly William S. Ewing, former head of the Manuscripts Section, and William L. Joyce, his assistant, I am also most sincerely thankful. I was made to feel a part of the Clements Library family; I was given access freely and fully to the materials contained in the library. It has been a joyful experience, and one made possible only because of the staff of the Clements Library.

As a librarian myself, I cannot forget the other librarians who willingly gave help and provided resources for my study. I spent many weeks in the Michigan Historical Collections working with archival materials there. I was provided with desk space, a place to leave my typewriter, and all needed materials from the collections by the courteous and helpful staff members. Librarians at the Bay City Public Library were helpful in giving

346

me access to early library records and information about Aaron J. Cooke, a nineteenth-century Bay City dry goods merchant, also one of Bay City's earliest librarians, whose collection of Americana served as the foundation for William L. Clements' own library.

I wish to acknowledge with thanks financial aid for the study provided by a grant for travel expenses given by the Horace H. Rackham School of Graduate Studies at The University of Michigan. I would be remiss if I did not also express my gratitude for the U.S. Higher Education Act Title II-B fellowship for doctoral work which has made my entire program possible, and to those in the School of Library Science who supported my application for the fellowship. For the substantial aid provided by friends of Clements, Morrison Shafroth of Denver, Colorado, and James Shearer II of Chicago, as well as by the Clements Library to insure publication of this work, I am indeed grateful. Special thanks go also to Mrs. Alice Gibson for editorial revision of the dissertation manuscript.

I mention my family last, and that not because I am insensitive to the debt of gratitude which I owe them, most particularly my husband. They have given encouragement and a listening ear; they have endured many things with patience and as much good humor as they could muster. Only occasionally have they asked how much longer the whole project would take. To LeGrand, to Robert, Brian, and Bruce I owe the greatest debt. Our years in Ann Arbor were fruitful ones.

Margaret Maxwell

BIBLIOGRAPHY

PRIMARY SOURCES

Unpublished Material

Most of the unprinted primary source material is located at
The University of Michigan, Ann Arbor, in one of the following
libraries: William L. Clements Library (cited as Clements Library), General Library, Michigan Historical Collections. When
these are cited, no further location is given.

Adams (Randolph) Papers. Clements Library.

Bay City Library. 'Proceedings for Building Library, 1919–21.' Scrapbook.
  Undated. Bay City, Michigan.
Bay City Library. Board of Trustees. Minutes of meetings, May 26, 1877 –
  January 19, 1922. Bay City, Michigan.
Beal (Junius E.) Papers. Michigan Historical Collections.
Bishop (William Warner) Papers. General Library.
Burton (Marion LeRoy) Papers. Michigan Historical Collections.

Clements (William L.) Papers. Clements Library.
Clements Library. Committee of Management. Minutes, 1923–29. Clements
  Library.
Cooley, Thomas M. Diary. Michigan Historical Collections.
Cross (Arthur Lyon) Papers. Michigan Historical Collections.

Demmon (Isaac N.) Papers. Michigan Historical Collections.

Hubbard (Lucius L.) Papers. Michigan Historical Collections; General
  Library, Rare Book Division.
Hutchins (Harry B.) Papers. Michigan Historical Collections.

Koch (Theodore Wesley) Papers. General Library.

Michigan. University. General Library. Papers. Michigan Historical Collections.
Michigan. University. Registrar's Office. Records.

Perry, Ernest B. Diary. Clements Library.
Pond, Elihu B. Diary. Michigan Historical Collections.

St. Andrew's Episcopal Church, Ann Arbor. Records. Ann Arbor.
Sawyer (Walter H.) Papers. Michigan Historical Collections.
Smith (Shirley W.) Papers. Michigan Historical Collections.
Stevens, Henry N. 'DeBry in the William L. Clements Library, June, 1924.' Clements Library.

Van Tyne (Claude H.) Papers. Michigan Historical Collections.
Van Tyne, Claude H. 'Report on Clinton Papers Already in Print or Known to Exist in Manuscript Copies in Public Repositories.' [1925] Clements Library.

Wenley (Robert M.) Papers. Michigan Historical Collections.
Whedon, Helen M. Diary. Michigan Historical Collections.

Contemporary Official Publications of The University of Michigan

Michigan. University. *Calendar*, 1878–1882. Ann Arbor, 1879–1883.
Michigan. University. Board of Regents. *Proceedings*, 1837–1926. Ann Arbor: The University, 1915–1927.
Michigan. University. General Library. *The Library Building, with the Addresses at the Dedication, January Seventh*, 1920. Ann Arbor, 1920.
Michigan. University. William L. Clements Library. *The Dedication of the William L. Clements Library of Americana at the University of Michigan.* Ann Arbor: University of Michigan, 1923.
Michigan. University. William L. Clements Library. *Reports, 1924–41.* Ann Arbor, 1926–1942.

City Directories and Newspapers

Ann Arbor, Michigan. *City Directory*, 1860–1884.
Ann Arbor Argus, 1879–1895.

Bay City, Michigan. *City Directory*, 1868–1894.
Bay City Times, 1934, 1937.

Michigan Argus (Ann Arbor), 1858–1879.
Michigan Daily (Ann Arbor), 1909–1934.

Washtenaw Evening Times (Ann Arbor), 1893.

Library Catalogs and Bibliographies of Americana

Brown, John Carter. *Bibliotheca Americana; a Catalogue of Books Relating to North and South America in the Library of John Carter Brown of Providence, Rhode Island.* Providence, 1865–71. 3 vols.

Brown, John Carter. *Bibliotheca Americana; a Catalogue of Books Relating to North and South America in the Library of John Carter Brown of Providence, Rhode Island.* Providence: H. O. Houghton, 1875–82. 2 vols.

Church, Elihu Dwight. *A Catalogue of Books Relating to the Discovery and Early History of North and South America, Forming a Part of the Library of E. D. Church.* Completed and annotated by George Watson Cole. New York: Dodd, Mead, 1907. 5 vols.

Harrisse, Henry. *Bibliotheca Americana Vetustissima; a Description of Works Relating to America Published Between the Years 1492 and 1551.* Chicago: Argonaut, 1967. Facsimile reprint of New York/Paris edition of 1866/72.

Ives, Brayton. *Catalogue of the Collection of Books and Manuscripts Belonging to Mr. Brayton Ives of New-York . . . to be Disposed of by Auction on Thursday, March 5, 1891 . . .* New York: DeVinne Press, 1891.

Michigan. University. William L. Clements Library. *Author/Title Catalog of Americana, 1493–1860 in the William L. Clements Library, University of Michigan, Ann Arbor, Michigan.* Boston: G. K. Hall, 1970. 7 vols.

Winsor, Justin. *Narrative and Critical History of America.* Boston: Houghton Mifflin, 1884–1889. 8 vols.

BIBLIOGRAPHY

The Works of William L. Clements

A Check List Preliminary to a General Catalogue of Books Published before 1700 belonging to the Library of William L. Clements, Bay City, Michigan. Bay City, 1920. Addenda. February, 1921.

[Facsimile Catalog of Books in the Library of William L. Clements. Bay City, 1914.] 3 vols.

A Friendly Letter and A Serious Letter from Henry Philip Tappan. Edited with a Preface by William L. Clements. Bay City, 1933. 2 vols.

Geographical Maps of the Periods of Discovery. Colonization and Revolution, Many from the Library of the late Henry Vignaud, Paris. Duplicates from the William L. Clements Library, University of Michigan, Ann Arbor, Michigan. Also important books pertaining to the discovery of America and later periods of American history. Sold by order of Mr. William L. Clements. To be sold Tuesday afternoon, February 28th, at 2 o'clock. New York: Anderson Galleries, 1928.

Jesuit Relations in the Library of William L. Clements, Bay City, Michigan. Corrected to June, 1931. Bay City, 1931. (Mimeographed)

Journal of Major Robert Rogers. Worcester, Mass.: American Antiquarian Society, 1918.
  Also published as 'Rogers' Michillimackinac Journal,' *Proceedings of the American Antiquarian Society*, XXVIII (October, 1918), 224–73.

[List of Newspapers in the William L. Clements Collection. Bay City, 1923?] 2 vols. (Typescript)

'Marion L. Burton, an Appreciation.' *The Michigan Chime*, VI (March, 1925), 15.

'Sketch of the Life of Judge Isaac Marston.' *Michigan History*, I (July, 1917), 1–13.

'Some Rare Americana.' *Michigan Library Bulletin*, XVI (January–February, 1925), 3–6.

'Source Books for the History of the Lake Region.' *Papers of the Bibliographical Society of America*, XVI, pt. 1 (1923), 1–5.

'Steam Excavators.' *Transactions of the American Society of Mechanical Engineers*, IX (1888), 515–33.

Uncommon, Scarce, and Rare Books Relating to American History During the Discovery and Colonial Periods, together with other Americana from the Library of William L. Clements, Bay City, Michigan. Bay City, 1914.

The William L. Clements Library of Americana at the University of Michigan. Ann Arbor: The University, 1923.

Interviews

Bishop, William Warner, Jr. Interview, June 3, 1971.

Finkenstaedt, Mrs. Betty Clements. Interview, July 31, 1969.

Parsonage, Douglas. Interview, November 27, 1970.

Peckham, Howard H. Various times.

Shearer, James II. Interview, May 29, 1970.

SECONDARY SOURCES

Books

Adams, Randolph G. *The Headquarters Papers of the British Army in North America during the War of the American Revolution.* Clements Library Bulletin, XIV. Ann Arbor: Clements Library, 1926.

Adams, Randolph G. *The Whys and Wherefores of the William L. Clements Library.* 2nd edition. Ann Arbor: University of Michigan Press, 1930.

Bay City Library. Board of Trustees. *History of the Bay City Public Library.* Bay City, 1966? (Mimeographed)

Beakes, Samuel W. *Past and Present of Washtenaw County, Michigan.* Chicago: S. J. Clarke Pub. Co., 1906.

Brown, R. B. *The Visitor and the Clements Library.* Clements Library Bulletin, LXI. Ann Arbor: Clements Library, 1950.

Cannon, Carl L. *American Book Collectors and Collecting from Colonial Times to the Present.* New York: Wilson, 1941.

Carlyle, Thomas. *Inaugural Address at Edinburgh*, in *The Works of Thomas Carlyle.* Centenary edition. New York: AMS Press, 1969. Vol. XXIX, 449–83.

Grolier Club, New York. *Grolier 75: a Biographical Retrospective to Celebrate the Seventy-fifth Anniversary of the Grolier Club in New York.* New York, 1959.

Hariot, Thomas. *A Brief and True Report of the New Found Land of Virginia. A Facsimile Edition of the 1588 Quarto, with an Introduction by the late Randolph G. Adams.* Ann Arbor: Clements Library Associates, 1951.

Industrial Works. *The Fiftieth Anniversary of the Industrial Works, 1873–1923.* Bay City, 1923.

Jones, Howard Mumford. *The Life of Moses Coit Tyler.* Ann Arbor: University of Michigan Press, 1933.

McKay, George L. *American Book Auction Catalogs, 1713–1934, a Union List.* New York: New York Public Library, 1937.

Marston, George Arthur, and Shearer, James, II. *William L. Clements: Some of the Events Prior to his Election as Regent of the University of Michigan.* Ann Arbor: Clements Library Associates, 1953.

Peckham, Howard H. *The Making of the University of Michigan, 1817–1967.* Ann Arbor: University of Michigan Press, 1967.

Peckham, Howard H. *Guide to the Manuscript Collections in the William L. Clements Library.* Ann Arbor: University of Michigan Press, 1942.

Ricci, Seymour de. *English Collectors of Books and Manuscripts, 1530–1930.* Cambridge: University Press, 1930.

Schad, Robert O. *Henry E. Huntington, the Founder and the Library.* San Marino, Calif.: Henry E. Huntington Library and Art Gallery, 1963.

Sparks, Claud Glenn. *William Warner Bishop, a Biography.* Unpublished Ph.D. dissertation, University of Michigan, 1967.

Tyler, Moses Coit. *A History of American Literature, 1607–1765.* New York: Putnam, 1878.

Tyler, Moses Coit. *The Literary History of the American Revolution, 1763–1783.* With an Introd. by Randolph Greenfield Adams. New York: for Facsimile Library by Barnes & Noble, 1941. 2 vols.

Winship, George Parker. *The John Carter Brown Library, a History.* Providence, 1914.

Wolf, Edwin, and Fleming, John F. *Rosenbach, a Biography.* Cleveland: World Pub. Co., 1960.

Wroth, Lawrence C. *The First Century of the John Carter Brown Library: A History with a Guide to the Collections.* Providence: Associates of the John Carter Brown Library, 1946.

Articles

Adams, Randolph G. 'Clements, William Lawrence.' *Dictionary of American Biography.* 1944. XXI, Suppl. 1, pp. 179–81.

Adams, Randolph G. 'GPW & WLC.' *The* [*Clements Library*] *Quarto* (April, 1946), [1–2].

Alloway, Henry. 'Bye the Bye in Wall Street.' *Wall Street Journal*, January 15, 1935.

Alvord, Clarence Walworth. 'The Shelburne Manuscripts in America.' *Bulletin of the University of London Institute of Historical Research*, I, no. 3 (February, 1924), 77–80.

Bishop, William Warner. 'Some Recollections of William Lawrence Clements and the Formation of his Library.' *Library Quarterly*, XVIII (July, 1948), 185–91.

'The Bloodless Battles for Books of the Bibliophiles.' *New York Herald*, January 14, 1912, III, 4.

Brigham, Clarence S. 'William Lawrence Clements.' *Proceedings of the American Antiquarian Society*, n.s. XLV, no. 1 (1936), 10–13.

Burgess, Gelett. 'The Battle of the Books.' *Collier's*, XLVIII (February 10, 1912), 17, 31.

Carlton, W. N. C. 'Henry Edwards Huntington, 1850–1927,' *American Collector*, IV (August, 1927), 165–67.

'Clements, William Lawrence.' *The National Cyclopedia of American Biography.* 1958, XLII, 669.

'Cooke, Aaron J.' *American Biographical History of Eminent and Self-Made Men ... Michigan Volume.* 1878. pp. 7–8.

Goodrich, Francis L. D. 'Theodore Wesley Koch, 1871–1941.' *College and Research Libraries*, III (December, 1941), 67–70.

Grannis, Ruth. 'American Book Collecting.' Hellmut Lehmann-Haupt. *The Book in America.* New York: R. R. Bowker Co., 1939.

Heartman, Charles F. 'Lathrop Colgate Harper.' *The Americana Collector*, I (January, 1926), 142–43.

'Henry Vignaud.' *American Historical Review*, XXVIII (January, 1923), 377.

'The Hoe Sale.' *Library Journal*, XXXVI (June, 1911), 297–98; XXXVII (February, 1912), 75–76; (May, 1912), 266; (December, 1912), 678–79.

Koch, Theodore W. 'Enlargement of the University Library Needed.' *Michigan Alumnus*, XXI (March, 1915), 302–05.

'National Records, Manuscripts Sold Abroad: Suggestions for Future Preservation.' *London Times*, October 6, 1924.

'The New Clements Library of Americana.' *Michigan Alumnus*, XXVIII (December 15, 1921), 96–97.

'Regent Clements' Gift.' *Michigan Alumnus*, XXVI (March, 1920), 13–15.

Robbins, Frank E. 'William Lawrence Clements.' *Michigan Alumnus*, XLI (November 17, 1934), 101–02.

Roberts, W. 'Recent Book Sales.' *Nineteenth Century*, LXXII (November, 1912), 1029–39.

Shearer, James II. 'Bay City and the Clements Library.' *Michigan History Magazine*, XXXVIII (September, 1954), 253–64.

Spaulding, Thomas M. 'Hariot's Virginia.' *Michigan Alumnus Quarterly Review*, LXIV (Spring, 1958), 198–207.

Stevens, Henry N. 'The DeBry Collector's Painefull Perigrination along the Pleasant Pathway to Perfection.' In *Bibliographical Essays, a Tribute to Wilberforce Eames*. Cambridge: Harvard University Press, 1924.

Troxell, Gilbert McCoy. 'The Elizabethan Club of Yale University.' *Papers of the Bibliographical Society of America*, XXVII, pt. 2 (1933), 83–88.

Watkins, Herbert G. 'Memories of a Michigan Town.' *Bay City Times*, August 14, 1949, p. 7.

'William L. Clements.' *Michigan History Magazine*, XIX (January, 1935), 157–59.

'William L. Clements.' *New England Historical and Genealogical Register*, LXXXIX (January, 1935), 66.

Wroth, Lawrence C. 'Americana for Americans; Collector's Story of the Clements Library.' *New York Times Book Review and Magazine*, July 22, 1923, p. 3, 25.

Wroth, Lawrence C. 'Lathrop Colgate Harper, a Happy Memory.' *Papers of the Bibliographical Society of America*, LII (Third quarter, 1958), 161–72.

INDEX